The Vandemonian Trail

Published in 2016 by Connor Court Publishing Pty Ltd

Copyright © Patrick V Morgan

All rights reserved. No part of this book may be reproduced or transmitted in any form or by any means, electronic or mechanical, including photocopying, recording or by any information storage and retrieval system, without prior permission in writing from the publisher.

Connor Court Publishing Pty Ltd
PO Box 7257
Redland Bay QLD 4165
Australia

sales@connorcourt.com
www.connorcourt.com

Phone 0497-900-685

ISBN: 978-1-925501-21-6

Cover design: Maria Giordano

Front cover illustrations: Dan Morgan's Capture at Peechelba Station, Victoria

Printed in Australia

THE VANDEMONIAN TRAIL

CONVICTS AND BUSHRANGERS IN EARLY VICTORIA

Patrick Morgan

CONTENTS

	Preface	9
	Introduction	11
	Part One: Crossing the Strait	23
1	Arthur Orton in Hobart	25
2	The Vandemonian Move to Victoria	37
3	Stockriding on Central Gippsland Runs	51
4	Lawlessness around Sale and Stratford	63
5	Delusions of Grandeur	75
	Part Two: The High Country	89
6	Miners, Traders, Stockmen and Squatters at Omeo	91
7	The Legends of Bogong Jack	103
8	The Disappearance of Ballarat Harry	121
9	The Murder of Cornelius Green	131
10	Henry Kingsley on the Trail	143
	Part Three: North of the Divide	157
11	Cattle Rustling in the Ranges	159
12	Wandering in the Riverina	171
13	Back to Britain	185
14	Literary Versions of the Basic Story	201
15	A Victorian Fable	215
	Acknowledgements	225

ILLUSTRATIONS

The Vandemonian Trail	17
Liverpool Street, Hobart Town	28
The Forestier and Tasman Peninsulas	30
Settlements on the Gippsland Coast	40
Squatting Runs in Central Gippsland	52
The Crimean War Appeal	54
The VDL Convict File of Thomas Toke (Tookey)	55
The Tichborne Case – The Claimant	77
Early Squatting Runs around Omeo	92
Omeo During its Mining Days	96
The Marriage Certificate of John & Ann Paynter	109
Possible Horse and Cattle Smuggling Routes	116
Cornelius Green and His Grave at Swift's Creek	134
Henry Kingsley	145
Castro's Travels in the Riverina	174
Tom Castro's House at Wagga Wagga	180
A Scene at the Trial	193
Marcus Clarke	204
Rolf Boldrewood	204
From Manaro to Gippsland	207

PREFACE

This study attempts to see as a whole a number of topics which are usually considered separately:

> Subject matter common to the writings of the three most prominent colonial novelists, Henry Kingsley, Marcus Clarke and Rolf Boldrewood
>
> The movement of Tasmanians to eastern Victoria in the 1850s, here called the Vandemonian Trail
>
> The initial population composition of Victoria, in comparison with its adjacent colonies of New South Wales and Van Diemen's Land
>
> Rapid upward and downward mobility in the early days
>
> The Bogong Jack and Tichborne Claimant stories
>
> The extensive literature, folklore and myths which grew up around early events

The Vandemonian Trail and the movements of the Tichborne claimant and Bogong Jack provide a basic structure into which the other topics are integrated.

INTRODUCTION

In its early decades the infant district of Port Phillip, later Victoria, spawned four mystery stories which gripped the imagination of its settlers. In 1835, the year European settlement began, a man named William Buckley emerged from the scrub. A convict at the abortive 1803 settlement at Sorrento, he had escaped, gone bush, and in succeeding years walked around the rim of Port Phillip Bay mixing with Aboriginal tribes, until he finally settled in the Geelong region, taking an Aboriginal wife. Though himself in a dependent position, he was treated by the Aborigines as a superior being, the revenant figure of an ancestor come back from the dead. In 1835, to the amazement of the new settlers, Buckley rejoined European society after thirty two years in the wilderness. Like the Aborigines, the new settlers saw him as coming back from the dead to civilization.

In the next decade, the 1840s, Melbourne society was engrossed by the unfolding drama of the supposed lost white woman of Gippsland. Stories filtered back that a distressed white woman had been seen with an Aboriginal tribe, which was presumed to have taken her captive. She was thought to be a survivor of a vessel shipwrecked on the Ninety Mile Beach. Melburnians were horrified that a women of their own race had been so rudely removed from civilized society and reduced, in their view, to a barbaric level of existence. Rescue parties were sent out to retrieve her, with messages distributed around the bush directing her how to escape. Gippsland Aboriginal tribes were asked to produce their captive, and harried when they failed to do so. The captive white woman was never found. Some said she had drowned in the Gippsland lakes, others that she was in reality a ship's prow carved in the shape of woman's head carried around by the Aborigines as a cargo cult trophy.

In the next decade, the 1850s, stories began to circulate of a daring cattle thief, Bogong Jack, originally of respectable origins, whose gang flourished in the mountains of north-east Victoria. When pursued by police he escaped into the remote high plain country. In one story he lived with an Aboriginal tribe near Omeo for a number of years. Always able to outwit police parties sent to capture him, Bogong Jack attained the status of a folk hero. In one version he returned after some years and settled back to his former life, but in other accounts he retreated to his mountain hideouts when police surveillance became too hot.

In the next decade, the 1860s, the great Victorian mystery story, the Tichborne saga, began to make its appearance. An English aristocrat, (Sir) Roger Tichborne, had disappeared while overseas; rumour had it that he had been seen on the Victorian goldfields. His mother advertised in Australian papers for knowledge of his whereabouts. Eventually a low grade Wagga Wagga butcher who called himself Thomas Castro claimed to be the missing heir, and proceeded to England to sue for the title. This development split public opinion in England and Australia, which became engrossed in the mystery of whether Castro was the true heir.

The reason these stories gripped the public imagination is not arbitrary. Merely to recount them in their basic form reveals a similar pattern in their structure. In each case an individual leaves England for Australia, the first step in a succession of exiles and social descents. Then he or she moves away from society in Australia and retreats into the bush, which, being strange and unknown, was a further retreat from civilization. Then a further descent, living with low-life criminals or nomadic Aboriginal tribes, the very lowest, to the Victorian mind, rung of existence. Then comes the reverse movement as the central figure slowly mounts the steps back to normality by leaving his low company, emerging from the bush, and rejoining civilized society, even aspiring to go the whole hog and return to England as an aristocrat, as in the Tichborne case. Only the lost white woman fails to return, which made her case more mysterious and frightening, but all the narratives had an air of the unexplained about them, which accounted for the public's fascination with them. These stories centered on the hopes and fears of a society in the process of settling, unsure of its tenure and social standing in a new land. Fears of a reversion to dissolution and death, or hopes of a more exalted station, jostled in the dreams of the settlers. The descent of the protagonist into Avernus, where he undergoes trials and challenges which have to be overcome before returning to the upper world as a hero, is a common mythic archetype. In his book *The Hero With A Thousand Faces* Thomas Campbell sees it as the prototype of many folk stories. The Victorian public seized on stories which could be embraced in a basic, satisfying form. Inconvenient details were elided, and as a result the events themselves have come down to us in a distorted form

In the Australian bush, that unfamiliar and ever-changing landscape where the normal rules of society did not apply, everything seemed up for grabs. People were fascinated at the time with the idea of an English aristocrat who throws off the shackles in Australia and descends the social scale, eventually disappearing into the mass of common humanity. Or by the contrary image of a working man in Australia discovered to be an English aristocrat. Or by two similar characters, one who descends as the other rises. But it wasn't necessarily a matter of making a clear choice between one style of life or another. In a normal society the gap between the disreputable and the respectable looms large. But in the Australian bush it was bridged by a peculiar mingling of refined and low-grade behaviour. One could move very rapidly from one mode to the other, as the Tichborne case seemed to demonstrate. People could combine disparate states – the lost heir, the ex-convict squatter, the distressed gentlewoman, the low-life aristocrat, the Englishman with a past, the gentleman bushranger. The real life Captain Melville, a former convict, was an early example of the 'gentleman bushranger' looked upon sympathetically by the public, as the entry on him in the *Australian Dictionary of Biography* reveals: 'Melville created the legend of the cultured gentleman of good address and scholarship turned highwayman, considerate to those whom he robbed, courteous and charming to women, and a nineteenth-century Robin Hood. Yet he was a swaggerer courageous behind a brace of pistols and a skilful confidence man destroyed by the penal system and his unbalanced character.' The Tichborne claimant, the legendary Bogong Jack, and

Boldrewood's fictional Captain Starlight in *Robbery Under Arms*, all have something of this aura about them.

The Tichborne case played up to the widespread nineteenth century hope of ordinary people that one day they might, without effort, suddenly improve their lot in life, like today's dream of winning Tattslotto. The English novelist Anthony Trollope believed Australians supported the claimant not necessarily because they believed his story, but because 'there was a pleasurable excitement in the idea that such a man should return home from the wild, reckless life of the Australian bush and turn out to be an English baronet'.[1] An ordinary workman could beat the English at their own game. The later mateship legend claimed Australians had embraced a new egalitarian style of life here, against the ways of old England. But for every Australian who embraced the mateship ethic, there was another who hoped to discover a genteel past which would confer status in a class-ridden society. People struggled to find, as the Victorian novelist Mary Braddon put it, 'equilibrium in the universal see-saw'.[2] The belief that one could straddle social extremes was one of the defining characteristics of 19th century Australia.

The four formative myths had their location in the new colony of Victoria, situated between New South Wales and Van Diemen's Land (VDL). The Port Phillip district, later called Victoria, was populated from two opposite directions by Europeans. It was founded by overstraiters, parties coming north from Van Diemen's Land across Bass Strait from the early decades of the nineteenth century. It was also settled by overlanders, squatters moving south from New South Wales with their flocks and cattle herds. The Port Phillip district was, in its early days before gold, a virtually convict-free wedge between the two originally penal colonies of VDL and NSW.[3] But the social gap between convict and non-convict colonies was even greater than might be expected, as a disproportionate number of Victoria's early settlers were 'Port Phillip Gentlemen', British-Australians of gentry status, some the younger sons of the minor aristocracy of Britain. Pre-gold Port Phillip citizens had pretensions to status. As a result Victorians considered themselves not just as cleanskins, but as markedly superior in social status to the inhabitants of the two adjacent colonies. Population exchanges between free and convict colonies naturally created opportunities for rapid movement up and down the social scale.

Port Phillip/Victoria had been founded much more recently than the two colonies which surrounded it. By 1850, NSW had been in operation for seven decades and VDL for five decades, whereas Port Phillip was only 15 years old. This meant its society was in a much more unformed and malleable state. Before Victoria had time to settle down, it was overwhelmed by the gold rushes which brought in up to half a million immigrants from overseas. Most of them made for the western goldfields and Melbourne. This led to a population disparity within the colony between its eastern and western halves. In the early 1850s Eastern Victoria had only about 3,000 inhabitants on thirty new squatting runs, with its biggest towns of little more than five hundred people. The first Gippsland electoral roll of 1856 contains less than a thousand names. A good deal of Gippsland's early increase in population came from Tasmania. Gippsland's tiny society was disrupted not so much gold rushes as by a Tasmanian influx which was disproportionately large.

The Port Phillip district's convict-free status ended when from the late 1830s onwards absconding convicts and ticket-of-leave men began quietly crossing Bass Strait and landing at Western Port, Wilson's Promontory, and along the Ninety Mile beach. This traffic of overstraiters increased considerably when Gippsland was opened up for squatting in the 1840s. The ending of transportation and the finding of gold in Victoria in the 1850s gave a further impetus to this population shift. Van Diemen's Land had virtually no gold and many convicts, and Victoria had gold but virtually no convicts, so Vandemonians began to come across the strait in large numbers in the 1850s. Many Tasmanians went to the large fields around Ballarat and Bendigo, but a smaller but distinct group moved to Gippsland as rural workers. Vandemonians (some free and some ex-convict), including the Tichborne claimant Arthur Orton and Bogong Jack, worked on Gippsland squatting properties owned by fellow Van Diemen's Land colonists. When gold was discovered in the mountains, the rough Van Diemen's Land mob moved north again along the Tambo River to the Livingstone Creek goldfield at Omeo, the centre of the northern fields. In addition to its goldfield, Omeo's location was crucial. It was the fulcrum of the road system in north Gippsland, being near the watershed of the ranges, and one of the few places through which one could get from the southern to the northern slopes with relative ease, and in some cases on to the Monaro and the Riverina in NSW. A witness at the Australian Commission on the Tichborne case, William Higgins, described the main demographic pattern in Gippsland at the time: 'The movement of population in Gipp's Land has generally been from the south towards the north; persons coming into Gipp's Land from Tasmania, or elsewhere by the lakes, or from Melbourne and the west over the mountains, mostly went northwards towards Bairnsdale and the Omeo'.[4] This distinctive migration pattern constituted the Vandemonian Trail.

As inhabitants of the different types of colony mixed more freely from the 1850s onwards, contamination and social advancement were both possible. Tasmanians flocked to Victoria with its twin attractions of freedom and gold, but Victorians feared an influx of the group they labelled Vandemonians. Ex-convicts from Van Diemen's Land were believed to look physically different from other groups, and to be different in temperament. They were regarded as hardened cockney criminals, inured to horror and murder, who scared the living daylights out of the more equitable mainlanders. As a result a considerable social gulf separated would-be aristocrats from would-be rogues and racketeers.

Some of best known 19th century Australian novels covered, in various fictional guises, events on the Vandemonian convict trail. The three principal colonial novelists – Henry Kingsley, Marcus Clarke and Rolf Boldrewood – all spent their formative years in mid-century Victoria. During his time in Australia, Kingsley was based in Victoria, Boldrewood moved from Victoria to NSW as a squatter and police magistrate, and Clarke visited and imaginatively inhabited VDL for his major writings. As Port Phillip gentlemen they were fascinated with the low-life activities of the denizens of the neighbouring convict-bushranging colonies. All wrote major fictions which included the Bogong Jack, Tichborne and

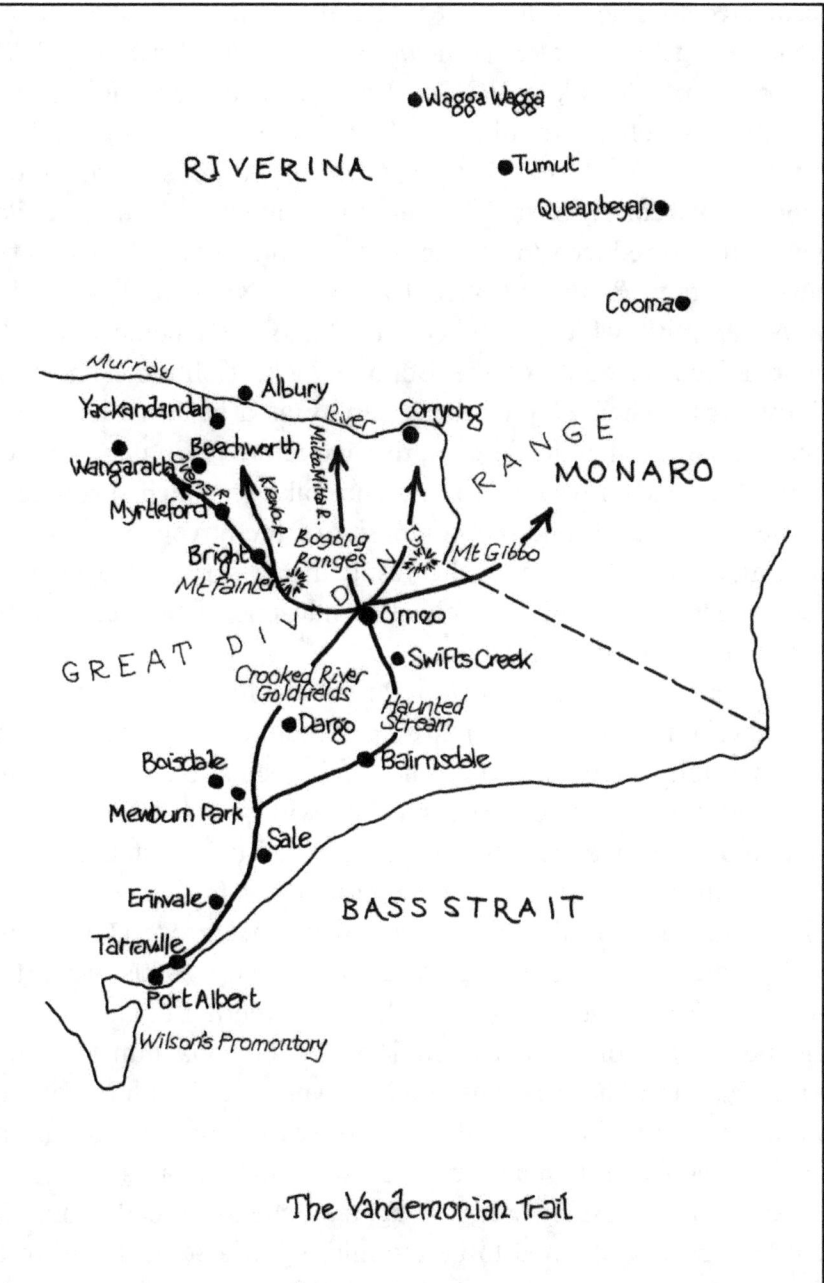

The Vandemonian Trail

associated complex of folk tales. The first major Australian novel, Henry Kingsley's *The Recollections of Geoffry Hamlyn* (1859), describes an outbreak by VDL bushrangers in eastern Victoria and the Alps, as well as providing the first account of the Bogong Jack fable. In *For The Term Of His Natural Life* Marcus Clarke wrote about VDL convicts, and in particular about a Tichborne-like gentry figure reduced to convict status. Boldrewood focussed on bushrangers in *Robbery Under Arms,* set in NSW, and especially in *Nevermore*, which is based on Omeo and includes lightly fictionalized accounts of the Bogong Jack, Tichborne and Ned Kelly sagas. Their major novels deploy as a basic structure the same sequence of exile, descent, rise and return to England noticed in the four early mystery stories. The folklore which surrounded events on the trail, and the popularity of the novels about them, amplified each other, with the result that a series of events on the Vandemonian trail were elevated into one of the best known narratives of colonial Australia.

Australians have a fascination for stories, like the recent Azaria Chamberlain and Peter Falconio ones, which remain mysterious – it is impossible to tell where fact ends and speculation begins. Many of these mystery stories are connected with people disappearing, and sometimes reappearing, in unexplained circumstances. This was an ingredient in the great international mystery story, the Tichborne saga, the alleged events of which occurred in Gippsland and southern NSW.[5] Its origins lay in the early 1850s, when the heir to the ancient Tichborne title in southern England, Roger Tichborne, left on a voyage in 1853 which took him to South America, where he was presumed drowned. His mother, holding out the hope that he was still alive, advertised for news of him in English and Australian newspapers from 1863 onwards.

An unprepossessing Wagga Wagga butcher, who called himself Thomas Castro, claimed to be the missing aristocrat. He went to England to claim the title and estates in 1866, and was accepted by the mother and a few family friends and retainers, but rejected by the rest of the family. In May 1871, with great popular backing, he sued to have the estates and title returned to him. After a trial lasting

10 months, the claimant was unsuccessful. He was immediately charged with perjury and other offences; another marathon trial ensued, with the claimant being found guilty and sentenced to 14 years' imprisonment. These trials and their preliminaries kept English and Australian newspaper readers engrossed for over a decade, just as the Azaria Chamberlain ones did a century later. When the English novelist Anthony Trollope visited Australia in 1872, he remarked that 'the name of Gippsland will be familiar to the ears of English readers, chiefly because that great hero of romance the Tichborne claimant for a while carried on there his trade as a journeyman butcher'.[6] Ironically at the time Gippsland was better known in England than in Australia, where it was considered an out-of-the-way place.

The movements of the claimant, who turned out to be a Hobart butcher, Arthur Orton, followed the Vandemonian convict trail from Van Diemen's Land to Victoria. Orton was not a convict but mixed with dubious elements in Hobart. He then crossed Bass Strait to central Gippsland squatting runs, where he worked with a large band of Vandemonian ex-convicts. When that group moved to the Omeo goldfields, Orton, because he had to avoid being arrested for horse stealing, found his way north to the Riverina by a different route. But his basic pattern of movement aligns itself to the Vandemonian trail, and much of his eventful life can be understood in its context.

The mystery of the Tichborne case was that no explanation sufficed. If the claimant was Sir Roger, he had too imperfect a recall of Sir Roger's past to be plausible. If he wasn't, he knew too much and had too many similarities to be dismissed out of hand. A family illegitimacy, or the possibility that Tichborne was murdered in Australia and his identity assumed by the claimant, were two explanations advanced to solve the conundrum. Neither turned out to be true. As far as can be established, the account given in this book of Orton/Castro is his actual life, not the one he retrospectively invented for himself by manipulating reality.[7] It is in many ways the life of a typical bush worker in mid-nineteenth century Australia. Apart from its intrinsic interest in relation to the Tichborne case, it is an exceptionally well-documented life story for the period. The emergence of Thomas Castro at Wagga Wagga was the natural culmination of his shady activities on the Vandemonian trail, and does not occur out of the blue, as it appeared to the rest of the world when he first made his astounding claim. This study reveals his many hidden escapades in Van Diemen's Land, Victoria and New South Wales. Those at his trials in faraway London naturally had a very imperfect understanding of this context. They were unaware that certain incidents, like the murder of Ballarat Harry, which figured prominently at the Tichborne trials, were closely connected with the Bogong Jack gang. Their notions of Australian geography, topography and habits of life were understandably hazy; even Douglas Woodruff's admirable book *The Tichborne Claimant*, published in 1957, has Boisdale mistakenly located in the middle of Victoria near Bendigo, instead of in Gippsland.

One discovery from which the present book grew was finding the real, a distinct from the mythical, origins of Bogong Jack. In his book *Bogong Jack: Gentleman Bushranger* Eric Harding described him born in England with a Leicestershire gentry background, and this has been generally accepted since. But the Bogong Jack who operated in the Omeo area was born in Hobart in 1830, the son of a poor butcher, William Paynter. Today Bogong Jack is a folk figure of some magnitude, and his ally Thomas Toke, an ex-convict from VDL, is unknown. But in the 1850s, when the relevant events were taking place, Thomas Toke was in the public eye as a notorious murderer and leader of the criminal 'Bogong Jack' gang, and his offsider Bogong Jack Paynter was hardly known at all. Why and how did their reputations reverse themselves over the next century?

An all-encompassing folk tale grew up at the time claiming to explain the variegated activities of the Vandemonian trail. A prime example of this kind is Rolf Boldrewood's novel *Nevermore* (1892), where many allegedly historical events (the Alpine cattle rustling gangs, Tasmanian ex-convicts, and the Tichborne heir) are fitted into a neat pattern. In this novel an Omeo miner, the heir to an English estate like the Tichborne one, is murdered by a member of the criminal Bogong Jack gang. An erstwhile friend from the gang elicits his story from him before his death and is thus able to impersonate him. Though this was thought a plausible scenario, it was not true to what happened, being based on rumour-driven speculation at the time. Boldrewood and many of his readers accepted it, and so it spread further, with the result that it was projected back on to reality. By such means the historical record has become distorted.

This study attempts to establish the chronological sequence of events that occurred on the Vandemonian trail, as distinct from the unreliable folklore version which has come down to us. By this means the complex layers of proliferating folk accretions can be peeled away, and confusions over time, place and identity sorted out as far as possible. Having separated out the discrete elements in the story, they can then be reconstructed as a new whole. This has the side effect of removing the mystery from the stories, the element which accounted for their great attraction in the nineteenth century.

Mythic patterns influence the way literature is written. Scene shifting occurs as events become jumbled in the process of being repeatedly recalled. Materials from history, literature, folklore and myth have different status as evidence, but they have become hopelessly entangled, so the 'record' is now very confused. Some of Henry Kingsley's writings served to predict events, not just to recount them. As the poet Thomas Campbell expressed it in a phrase common at the time: 'Coming events cast their shadows before'. This further blurred the line between fact and imagination. Archetypal images affect both the way people behave, and the way they interpret historical events. Actual events were, as always, much messier and less romantic that the received version of them.

The more these inter-related legends proliferated, the more folk memory tried to standardize them to render them more easily explained, and more emblematic. Henry Kingsley wrote of 'a mist of incidents and anecdotes which the younger folks took to be original, but which the older hands recognized as mere replicas of old stories.'[8] The public reshaped the material of old myths into new forms. The underlying pattern was repeated, though the details changed over time. As a result the mysteries deepened, not lessened. The real puzzle in the Tichborne case was not who the claimant was, but why the confusion persisted for so long. The public read into these events what they wanted to see. Many commentators at the time who were trying to decipher these mysteries were in fact conniving in and adding to them.

NOTES

1   Anthony Trollope *Australia and New Zealand*, 1873, repr. as *Australia*, ed. P.D. Edwards & R.B. Joyce, University of Queensland Press, St Lucia, 1967, p. 412.

2   Part of a quote from her novel *Aurora Floyd*, which the Tichborne claimant had copied into his notebook.

3   A.G.L. Shaw has shown in *A History of the Port Phillip District: Victoria Before Separation*, Miegunyah Press, Melbourne, 1996, that Victorians created the belief that their colony didn't have convicts. It didn't, apart from the short-lived Corinella venture of 1826-8, have convict settlements, but it wasn't entirely convict free.

4   *Commission for the Examination of Witnesses in the Colonies of Victoria, New South Wales, and Tasmania, in the Common Pleas Tichborne v. Lushington* (hereafter called *The Australian Commission*), 1868-9, p. 132.

5   Books on the Tichborne case include Michael Gilbert *The Claimant: The Tichborne Case Revived*, Constable, London, 1957; Douglas Woodruff *The Tichborne Claimant: A Victorian Mystery*, Hollis and Carter, London, 1957; Lord Maugham *The Tichborne Case*, Hodder & Stoughton, London, 1936; Michael Roe *Kenealy and The Tichborne Cause*, Melbourne University Press, Carlton, 1974; and Robyn Annear *The Man Who Lost Himself: The Unbelievable Story of the Tichborne Claimant*, Text, Melbourne, 2002. Gilbert treats the claimant Orton/Castro as an imposter, which people now accept as accurate. Woodruff still hankers after the belief that the claimant may have been genuine. Although untrue, this makes his book more enthralling, as he can recreate the genuine sense of mystery to which the endless possibilities of the case gave rise, which was how the public felt about it at the time.

6   Trollope, op. cit., pp. 412-3.

7   The claimant's narrative *The Entire Life and Full Confession of Arthur Orton*, published in the London magazine *People* in 1895, is, though later retracted, an accurate short summary of his life, with some notable omissions. It is hereafter cited as *The Confession*.

8   Henry Kingsley, 'The Two Cadets', *Old Margaret and Other Stories*, Ward, Lock and Bowden, London, 1895, p. 349.

PART ONE: CROSSING THE STRAIT

1

ARTHUR ORTON IN HOBART

If the real Tichborne saga starts at any one time, it is the day on which Arthur Orton reaches Hobart in April 1853. In the second Tichborne trial the claimant was found to be Arthur Orton, born in 1834, the son of a cockney butcher and trader from Wapping in the East London docks. The twelfth and last child in his family, he was known as 'Bullocky Orton' because of his large frame. During his youth he was badly affected by watching a fire, which caused him to get St Vitus Dance, a twitching of the face. To cure this affliction his family, whose business included provisioning ships, sent him to sea in 1848 apprenticed as a ship's hand. But he didn't enjoy the work and jumped ship at Valparaiso in Chile in South America, the first of many occasions in his life in which he cleared out of situations he didn't like. He spent some time as an adolescent at an inland town in Chile called Melipilla, curiously in the same area that the real Roger Tichborne was to visit five years later in 1853. Here Arthur, being poor, was befriended by the family of Thomas Castro and by an English couple, Dr Hayley and his wife. Orton learnt to round up stock while on horseback, an occupation he was to pursue in later life. After returning to England and his family in 1851, he worked in his father's business at markets in London, driving Shetland ponies and carting meat. During this period he walked out, dressed up in a natty naval uniform he had designed for himself, with his girl friend, Mary Ann Loder.

Dealing with ponies and cattle was part of the family business. In late 1852 Arthur, then 18 years old, was selected by his father to look after two Shetland ponies on their journey to Tasmania in the ship *Middleton.* The ship arrived in Hobart on 27 April, 1853, and the ponies were delivered to their buyer, Thomas Chapman, a merchant and later Colonial Treasurer of Tasmania. Arthur Orton arrived in Australia as a groom or horse attendant, and as a free man, not a convict.[1] Mrs Mina Jury, his brother-in-law's wife, met him when he arrived. From his letters it appears he kept changing his mind about whether he would stay in Australia permanently. He wrote to Mary Ann Loder on September 18, 1853: 'My dear girl, I hope you will be comfiteble until i come home that will be in about 15 month'. He added that in the meantime he would try his luck on the Victorian goldfields before returning to England. But later, in a letter to his sister Elizabeth on March 31, 1855, he wrote: 'I shall never go to England again Dear Lisy. I have made my mind to that.' He did return to England, but not as Arthur Orton. He didn't particularly take to life in Hobart, if we can judge by a comment he made in a letter to Mary Ann Loder: 'this is a Dredful place to live in. I should not have been able to make you comfortable and I would sooner luse all I got than make you un so'.

Van Diemen's Land was then in a period of gradual transition from convict colony to free society – Arthur Orton arrived in Hobart a month before transportation ceased. But the Hobart which greeted him in 1853 was still a fairly lawless place. Drunkenness, larceny and people acting as public nuisances were common. Convicts regularly absconded from assigned employers and were pursued by the police. Bushranging was still occurring on the island – a bushranger named 'Dido' (William Driscoll) flourished in the countryside around Oatlands during Arthur Orton's time in Hobart. The authorities were trying to stamp out the old, rough ways. Attempts were being made to suppress sly groging. The streets were cleaned up – carters and hawkers couldn't sell their wares in public any more, nor could cattle be driven willy nilly through the streets.

A month after Orton arrived the Governor, Sir William Denison, lamented that the discovery of gold in Australia had turned his world upside down. The chronicler George Dunderdale commented on this in *The Book of the Bush*:

> [The Governor] rejoiced that no gold had been discovered in *his* island. Then the Legislature perversely offered a reward of five thousands pounds to any man who would discover a gold field in Tasmania, but, as a high-toned historian observes, "for many years they were so fortunate as not to find it".[2]

Lack of gold meant the prosperity and rapid changes noticeable on the mainland were not evident in Van Diemen's Land.

Arthur Orton worked as a butcher and in allied trades in Hobart during the time he lived there. He was first employed by a butcher, Mr Josiah Knight. Of this job, Orton wrote in his 1895 *Confession*: 'Of course, I knew nothing about the slaughtering business, never having dressed an animal in my life. Mr. Knight used occasionally to kill and dress a few sheep, and taught me'.[3] Orton then took employment with another butcher, Samuel Loring, after which he worked in the same occupation for William Wilson in lower Macquarie St, as well living in Wilson's house for over a year. Wilson was in partnership with Samuel Bendall of Liverpool St. Many of these butchers had stalls in the New Market in Macquarie St, which had been designed by Governor Dennison and opened in December, 1853. Loring, Wilson and John Dight, a butcher and poulterer whom Orton later worked for, all had stalls there. Orton's tasks for Wilson were slaughtering, driving cattle from the Domain jetties and carting meat to customers, as well as looking after Wilson's horses. This combined interest in butchering and horses was a feature of Orton's Australian career. During this period he was known by the nicknames 'Long Arthur' and 'Arthur the Butcher'. Most acquaintances thought him an indifferent butcher, but a good horse-rider.

His physical features (he was now around twenty years old) were remembered from the time as: raw-boned, stout, full-chested, no beard, smooth skin, fairish brown hair pushed back, eye twitch caused by St Vitus Dance, a bumped nose and husky voice. His manners were coarse, his movements clumsy, and he walked with a slouching gait. He was described by a fellow butcher 'Long Tom' Hales as a 'harum-scarum sort of young chap', he mixed in roughish company and liked to drink. Hales was a former guard of the Scots Fusiliers who had been sentenced to seven years in Leicester in 1840, and had repeat offences in Van Diemen's Land.[4] In Hobart Orton claimed, as he did during his time in South America, to have come from a wealthy family.

LIVERPOOL STREET, HOBART TOWN

After leaving Wilson, Orton worked in 1855 for the butchers Richard Lord and William Paynter. Paynter had one of the 'low butchers' shops in Liverpool St.', to use the expression of Mrs Mina Jury. Liverpool St had shabby little stores, wooden shanties, including greengrocers, butchers and fishmongers. William Paynter had been transported for seven years for embezzlement and arrived in 1821. His gaol report deemed him to be of bad character, but he had only one minor misdemeanour while serving his time here. William and Elizabeth Paynter had a son, John Paynter, born in 1830, and so four years younger than Arthur Orton. John Paynter was to become Bogong Jack, an important figure in this story. Young John Paynter would have known Orton in his teenage years in Hobart when Orton was working for his father. So even at this early stage the Tichborne and Bogong Jack sagas were intertwined.

From mid 1855 Orton worked for the butcher John Dight. He wrote at that time: 'Beef and Mutton is very dear at present not for the want of it for there is plenty in But the Butchers run one other up so much at Sales'. He also wrote: 'I have taken a Shop in the new Market No. 25 witch will answer me better has i am better known in this neighbourhood. I have got a fue very good customers that will keep me going for a while till I get a fue more'. Orton seems to have been a struggling butcher at this stage.

In early 1854 Orton worked intermittently on the Forestier and Tasman Peninsulas, which contained the large convict settlement of Port Arthur. Orton's job was centred on the slaughterhouse at King George's Sound on the western side of the Forestier Peninsula. For much of the year Tasmania was too cold to raise beef cattle to feed the large convict population, so ships loaded with cattle came in from mainland ports such as Port Albert in Gippsland. Some of the livestock were landed ashore by swimming them from the ships that anchored at Wilmot Harbour, also known as the Lagoons or Lagoon Bay. The animals were then fattened on drained marshes nearby, prior to being driven across the peninsula to the slaughterhouse at King George's Sound, which Orton referred to as The Sounds. The meat was then packed and sent to the Commissariat Store at Taranna on the peninsula for distribution

The Forester and Tasman Peninsulas

to the various convict settlements on the Tasman Peninsula. Other ships from the mainland were landed at Hobart, where the cargoes were sold to Hobart butchers.

Orton was employed by merchants who had government contracts to provide meat for convicts and others. His relative, Frank Jury, who was in a similar trade and lived for some time at Eaglehawk Neck, arranged for the merchant John Johnson to employ Orton. Johnson, like Orton's father, provisioned ships among his many other activities. John Johnson was a Norwegian, christened Knud Olai Boe, and had become a prosperous grazier and shipper. Orton worked at various times for the contractors Johnson, Brown and Field. He also worked for William Ladds, a contractor to the military. Orton would go down to the Sounds from Hobart once every ten days, which suggested he was driving cattle or meat from there to Hobart, or from a cattle station to the slaughterhouse. Frank Jury used to see him regularly at The Sounds, which was about 40 miles from Hobart by road. Later Orton worked for Ladds in Hobart, living in his house in Elizabeth St, probably in early 1855.

It was while he was working for Dight the butcher that Orton became involved, over a short period in the later months of 1855, in six court cases which resulted in unwelcome publicity for him.[5] Orton was working at a stall which was sub-let from Dight, who was an ex-convict. Originally sentenced to 14 years for receiving stolen poultry in England, Dight was charged with a number of minor offences and one serious stealing charge while serving his sentence in Van Diemen's Land. Because Orton was behind in his rent, Dight had taken some meat off him in lieu of payment. All the evidence points to Orton being at a low ebb as a butcher at this point, as the meat he was selling was well below grade. On 31 July, 1855, a city inspector named Fane charged Orton in the Mayor's Court with selling unwholesome meat, the fine being a penalty of up to £50. Orton was defended by a lawyer, Mr. Brewer, and pleaded not guilty. The meat in question was produced in court and was described as having a most disgusting appearance, being black, sticky and full of blood. The Inspector of Stock, Mr Dossetor, said the animal from which the meat came had all the appearance of having died, and, if it had been killed, it must have been to save its life (at which those present in court laughed). Evidence was given that dead cattle arriving on ships were often sold to butchers. The meat in question probably came from a diseased animal, and Dossetor concluded that the meat had never been fit for human food. The butcher John Dight gave evidence that he had taken meat off Orton in payment of rent. It was shown in court that Dight was the real lessee of the stall, which he sub-let to Orton, who acted as his employee. On these grounds the court found that, although the meat was undoubtedly unwholesome, the selling of the meat was the responsibility of Dight, who was answerable for the acts of his servant. So the case against Orton was dismissed, and the meat ordered to be destroyed. One can understand that in this matter Dight would have been annoyed with Orton, who both owed him rent and got him into trouble over bad meat. In its 'Local Intelligence' column on 3 August, the *Hobarton Mercury* focussed on Orton in connection with the case, in which 'some beef was produced, scarcely fit for a dog to eat'; the paper hoped the City Inspector 'will not relax in his exertions to bring to punishment all persons, who thus attempt to poison the public'.

The next cause of contention was a horse. The butcher Wilson had lent Orton a mare, and then Dight borrowed the horse from Horton (as he was referred to in this case) and refused to return it, on the ground that Orton owed him £40, and Dight was taking it in lieu of payment, as he had done with the meat. Dight thought Orton owned the horse. The sequel to this squabble was another court case, this time in the Supreme Court before Mr Justice Horne and a jury on 19 September. This was a civil action in which the butcher John Wilson tried to recover £30, the value of a mare, from the butcher John Dight, both of whom had employed Orton. Orton, though appearing here as a witness, was once again the focus of the case. Dight stated that he was present at Wright's hotel where he saw Orton pay Wilson a pound, saying 'Here is another £1 for the horse, that I brought of you for £16'. This was corroborated by another butcher, Samuel Bendall, Wilson's partner. Dight admitted that he had had Orton arrested for the full amount of his debts, and that he had paid neither Orton nor Wilson for the horse. The judge in summing up said the crucial question was who was the owner of the horse. The jury found for Wilson, to whom Dight was forced to pay £30 damages. Once again Dight must have been annoyed that Orton had caused him such trouble. Though Orton was the cause of the problem in both instances, he had cunningly avoided any legal penalty, even though Dight had gone to the trouble to have him arrested for his debts.

Immediately following this case was a similar one involving a dispute also over the ownership and keep of a horse. The plaintiff in this matter was John Sheehan, who had gone over to the Port Phillip district, who successfully sued a John Wheatley. In a sequel to this case Wheatley unsuccessfully sued Sheehan for assault, in a case in which two men named John Jones and Richard Whittacker gave evidence.[6] Referring to these 'horse cases' the Judge said the character of those appearing before him was crucial in judging their cases. The *Mercury* commented that 'in a community like this every man's character is sure to be known'. Jack Sheehan, John Jones and Richard Whittacker were all later associated with the Bogong Jack horse-stealing gang at Omeo.

In another case during the same month, Orton appeared in court for a third time, here as a witness, when the Government Meat Inspector, William Dossetor, charged the butcher Samuel Bendall in the Mayor's Court with driving cattle from Macquarie St through the streets to Wilson's, a practice the authorities were trying to restrict. From the evidence it seems Orton let the cattle out of the yards in the first place, and so was responsible for their presence on the streets; he then borrowed a horse and rode after them to control the wayward beasts in the interests of public safety.

The skirmishing between Dight and Orton had not ended. Dight subsequently left four of his own sheep skins with Orton to be taken to Elliot's tannery, but Orton kept the money (10 shillings) paid for them. Elliot had thought the skins belonged to Orton. A fourth legal case involving Orton followed, this one a sequel to the first two. In early October, 1855, Orton appeared in a Magistrates Court to answer a charge of obtaining the sum of 10 shillings from the tanner, Mr Elliot, under false presences, Mr. Brewer again appearing for Orton. Dight said that he had not taken action sooner, as he had already had Orton arrested for his debts, and that a further charge might look spiteful. Dight described his entanglements with Orton in the two previous court cases, but denied he had gone around saying he would 'lag' Orton, right or wrong, but he had decided to punish him for taking the proceeds of the sheep skins. Dight had told other people in business not to pay Orton any bills owed to Dight. When Orton was arrested, he claimed that Dight had made the charge in revenge for the evidence Orton had given in the Supreme Court case which Dight had lost. Mr Brewer, summing up for Orton, maintained that the prosecution was a malicious one. The prosecutor said the issue was not malice, but one driven by the facts of the case. The Magistrates, after a short consultation, dismissed the charge. Once again Orton had escaped scot free.

In a fifth case in early November Orton gave evidence against Dight in a case in which a bootmaker, Fardell, sued Dight for a debt. The transaction at issue once again involved Orton, who said, as a witness in this case, that he did not understand the account books, and then went on to imply that Dight had maliciously tried to get evidence against Fardell. Dight lost the case. A month later Dight counter-sued Fardell for payment over a related transaction, which involved meat supplied by Orton, who had by the time of the court case left the colony for Victoria. Fardell repeated Orton's previous claim that Dight had offered money to Orton for evidence against Fardell. In spite of this, the judgment in this case went in favour of Dight.

Orton does not come out of these cases well, as his shaky financial situation and dealings were the root cause of all the litigation. His feckless behaviour in dodging debt and fleeing from his problems set a pattern for his future life. In Australia he kept moving on. At many places where he lived he got himself entangled in debts or the threat of court charges or both, and cleared out rather than face the music. This was perhaps a sign of some temperamental inability to cope with reality. These Hobart cases are the first of many in which Orton/Castro was involved in Australia. He was to become familiar with the law as plaintiff, defendant and witness, and usually contrived to come out unharmed. The six cases were, though on a tiny scale, the beginning of a long career in the courts which would eventually lead to the immense Tichborne litigation.

Orton had another debt problem during this period. In May, 1855, he had borrowed £14 off his relative by marriage, Mrs Mina Jury. She used to give him geese to sell at Dight's stall where he worked. She lent him money after her husband refused to lend him anything. In return Orton wrote a note which said: 'Three months after date I promise to pay to Mr. Francis Jury the sum of Fourteen pounds for Cash advanced to me. Arthur Orton'.[7] By mistake she lent him £18 instead of £14, mistaking a five pound for a one pound note. This money was ostensibly to set up his own stall in the New Market, but from the evidence in the first court case, he never did this, merely looking after Dight's stall. The debt was due to be paid in August, but Orton left Hobart in November, 1855, without paying off the debt to Mrs Jury. He must have laid low between August and November to avoid the Jurys. Mrs Jury later said: 'He was a scoundrel; he had gone away and cheated me and my orphans'.

Late in 1855 the merchant Johnson advertised in the Hobart press for splitters, fencers and stockriders to work for him in Gippsland. At this time Orton engaged with Johnson, whom he had worked for at the Sounds, to take employment on Johnson's Mewburn Park run in central Gippsland in Victoria. Orton left Hobart on 17 November, 1855, on the schooner *Eclipse* bound for Port Albert. He went to Gippsland with a Hobart butcher of German origin named Alfred Schottler. John Dight, whom Orton had worked for, also went to Gippsland, setting up business as a butcher at Port Albert. John Higgins, a butcher who knew Orton in Hobart, took employment (like Orton and many other Tasmanians) with John Johnson at Mewburn Park in Gippsland. John Paynter, son of the butcher William Paynter, also travelled, like many others, to work in Gippsland on the Vandemonian trail.

Later as Castro, Orton was forced to completely suppress his Hobart period, as he claimed that as Castro he had arrived in Melbourne directly from South America and then had gone straight to Gippsland. It would have been too risky for him to have retrospectively claimed to have been in Hobart, where his movements could have much more easily been traced than in the bush of Gippsland. Moreover his landing in Hobart could be traced back to Arthur Orton from Wapping. There had to be some gap to establish a new identity.

NOTES

1   This chapter is indebted to Michael Roe 'Arthur Orton, The Tichborne Case, and Tasmania', *Tasmanian Historical Research Association, Papers and Proceedings*, Vol. 18, 1971, pp. 115-136.

2   George Dunderdale *The Book of the Bush*, Ward Lock, London, 1898; repr. Penguin Books, Ringwood, 1973, p. 282.

3   *The Confession*, op. cit., p. 5.

4   *The Australian Commission*, op cit., p. 36.

5   The court cases were reported in the Hobart press in 1855. First case: *Hobarton Mercury*, 1 August, and *Colonial Times*, 2 August. Second case: *Hobarton Mercury*, 21 September, and *Colonial Times*, 20 September. Third case: *Colonial Times*, 12 September. Fourth case: *Hobarton Mercury*, 12 October. Fifth case: *Colonial Times*, 5 November. Sixth case: *Colonial Times*, 7 December.

6   *Colonial Times*, 27 October, 1855.

7   *The Australian Commission*, op cit., p. 214.

2

THE VANDEMONIAN MOVE TO VICTORIA

The European founders of the Port Phillip district were Van Diemen's Landers, and the district continued to be settled from the south by overstraiters in the 1840s and 1850s. Trade between Gippsland and Van Diemen's Land began in the 1840s. Because of its cool climate Van Diemen's Land farmers produced sheep for wool more than for mutton. As a result animals intended for consumption in VDL were raised in Gippsland and shipped to Hobart, and also to Wilmot Harbour to feed the Port Arthur convicts. Most trade was in live cattle, but some wool and dairy products were also brought south from Gippsland. These exports helped the Gippsland squatters, as there were few markets for their produce in the Port Phillip District. Gippsland had a very small population, and the pre-gold Melbourne of the 1840s was not a big city. In contrast Van Diemen's Land had relatively large populations at Hobart and at convict institutions.[1]

Port Albert, being the nearest mainland port to Van Diemen's Land, was the outlet from which the Gippsland trade was conducted. By the late 1840s, at the peak of the trade, up to three-quarters of vessels leaving Port Albert were undertaking the three-day voyage to Van Diemen's Land. Some Hobart merchants developed a vertically integrated trade. They purchased properties on the central plain of Gippsland, which was excellent country for raising beef and sheep. Their livestock were driven to Port Albert, where salting down works produced meat for ship's provisions. In addition these merchants owned the ships which took stock to various Van Diemen's Land ports. Of the Hobart merchants, John Johnson owned ten and John Foster four of the twenty five vessels registered in Hobart for the mainland trade. Some of these traders also owned butcheries in Hobart and on the Forestier Peninsula to handle government contracts to distribute meat. On the return journey from VDL to Gippsland, basic items for daily living and some construction materials were brought to Gippsland. This trade led to Van Diemen's Land immigration into Gippsland.

An earlier source of Van Diemen's Land immigrants to eastern Victoria was escaped and ex-convicts. As Gippsland is directly north of Tasmania, convicts escaping by boat landed on its coast from the 1830s to the 1850s. This was happening even before Europeans had settled in the Port Phillip district. 'Old Joe' Green, a Van Diemen's Land policemen in the very early days, recalled chasing a whaleboat commandeered by two bushrangers across Bass Strait in 1832. Later on, when Green was working in northern Van Diemen's Land, twenty convicts escaped. To prevent them sailing across the strait, Green and another policeman requisitioned a boat on the coast which they knew the escapees would try to steal.[2] In 1836, the second year of Melbourne's existence, two convicts stowed away on the *Caledonia* from Launceston and hid in the bush near Melbourne. In 1844 four prisoners escaped from Hobart and lived on the Kent Island group in Bass Strait for a time; two of them reached the mainland but were caught by police after landing near Cape Paterson. Such were the strength of the horror stories emanating from Van Diemen's Land that they were suspected of having eaten their two comrades. Eventually taken to Commissioner Powlett, they were arraigned in Melbourne and returned to Hobart.[3] Mrs McLean, wife of Charles McLean of the Glenaladale run in Gippsland, recalled being accosted by a stranger in 1851 who was soon identified as 'one of a band of convict escapees wanted by the police. While on a small vessel in Bass Strait the gang had murdered the captain and reached the mainland in a rowing boat, which was afterwards found on the Ninety Mile Beach'.[4]

The coast from Wilson's Promontory to the Mornington Peninsula was the scene of so many landings by escapees that the authorities sent a constable, Old Joe Green of previous Van Diemen's Land experience, to act as a one-man garrison at Yanakie north of Wilson's Promontory. This was a narrow neck of land which would hopefully trap escapees in the same way that Eaglehawk Neck did on the Tasman Peninsula. Another constable was situated on the Barker's run at Cape Schanck; the Barkers were a prominent Melbourne family with holdings on the Mornington Peninsula. Henry Kingsley described policemen hunting bushrangers on the Barker's run in two of his novels. On one occasion a cutter arrived at Corner Inlet, and the resident squatter, Richard Bennison, Constable Green and a helper unsuccessfully tried to arrest its four convict occupants. Instead they were compelled to give them food and show them the road to Melbourne; the escapees were later captured at Dandenong. A woman found in the bush on Wilson's Promontory was the survivor of a party of three which had crossed the strait. The squatter George Black of the Tarwin Meadows run encountered escapees a number of times. On one occasion when mustering he came across three convicts. He gave them food, but not the firearms they wanted. In the early 1850s a schooner ran aground at Morgan's Creek near Cape Liptrap. Black, warned that its convict occupants were going to raid his stores, burned the boat to prevent them sailing with their loot to King Island. In 1850 seven men landed in a boat near the Boneo run on the Mornington Peninsula and travelled inland looking for food. They took some ammunition and shot a beast for food at Barker's nearby Cape Schanck run, eventually returning to their boat. This illegal influx of boats caused much unease in the Port Phillip community.

Tasmanians coming into Gippsland from the Melbourne area were also feared. The Chief Protector of Aborigines, George Augustus Robinson, brought five Tasmanian Aborigines with him to Melbourne when he was appointed there in 1838. They gradually drifted out to the Dandenong and Western Port regions, engaging in minor crimes like pilfering. By late 1841 they were in the Cape Paterson area. Two whalers were shot by this group of VDL Aborigines, who then captured two resident white women from a family of coal miners in the area. The two women soon escaped, and the Aborigines, pursued by parties composed of police, settlers and black trackers, were eventually captured near

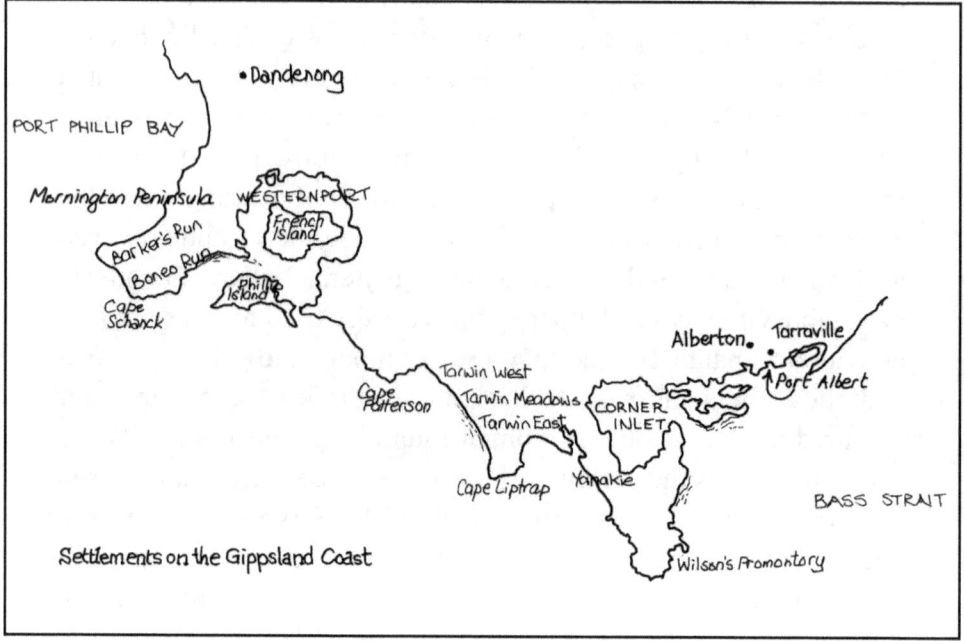

Settlements on the Gippsland Coast

today's Wonthaggi. An Aboriginal women, the famous Truganinni, was found wounded. Two of the Aborigines were found guilty of murder and hanged at Melbourne.

By the late 1840s there were former convicts in Victoria, most from Van Diemen's Land, though a few had come from New South Wales. The traffic from Van Diemen's Land increased markedly with the discovery of gold in the 1850s. The chronicler George Dunderdale records that in the early gold-rush years 45,000 people left Van Diemen's Land for Victoria, including 10,000 convicts and ex-convicts. William Howitt recorded that over 9,000 ex- and conditionally pardoned convicts came from Van Diemen's Land to Victoria in an eighteen months' period in 1852-3, figures which tally with Dunderdale's. Most went to Melbourne and to the western goldfields of Victoria. There the Van Diemen's Landers got a bad reputation. The Melbourne *Herald* of 28 January, 1852, reported that 'a gang of Vandemonians have kept the road between Bendigo and Eaglehawk Gully for three days, robbing all who passed'. Murder was not unknown on the fields. The gentleman bushranger

Captain Melville, who terrorized parts of western Victoria, was a Van Diemen's Land felon, with many convictions and attempts at absconding. The movement of a large group of Tasmanians to Victoria during the goldrush decade meant that two quite different populations – convict and respectable – were mingling for the first time.

The police magistrate at Bendigo, Mr Lachlan McLachlan, popularly known as 'Bendigo Mac', claimed he could spot old Van Diemen's Land hands on sight by their features. So did one witness at the second Tichborne trail, who, referring to his time in Victoria, said: 'We say there "from the other side", that is what we mean by the Hobart Town side, and we put them all down as ticket-of-leave men...We can always pick those characters out.'[5] The visiting English writer William Howitt changed his usually liberal ideas and came to believe that the convict-bushrangers were incorrigible: 'Since I have come out here and seen the *quality* of the scoundrelism which abounds here – that which has passed through the *annealing* process of home correction and transportation – I begin to grow Carlylish, and to think, "once a scoundrel, a scoundrel for ever," and that the only thing is to squash them as we do snakes and scorpions'.[6] An article in the *Gippsland Guardian* of 19 April, 1861, expressed similar sentiments:

> Van Diemen's Land, that pandemonium of the most wicked and debased of England's children, opened her hell gates and overflowed us with the unrestrained iniquity of those who, freed from the chains which they wore for years, returned to their evil courses trained in all the villainy which the constant intercourse of those perfect in crime had invested with a romantic boldness.

The public believed most crime was committed by old Van Diemen's Land hands. Norfolk Island prison, which housed the worst offenders, was closed on 1850 and its inmates sent to VDL, which increased the mainlanders' fears. There was suspicion between bonded and free people, the respectable not wanting to be linked with the desperado minority. People from Van Diemen's Land were demonised. Their more benign group names included 'Derwenters' and 'T'othersiders', but the spelling and pronunciation of the word 'Van Diemenians' gradually changed to 'Van*demon*ians', illustrating how reviled and scapegoated they had become. These memories lasted. In a bushranging incident near Albury in 1857, the papers reported that one of the bushrangers 'has been recognised as a person who formerly filled the post of hangman in Hobart Town'.[7] In Moe early in the 20th century a folk story grew up that a famous Tasmanian bushranger was buried there, named George Sexton, alias 'Three fingered George'. In a bid to eradicate the memory of past horrors, the name Van Diemen's Land was discarded in December, 1855, and Tasmania substituted for it.

By the early 1850s the law and order situation in Victoria was getting worse – bushranging and murder were becoming more common. Two incidents which began at Western Port particularly outraged public opinion. In December, 1852, James Dalton and Andrew Kelly were the only survivors of a group of convicts who escaped from Port Arthur and swam past Eaglehawk Neck. Both had been in constant trouble at Port Arthur and had been sent to the notorious Norfolk Island, from which they had been recently returned. After bailing up people in inns and on farms in southern Van Diemen's Land, they eventually shot dead a watch-house keeper during a raid on a farm, and murdered a Constable Buckmaster during another raid. They then seized a whaleboat and eventually reached Western Port, from where they proceeded separately overland to Melbourne, where both were captured. After being returned to Launceston, they were hanged for the murder of the constable in April, 1853.

A similar but more frightening escapade happened some months later in September, 1853. Henry Bradley and Patrick O'Connor, two convicts also originally from the Norfolk Island, were working on farms near Launceston. They went bush, joined forces and held up a number of farms in the vicinity, killing a man in the process. At Circular Head they boarded the schooner *Sophia* and forced the captain at gunpoint to take them across the strait. A rowboat was commandeered on board ship and they were landed at Cape

Schanck, at a cove still known as Bushranger's Bay or Cove. After paying visits to the Barker's Cape Schanck run and the Boneo run nearby, they then journeyed to Melbourne. At Brighton they held up and pointlessly shot a ploughman. Melbourne was in fear as they moved inland, terrorizing farms in the vicinity of the city and as far north as Gisborne and Kilmore, where they wounded a police cadet in a hold-up, and were later captured. They were hanged in Melbourne in October. During the episode they were dubbed the 'piratical bushrangers' by the Melbourne press, receiving much adverse publicity, and solidifying the already strong feeling against all such Vandemonian desperadoes. After their execution the *Argus* of 26 October, reporting on a phrenological examination on their skulls, concluded that reduced cranial capacity led to their crimes: 'The career of these men since landing here fully coincided with the development of their brains...Nothing but the scientific measurement of their heads could explain their infatuated proceedings. They were murderous ruffians, but they were also incapable fools, in fact, little else than criminal idiots'. The Vandemonians were looked upon as a lower species of the human race, biologically programmed for crime and therefore irredeemable.

The Port Phillip gentlemen were shocked – they didn't want this sort of behaviour in their colony. Papers constantly complained about 'T'othersiders'. As an historian of Tasmania, Lloyd Robson, commented: 'Melbourne grew frightened when rumour had it that the city was threatened by hundreds of escaped Van Diemen's Land convicts'.[8] As a result the Legislative Council of Victoria introduced a Convicts Prevention Act in 1852. The Act treated those who had been pardoned as though they were still felons with a ticket-of-leave – both categories were to be prevented from entering Victoria. This was intended to keep out the Van Diemen's Land element. The Act had some success at major Victorian ports, where ex-convicts were turned back, but the flow continued. However the British government, to the disgust of the Victorian colonists, ruled the Act improper, as British subjects had freedom of movement, so conditionally pardoned people had the right to enter. The Legislative Council was forced to amend its Act. It was at this time, in late 1853, that the Bradley-O'Connor escapade occurred, which steeled Victorians in their desire to keep their colony free from the convict stain. The aspiring novelist, Henry Kingsley, arrived in Melbourne during this period, and his first impression was of Melburnians being worried that an armed outbreak of terrorism in Victoria, led by seasoned Vandemonian criminals, would destroy incipient civil society. Fear of an organized disturbance by VDL villains remained subterranean in Victoria. Kingsley used it as a main theme in his novel *The Recollections of Geoffry Hamlyn*.

The 1850 decision to repatriate Norfolk Island prisoners to Van Diemen's Land meant multiple offenders, like Dalton and Kelly, and Bradley and O'Connor, could now escape to Victoria. William Howitt wrote in reference to these Norfolk Island convicts: 'Victoria will now get these, – the devils of devils, the most hardened and diabolical wretches who curse the earth. They are the vilest of the vile, the incorrigible, the refuse of the mass of convict scoundrelism, who are sent thither from Sydney or Van Diemen's Land to work in chains, whence Norfolk Island is styled the Ocean Hell'.[9] The *Argus* editorialized on 28 September, 1853: 'The consequences of importing the felons of Van Diemen's Land, whether unpardoned or only half-pardoned, have been written in lines of blood in the criminal records of Victoria'. It spoke of 'the frightful crimes which our pages have recorded...nine-tenths of which have been the work of the Van Diemen's land felonry'. After referring to the two recent outrages, it asked:

> Is this the time for Victorian to relax her vigilance? Will she throw open her coasts to the most demoralized band of ruffians that, perhaps, ever existed on earth; and place the lives and property of her people at the mercy of the criminals of Norfolk Island?

At this time Arthur Orton was observing Victorian events from his location in Hobart. On September 18, 1853, he wrote to his former girl friend, Mary Ann Loder, of Wapping: 'The gold diggers and solgers are fighting like tagers in Melbourne as soon as they have done I shall go over and try my luck They sent here last week for 500 more solgers to guard them'. This was a reference to the

Red Ribbon agitation on the Bendigo goldfields in September 1853, where diggers staged a number of demonstrations against the hated licence tax, a dress rehearsal for the Eureka Rebellion a year later. Arthur Orton did join the Van Diemen's Land exodus to Victoria, but did not try his luck as a digger on the goldfields.

Workers and gold-seekers from Van Diemen's Land, including ex-convicts and escapees, usually entered Gippsland through Port Albert. Many brought their Van Diemen's Land lawlessness with them. Most stayed at first near the port at Tarraville, which acquired the nickname of St Giles, after a suburb in London notorious for its criminal element. Some of group became cattle stealers; the Chief Protector of Aborigines, George Robinson, said it was they who inflicted outrages on Aborigines in the area in the early days. George Dunderdale wrote about 'white men who assisted the squatters to diminish the number of their stock. They were principally convicts who had served their sentences, or part of them, in the island, and had come over to Gippsland in cattle vessels...a few of the more enterprising spirits adopted the calling of cattle stealers'.[10] Much later the author Katharine Susannah Prichard remembered that some Port Albert families shrunk when they heard chains, which reminded them of their convict origins.

The *Port Phillip Patriot* reported on 21 September, 1843, that the Port Albert area 'is at present infested with a set of villains recently imported from Hobart Town who commit crime with impunity and then bolt overland'. Three years later the *Argus* reported: 'It would appear that the district is in a most lawless state. The police are exceedingly limited in their numbers, and cannot afford a tythe of the protection required by the inhabitants. It has been known for a cargo of ruffians just imported from Hobart Town, to keep Alberton in a state of riot and dread for a week together, putting the constituted authority at defiance'.[11] Ex-convicts still continued to enter Victoria through Port Albert. In December 1855, two men, John Martin and Edward Grimes, were charged at Alberton with being prisoners of the crown illegally at large. Martin explained that his term had expired before he left Tasmania. But the magistrate, Captain Carey, claimed that under the Convicts Prevention Act an emancipated convict could not come to Victoria until three years after this term of punishment had expired. Martin was sent back to Hobart at the first opportunity.

The *Gippsland Guardian* reported on 15 June, 1860, that 'for some time it has been suspected that a system of wholesale cattle-duffing has been going on in Gipps Land, and parties have been constantly on the watch to detect the plunderers'. The case it was referring to involved the former Hobart butcher, John Dight, who had employed Orton in Hobart. Dight had settled as a butcher at Tarraville near Port Albert, and appeared in a number of court cases there. A dealer named William Morris, assisted by Dight, had delivered a herd of cattle to a Sale butcher, Joseph Taylor, which included a beast belonging to the squatter Turnbull of Rosedale. Dight was 'most anxious to assist in killing the cow in question and afterwards of purchasing the hide.' Taylor was fined £10 for defacing the brand of Turnbull's beast, even though Dight had actually done the defacing. Dight and Morris were charged with cattle-stealing. At their trial at the Palmerston Criminal Sessions at Port Albert in September, 1860, evidence was given that Dight had removed the brand. Taylor stated that the defendants were anxious to have the beast killed quickly. Turnbull gave evidence that Morris had come to him and said he would rather pay £100 than get into trouble about the matter. Nonetheless the jury found Morris and Dight not guilty.[12] John Dight faced a series of minor charges including using obscene language and letting his sheep wander. The VDL lawlessness prevalent at Port Albert later spread to the central plains and to the Gippsland goldfields.

Hundred of thousands of people did arrive in Victoria in the 1850s. But we have also to trace the alleged history of one, Sir Roger Tichborne, who didn't. The claimant, Thomas Castro, alleged he arrived at Melbourne on the ship *Osprey* in 1854, the year before Orton arrived in Victoria. He claimed to be a survivor of a wreck of the *Bella* in the Atlantic Ocean, and had changed his name from Tichborne to Castro on arrival. This led to the supposition that Sir Roger Tichborne had survived his South American disappearance and somehow surfaced in Australia. People surmised that Orton and Tichborne may have known each other in South America, and then independently made their way to Australia and joined up again there. No evidence for this exists, and the known South American dates and movements of Orton and Tichborne show they couldn't have been together there.

After the initial claim by Castro in 1865, alleged memories of Tichborne's existence in Victoria came from many quarters over the next two decades. The main stories were that Tichborne was seen on the Australian goldfields (Ballarat was sometimes mentioned), or that he lived in the Australian bush under an assumed name and was involved in criminal activiries. No evidence of any substance was ever brought forward to show that Tichborne came to Australia. Most claims were made many years later when memories were subject to the massive publicity the case had already generated. Also the variety of the claims and the number of people he was linked with made them dubious, on the grounds that a single claim may be compelling, but a multitude of different claims means people are searching for one. As some members of the Tichborne family had feared, the mother's advertisement became after a time to be a self-fulfilling prophecy: it attracted numerous claims from people who seem, consciously or otherwise, to have rearranged their lives or their memories to fit in with the advertisement's specifications. People desperately wanted Tichborne to have survived and arrived here, since it confirmed a wonderfully mysterious archetype – the aristocrat who goes down to the depths, survives innumerable perils, and then resurrects himself and regains his rightful inheritance. Australia could make or break you, or both.

Castro's story of his arrival in Melbourne had many improbabilities, which were fully exploited by the opposition lawyers in the two Tichborne court cases. His description of the sinking of the *Bella* was not consistent with what experienced mariners knew would happen in such a circumstance. He could not recall the names of the crew and other passengers on the *Osprey*, even though he claimed to have sailed with them from the middle of the South Atlantic Ocean through the Pacific to Melbourne, an immense journey. He said he was suffering from loss of memory and disorientation after the wreck, but by his own account recovered his wits very quickly in Melbourne. No *Osprey* was found to have landed in Melbourne at the stated time, much less one with shipwrecked passengers from the *Bella*. No other *Bella* shipwreck passengers were ever found in Melbourne, in Australia or elsewhere. And the few details Castro did give, like the captain's name, corresponded with details from other sea voyages Arthur Orton was known to have made. Castro didn't arrive in Victoria the way he said he did.

The most plausible story of Tichborne's supposed whereabouts in Australia came from a witness at the 1869 Australian Commission, Benjamin Haywood.[13] Haywood said he had known Tichborne at Cheltenham in England from 1853 onwards. Haywood managed the Sydney Arms Commercial Hotel there, and during the season he would often leave the hotel open all night, serving wine, coffee and grilled turkey, when balls and other festivities were on. A rakish set of young rich layabouts who would drink, gamble, play cards, and go to the races and hunts, and to social occasions like the Bachelors' Ball, frequented Cheltenham. Tichborne was part of this group, and was sometimes, in Haywood's phrase, 'champagne tight'. Haywood was sure he met the same man outside the Ballarat Mining Exchange some years later, about 1863. 'When I saw him in Ballarat', testified Haywood, 'he looked something more like a man wanting five pounds than one able to pay five pounds.' He also met Tichborne some months later in Collins St, Melbourne, when Tichborne was living in Carlton and going by the name of Tom de Castro; Castro had spent, he said, several years on stations stockriding and butchering. Haywood invited Tichborne to his place in Hotham (North Melbourne), and Tichborne promised to visit, but never came. Haywood described Tichborne as having twitching of the eyes, a strange voice and bent knees, all characteristics of Orton, but not of Tichborne.

NOTES

1. This trade is described in Jane Lennon 'Trade and Communications across the Straits: Gippsland to Van Diemen's Land 1814-1851', *Victorian Historical Magazine*, Vol. 44, No. 3-4, 1973, pp. 93-107.

2. Melbourne *Herald*, 14 February, 1902.

3. *Port Phillip Gazette*, 9 March, 1844.

4. *Argus*, 17 July, 1920.

5. *The Trial at Bar of Sir Roger Tichborne,* ed. Dr. Kenealy, 9 vols, 1874-79, Englishman Office, London, Vol. 5, p. 384.

6. William Howitt *Land, Labour and Gold, or two Years in Victoria*, 1855; repr. Lowden, Kilmore, 1972, p. 245.

7. *Argus,* 1 August, 1857.

8. Lloyd Robson *A History of Tasmania*, Oxford University Press, Melbourne, 1983, Vol. 1, p. 511.

9. Howitt, op. cit, p. 232.

10. Dunderdale, op.cit., p. 238.

11. *Argus*, 8 December, 1846.

12. *Gippsland Guardian*, 7 September, 1860.

13. *The Australian Commission*, op. cit. pp. 198-202.

3

STOCKRIDING ON CENTRAL GIPPSLAND RUNS

The Vandemonians moved north along the road from Port Albert to Sale to find work on squatting runs on the central plain of Gippsland, particularly on stations runs owned by Van Diemen's Land businessmen. On the way to Sale they passed the Erinvale property, owned in the 1850s by John Foster of Hobart. His nephew William Foster, and William's wife Sara, managed the property from 1853 to 1856. Squatting properties began in Gippsland after Angus McMillan's European discovery of the province. Gippsland's central plain, open country dotted with trees and crossed by rivers, was ideal for cattle and sheep grazing. The town which evolved on the plain as the pivot of the squatting district was Sale, about 75 kilometers north of Port Albert. The population of Gippsland by the mid 1850s was small, numbering in the low thousands, and the towns were in their infancy. McMillan set up the first two Gippsland properties, Bushy Park and Boisdale, for his patron Lachlan Macalister in 1841; they were to the north of Sale under the lee of the mountain range. Boisdale, between the Macalister and Avon rivers, and Mewburn Park adjacent to it between the Thomson and Macalister rivers, were established soon afterwards. The township of Maffra, originally an outstation of Boisdale, was situated on the boundary between the two runs.

At these and other stations people were employed as horsebreakers, storekeepers, boundary riders, butchers and in similar occupations. Mrs Jessie Harrison, daughter of the pioneering Presbyterian clergyman Rev. W.S. Login, remembered: 'The work was done by labour obtained chiefly from Tasmania...Indeed, at most of the stations, there was some 'old hand' identified with the place, and more firmly fixed than the owner himself...These old

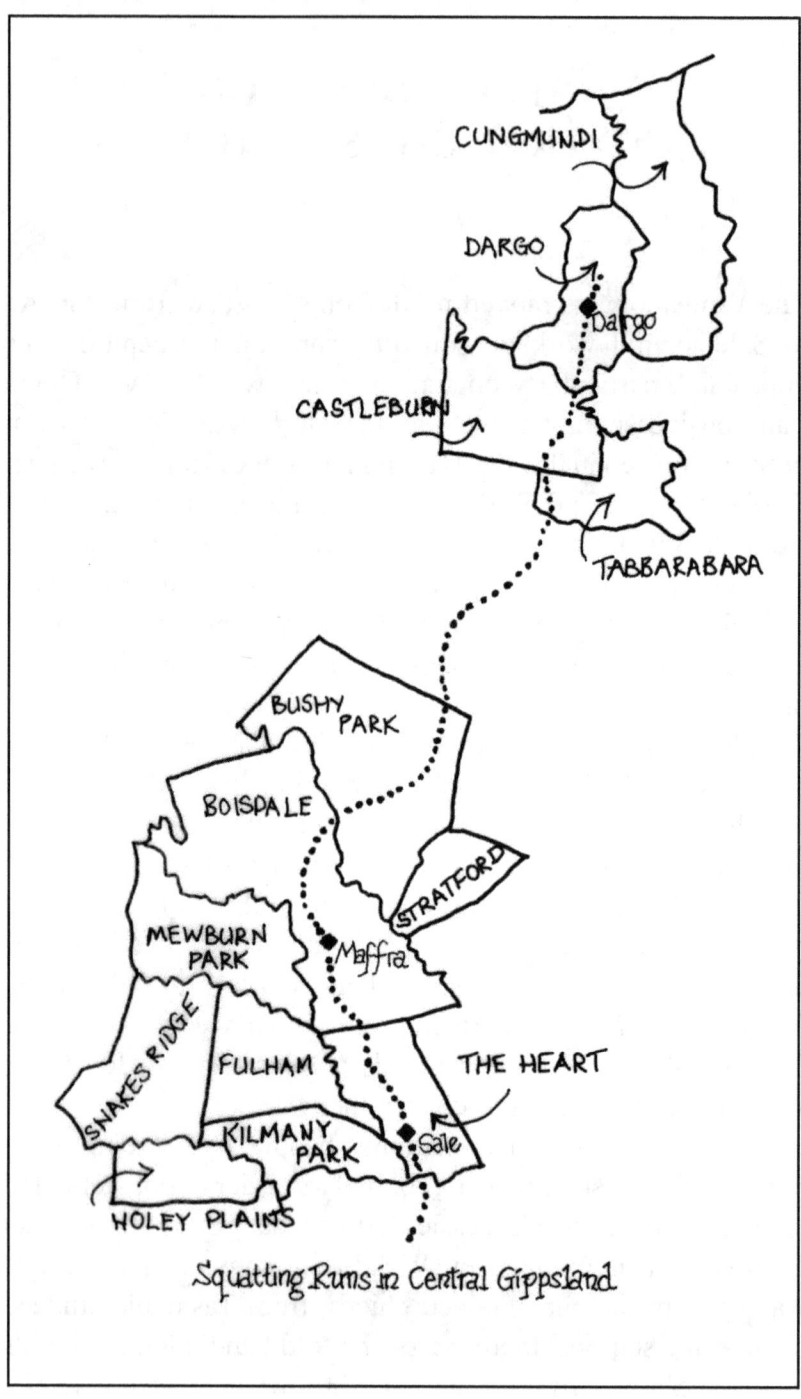
Squatting Runs in Central Gippsland.

station hands were handy men who could turn their hand to any work that had to be done, splitting, fencing, gardening, bullock-driving, cooking, or waiting at table'.[1] By the 1850s Mewburn Park and Boisdale were owned by John Johnson and John Foster, both of whom resided in Hobart. In addition Johnson had a salting down works at Port Albert. William Foster moved from Erinvale to manage the Boisdale run from mid 1865. After his death, his wife Sara married Matthew Macalister, and was an important witness in the Tichborne trial. Her maiden name was Sara du Moulin; she was the sister of the Mewburn Park overseer.

In late 1855 the Tasmanian businessman-squatter John Johnson contracted Orton, as he did other Hobart inhabitants, to work as a butcher and stockrider (Orton's two occupations) on his Gippsland run Mewburn Park. The claimant later described his arrival on the mainland: 'At Port Albert, a cargo of cattle was waiting for the ship. The men bring an extra horse, saddle, and bridle for me to go back with them. The next morning we started on our way to Newburn Park station, where we arrived at 8.30 pm, the distance being about 72 miles'.[2] As part of his duties at Mewburn Park, Orton would on occasions drive cattle to Port Albert with Jacobus Du Moulin, the overseer, for shipment to Hobart. En route he was seen by the Fosters at Erinvale station.

Mewburn Park was a run of 38,000 acres west of Maffra. Originally owned by Lachlan Macalister, it was purchased by Johnson in 1848. The Mewburn Park employees, numbering up to thirty, were a close-knit group, which included former Vandemonians, including some ex-convicts. They were usually rough and ready single males who had their own mores, and often lived on the borderline between legitimate and dubious activities. The Police Inspector Slade wrote on 9 May, 1857: 'Many ticket of leave holders have been sent to Gipps' Land: – such elements are infectious and most seriously influence the moral state of the district'.[3] Many of those in central Gippsland stuck together and later went as a group to the north Gippsland goldfields, where some will reappear in the story. Those at Mewburn Park included: John Higgins, Nicholas Ray and

SUBSCRIPTIONS to the PATRIOTIC FUND from the Upper District of Gipps Land, Victoria, collected by J. Johnson of Mewburn Park.			
James McFarlane	£50	0	0
John Johnson	50	0	0
William Pearson	25	0	0
Isaac Buchanan	10	10	0
J. W. Jones	20	0	0
William Thomson	5	0	0
William Montgomery	5	0	0
B. Cunningham	3	0	0
M. Macalister	2	2	0
A. Campbell	2	0	0
H. M. D. Pearson	2	0	0
From the men on Mewburn Park.			
Jacobus de Monlin, overseer	3	3	0
Neil Were, carpenter	2	0	0
John Luckman, stockman	2	0	0
Colin McLaren, stockman	2	0	0
Arthur Orton, stockman	2	0	0
James Walker, stockman	2	0	0
Thomas Ryan, stockman	2	0	0
Joseph Atkins, gardener	2	0	0
Joseph Freeman, farm servant	2	0	0
William Pritchard, stockman	2	0	0
James Patten, cook	2	0	0
William Rose, cook	2	0	0
John Clothier, sawyer	2	0	0
Henry Hall, sawyer	2	0	0
George Griffith, brickmaker	2	0	0
John Thomas, brickmaker	2	0	0
Thomas Daniel, fencer	2	0	0
James Welsh, fencer	2	0	0
Robert Bell, fencer	2	0	0
Thomas Macnight, fencer	2	0	0
James Wilson, fencer	2	0	0
Thomas Dea, fencer	2	0	0
	£219	13	0

THE CRIMEAN WAR APPEAL

Dunchize, all former Van Diemen's Land butchers like Orton; Thomas Toke, an ex-convict from Van Diemen's Land with many convictions, who worked at Mewburn Park driving a bullock dray; John Luckman, a stockrider, James Andrews, a sawyer, and George Gregory, all three also from Van Diemen's Land. Aleck Nielson, a carpenter from VDL, was a companion of Arthur Orton. Those not from VDL included: William ('Billy the Groom') Robertson; Colin McLaren, an old stockman of McMillan's; Charles Whitburn, horsebreaker and dealer, later a partner of Orton; and 'Flash Harry' Osborne. Orton's existence at Mewburn Park at this time, and that of many others, is confirmed by their listing as subscribers to a Crimean War Appeal in the *Gippsland Guardian* of 30 May, 1856. There is no hard (that is, contemporary or documentary) evidence, as distinct from later word-of-mouth accounts, of a Thomas Castro at Mewburn Park or any other Gippsland property.

The most important of these figures is Thomas Toke, soon to become the leader of the Bogong Jack gang. Toke had a grim previous history.[4] He was raised in Kent, where he was first charged with larceny, and then at the age of fifteen in 1825 was sentenced at Maidstone, Kent, to seven years' transportation for stealing, his

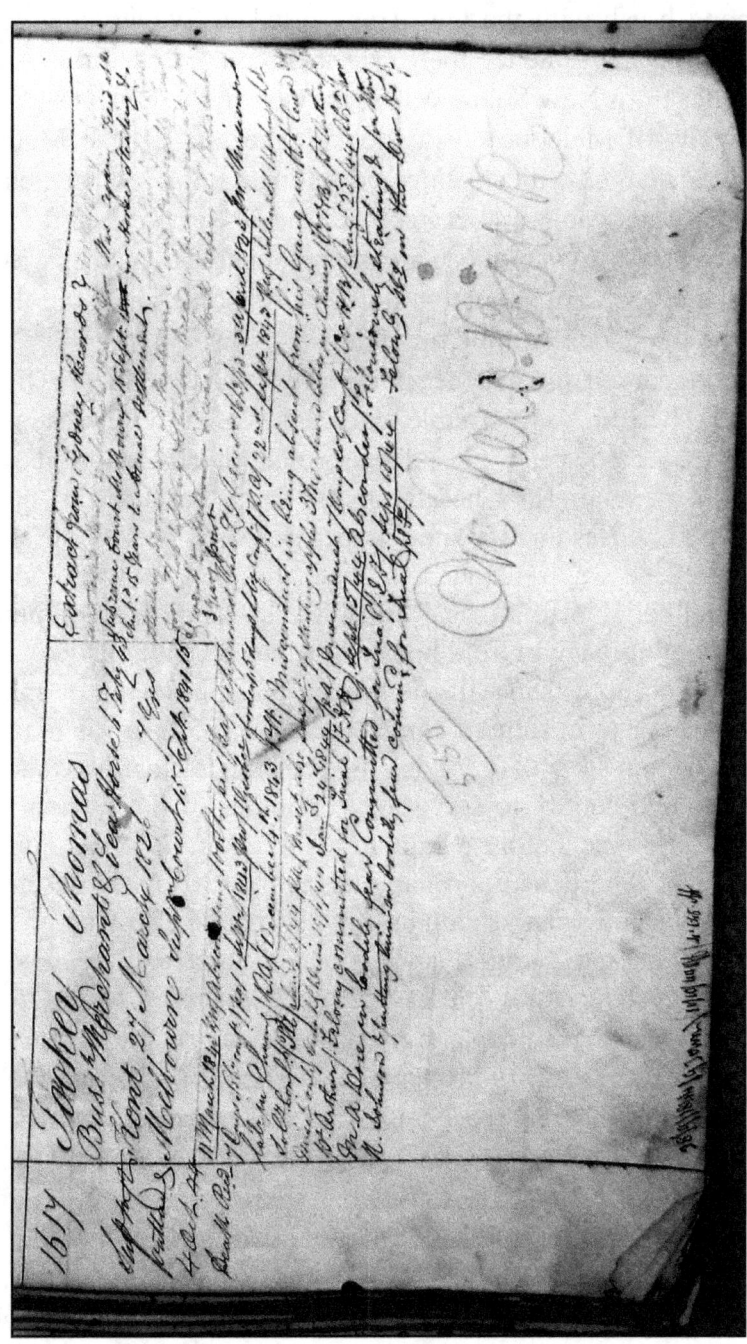

THE VDL CONVICT FILE OF THOMAS TOKE (TOOKEY)

second brush with the law. Transported to Sydney as a convict, he served his sentence there. He then entered Victoria as an ex-convict from New South Wales, moving in the early 1840s to the new city of Melbourne as a stock-keeper. In 1841 in Melbourne he was charged with stealing and selling a horse, and sentenced to fifteen years gaol. At this stage he was 30 years old, 5 ft 6 inches in height, swarthy, tattooed and scared, unable to read or write, and with a speech impediment – not very prepossessing, and the very image in the public mind of a felon.

Toke served this sentence initially at Port Arthur in Van Diemen's Land. There he was in trouble for breaches of discipline, absconding and suspected stealing, and was often in chains or in solitary confinement. In 1844 he absconded from the barracks, breaking into two houses and threatening people while on the loose. When captured he was sentenced to death, but was sent instead to the convict hell, Norfolk Island, in 1845. Here his woes continued; he was continuously in trouble, with further convictions like assault, and spent more than half his time at Norfolk Island in chains, at hard labour or in solitary confinement. In 1850 he was returned to Van Diemen's Land, following the decision to close Norfolk Island as a prison centre, to serve the remainder of his original fifteen years' sentence, before regaining his freedom in 1856.[5] This is the record of a hardened and habitual criminal. He was described in the Gippsland press as having 'long borne the character of being a doubly convicted expiree and a reputed horse and cattle stealer'.[6] Toke played a central role in subsequent events.

Many of these people were shady characters who resorted to assumed names to avoid the law. Convicts who had served their time and did not want their past known often changed their names, as did escapees. Nicknames were common, as people assumed fluid and often multiple identities. At Mewburn Park, for example, there were workers called 'Bristol Jack', 'the old milkman' and 'Possum Jack'. Many changed their names as they changed their localities, which was quite frequent. John Riley, book-keeper at the Royal Exchange Hotel in Sale, recalled: 'I knew the customers better by their nicknames than their real names...some men remain unknown to me by their real names to this day; they were entered by such names as Jemmy the Native, Old Damn your Skin, Greenhide Jack, the Man with the Cabbage-tree Hat, the Wooden Leg, Pack Bullock Jack; some word or name taken from what they said or what described them'.[7] People who wanted an alias found it best not to use an invented surname, which drew attention to itself, but one already in circulation. This creates great difficulties in trying to pin down such chameleon characters. Did the same surnames or nicknames always attach to them? Arthur Orton himself was known on central Gippsland properties variously as the 'the butcher' or 'Arthur the Butcher'.

It is noticeable how many people of shady reputation in this era are dealers in cattle and horses. In the economic slump of the 1840s, sheep and cattle were boiled down for tallow, and people in this unskilled occupation were loosely called 'butchers'. Butchers on goldfields were often suspect, as it was easy to steal cattle, cut them up and then sell the meat to the large goldfields' populations; no identification of the original beast was then possible. Similarly people in trades connected with horses – ostlers, grooms, horse dealers, pound keepers, jockeys, horse breakers – were often engaged in suspicious activities. Horses would be stolen, rebranded at a hideaway, and then taken to another district to be sold. Horses were relatively expensive items, and stealing them was a serious offence. At the time an ordinary horse could be worth £5-£10, a fair one £20, a good one £40-£50, and champion up to £100. When annual wages for an unskilled worker were maybe £100 per annum, horses were valuable property; like a car today, they were worth roughly a third of a year's wages. Horses once sold were supposed to have a receipt of sale, but this was often missing or forged. So horses often had flexible identities, like their owners. Many individuals had a past they were concealing or getting away from. Identifying both horses and humans was therefore often difficult. This is one of the problems – and fascinations – of this story.

Orton remained working at Mewburn Park run for sixteen months till December, 1856, when he left under a cloud. Orton and his friend Alex Nielsen injured one of Johnson's horses while riding it as a prank, or perhaps filching it. Nielsen absconded from the property and ran away to the Nicholson River because Johnson was 'in such a way about it'. A correspondent, J. Le Sage, later wrote about this incident: 'the groom [Nielsen] bolted, to avoid Mr. J[ohnson]'s wroth, and as Arthur Orton was known to be implicated he never dared to show up on that station afterwards'.[8] If so, it was a characteristic Orton exit – absconding from an uncomfortable situation created by himself.

In December, 1856, Orton moved to Foster's nearby station, Boisdale, where he worked initially for about six months till May, 1857. Foster had brought this 57,600 acre property from Macalister in 1847-8. It was perhaps the finest property in Gippsland, carrying 4,000 cattle and 8,000 sheep in 1856, the heaviest stocking of any run. At one stage Foster had eight stations in Gippsland, totalling 180,000 acres. Orton had similar work to that at Mewburn Park as a butcher, stockman and sheep-washer. There were ten to fifteen employees on the station. At Boisdale his workmates included: William Hopgood, an ex Vandemonian convict; William Higgins and Dunchize from Mewburn Park; and James Davidson, later connected with Orton. But there was not as extensive an ex-Vandemonian network at Boisdale as at Mewburn Park. The storekeeper at Boisdale in the mid 1840s was called John Paine, probably the John Paynter, the son of the Hobart butcher who employed Orton, who was later prominent at Omeo. Once again Orton drove cattle to Port Albert, and Andrew Hutton, a pioneer Gippsland stockman, remembered driving cattle to Melbourne with Foster, Orton and others. As a result of the goldrushes, Melbourne had a large population by the mid 1850s and gradually began to supplant Van Diemen's Land, where convict numbers were declining, as the prime market for Gippsland cattle. Horses were bred by Foster at Boisdale and at other properties for the growing Victorian population. Mrs Foster remembered treating Orton at Boisdale for minor illnesses, like the flu, and giving him books to read from the Boisdale station library.

After Gippsland's central plain had been filled up, properties in less accessible areas were sought out. On the Dargo spur in the mountains to the north of central Gippsland four remote runs were set up: Dargo and Castleburn, owned by Foster, and Cungmungi and Tabberabbera, owned by Angus McMillan, all nominally of about 16,000 acres. Like later mountain leases, they were used as back-up properties well away from the main stations, where heifers could be raised away from bulls, and weaners finished off. They were isolated runs, with no settlements in the area; the workers lived in huts. In May, 1857, Orton, still in the employ of the Fosters, was sent to manage their outstation at Dargo. Orton's job was to take up mobs of weaners and heifers for a few months and then bring them back. One of the tracks leading north from Boisdale to the Dargo area was known locally as Arthur's Track. For his work Orton received a rise of pay to £80 or £100 pounds a year (it was later a matter of dispute), not the usual pay of 25 shillings a week. Among those he mixed with at Dargo were workers, mainly Highland Scots, from McMillan's adjacent run of Cungmungi, including Samuel Campbell, Norman Nicholson and Archibald McDonald. They remembered Orton used to shoot at cherry trees and hunt game. This shooting practice in the wild uplands of Australia was later to stand him in good stead among the gentlemen of England.

At Dargo a curious incident occurred. Orton received a letter, but the seal had been broken. So he inscribed a novel *The Rivals*, which he had borrowed from the Boisdale library, in the following way:

> This day i have received a Letter from Donald MacDonald With the Seal Broken I Arthur Orton here make a vow on this Book Although not a Bible. It bear a cross. That has i am a man of Bone Bloud and flesh. That i will find out the Man if possible. That broke the said Seal. And that i will punish him according to the laws of. My Countrie
>
>   Sined   Arthur Orton
>
>   Dargo
>
> 11 March 1858.[9]

This letter reveals a ferocity and litigiousness out of proportion to the imagined slight. It also doesn't read like a letter written by an English aristocrat.

A much more serious event occurred immediately after this. A worker at Dargo, Norman Gillespie, saw the ex-convict Thomas Toke, now based at Omeo, with a miner named Ballarat Harry in Orton's hut at Dargo in March, 1858. Both had come from the Omeo diggings, where they had been with other Mewburn Park old hands. This was an important sighting, as it was one of the last times Ballarat Harry was seen alive – he was soon presumed murdered. The letter with the broken seal, to which Orton attached so much importance, may have been connected with the Ballarat Harry affair, as it occurred only a week before Toke and Ballarat Harry arrived. After Harry's disappearance in suspicious circumstances, Orton suddenly left Dargo and returned to Boisdale unannounced. William Foster's wife, Sara, recalled the incident: 'When [my husband] saw a man coming towards the house, he said, "Why that's roan Tommy, Arthur Orton's horse, what can he want down here, there must be something wrong, as he would never come without permission unless there were". When he came near, my husband asked him why he left, he said he could not stay at Dargo after the reported disappearance of a man named Ballarat Harry, it was too lonely'.[10] Orton may have reasonably feared being bumped off himself by Toke at the remote Dargo outstation in order to eliminate a witness to Ballarat Harry's disappearance. In June Thomas Toke was arrested on suspicion of having murdered Ballarat Harry. Orton told Norman Gillespie after returning to Boisdale that he was surprised that he [Orton] hadn't been subpoenaed in connection with this case. The disappearance and apparent murder of Ballarat Harry was to become an issue at the claimant's later trial in England, as his suspected involvement didn't do his reputation any good. This incident is a further connection between the Tichborne and Bogong Jack cases, as Toke was the leader of the Bogong Jack gang at the time.

When Arthur Orton arrived back at Boisdale after Ballarat Harry's disappearance in mid 1858, he continued to work for the Fosters on the property. However a dispute developed between him and his employer over his wages, which Foster maintained had to be reduced, now that he was not in a foreman position as at Dargo. As a result of the dispute, Foster discharged Orton for insubordination and want of skill on 8 October, 1858. The last date he is recorded in the Boisdale account books is 5 October. Orton, familiar with litigation, then took court action against Foster for £158 9s 2d. in lost wages. Both parties appointed arbitrators, who in turn handed the case over to a referee, Mr Robert Cunningham. He concluded in January, 1859, that there was no evidence that Foster had offered Orton £100 per year at Dargo, and awarded Orton £18 14s in discharging him from the job. This meant Orton had effectively lost the case.

Orton had left Mewburn Park, Dargo and Boisdale when trouble ensued at each place. After leaving Boisdale there was still the court case over wages, his own threat of a case over the broken seal (a minor matter), and the Ballarat Harry murder (a major matter). Orton was continuing his Hobart pattern of getting into trouble, then moving on to evade the consequences. To the world at large he was later known only as the Tichborne claimant, but concealed from public view was an extensive prehistory of debt problems and minor court cases. The Tichborne case was a much larger version of his earlier behaviour patterns. In this he was like another Australian figure of mystery and legend, Louis Lasseter. Known only to the public in his later life when he set out on his famous journey to find his lost reef – his Tichborne claim – we now know from Murray Hubbard's researches in *The Search for Harold Lasseter* (1993) that Lasseter's earlier life included a whole series of minor deceptions, as well as extravagant and unrealistic claims. Orton and Lasseter had similar fantasy-addicted personalities.

The claimant said that he had been rescued by the ship *Osprey* and taken to Melbourne in July, 1854. At a horse bazaar in Melbourne, he claimed, he had met the manager William Foster who had offered him a job at Boisdale station in central Gippsland, saying it 'was a very jolly life to lead in the bush – plenty of hunting and shooting'.[11] He had accepted the offer and claimed he had worked at Boisdale from that time till February, 1856, when he moved as a station hand to Dargo. There he worked, he said, till August, 1857, when he returned to Boisdale, where he worked until November, 1857.

After that he lived around Sale till May, 1858. Castro's account of his activities in Gippsland closely parallel those of the butcher from Wapping and Hobart, Arthur Orton, which led to the strong suspicion they were the same person. The list does get the sequence of Orton's work at Boisdale, Dargo, Boisdale again and then Sale correct, but the dates are wrong.[12] This was because at the start of his story he had to cover up his Hobart period, and at the end to cover up his disappearance from Gippsland and his surfacing in the Riverina under a new name.

NOTES

1 *The Wind Still Blows,* eds. John Leslie and Helen Cowie, Sale, 1973, pp. 26-7.

2 *The Confession*, op. cit., p. 6.

3 Public Records Office Victoria (PROV), Police Correspondence, VPRS 937, Unit 227, Bundle 4.

4 In an unpublished paper held at the Omeo Historical Society Jenny Cowans has provided a history of Thomas Toke and his connections with the Toke-Paynter gang.

5 Toke's convict record, under the name Thomas Tookey, is No. 1617, p. 550, in the Tasmanian Convict Records.

6 Edward Watson, Letter to the Editor, *Gippsland Guardian*, 15 April, 1859.

7 *The Australian Commission*, op. cit., p. 193.

8 *Gippsland Mercury*, July 30, 1874.

9 *The Australian Commission*, op. cit., p. 204.

10 Ibid, p. 93.

11 *The Trial at Bar of Sir Roger Tichborne*, op. cit., Vol. I, p. 63.

12 This was known in Irish legal circles as a Kerry alibi, as it was prevalent in that county: 'Its essence was that the story was true in every respect except one: the date.' Maurice Healy *The Old Munster Circuit*, Michael Joseph, London, 1939, p. 168.

4

LAWLESSNESS AROUND SALE AND STRATFORD

After leaving Boisdale in early October, 1858, and waiting for his court case against Foster, Orton led a desultory life around Sale for the next nine months. Sale was emerging as the focus of the province, though still only small, with about five hundred people in the town and the same number in the district surrounding it. It commanded a prime position on transport routes, where the north-south road from Port Albert to Omeo crossed the east-west road from west Gippland to the Gippsland Lakes. Orton, moving into a low-life phase, was observed working in various occupations and odd jobs around the Sale area. At one stage he was charcoal burning on the morass formed by Flooding Creek near the town, at another he sank a waterhole on a property on the Stratford road, and was employed splitting logs at the backwater near Sale.

But most of Orton's jobs were connected with horses. He partnered Charles Whitburn, an old Mewburn Park hand, in horse-breaking. He also worked as a groom looking after the stables at Duncan Clark's Royal Exchange Hotel in Sale, and at the same time took a stallion around to local farmers for a service. At this hotel his fellow boarder was Harry Pearson, then working as a pound-keeper. Pearson had been a Senior Sergeant in the Mounted Police Detective Force. Before that he had been a member of the Native Police, and had served at the McIvor diggings.[1] Pearson had been discharged from the police by Inspector Slade, the superintendent in charge of Gippsland police, for making false entries while running the Tarraville police station.[2] Orton and Pearson sold Gippsland and Murray River horses together at Bendigo and Castlemaine later on in the 1850s. Pearson's subsequent history was dodgy. After leaving Clark's hotel Orton moved to the house of James

Davidson, an old Boisdale hand, and broke in horses with him. He also broke in horses with a man called 'Jack the shepherd', and had a mate called 'Jack the devil', perhaps the same person. Orton frequented the Turf Hotel. Jacob Greenwood recalled him there: 'While at the hotel he was a rowdy, fast sort of fellow, would just as soon fight as not, could use his hands'.[3] John Hull described him from those days: 'He was very ungainly-looking, slobberly made, rough and uncultivated...very fond of expressing his mind by continuous talking...Orton never had much brains; but he was very cunning.'[4]

At the later Australian Commission of 1869 investigating the Tichborne claim those who supported the claimant had to show that there were two separate people, Orton and Castro, as Orton's real background was becoming known by this time. As a result many witnesses remembered, about fifteen years after the events, two people who went around as mates at the time. Some people remembered Orton during this period around Sale in the company of a mate who was like him, but slighter. Sometimes the two were said to be known as Tom and Arthur, presumably representing Castro and Orton. At other times the second person was known as George Smith, nicknamed 'George the Butcher'. But in some accounts Orton himself was said to have passed under the name of George Smith, which further confuses the picture. Arthur Orton, it was said, used the names Morgan, Horton, Alfred and George Smith, 'George the Butcher', Brown, and Arthur Graham during his Australian career, and of course, later and famously, Tom Castro. But these memories were retrospective, and may have been subconsciously adjusted to fit in with current theories. The mysterious concept of the *doppelganger*, the alleged coexistence of two allegedly similar types, secret sharers in each other's fate, here comes into play. Twins and doubles are a common element in folk tales, sometimes as similar types and sometimes as opposites. These neat, symmetrical patterns appeal to the folk imagination, and seem to have proliferated in the retrospective accounts of Orton/Castro and his alleged mate. In these speculations the notion of the *doppelganger* merges with the common notion of two mates wandering around the Australian bush.

The presence of a 'foreigner' was often mentioned in these later memories. William Hopgood and William Higgins said there was a Frenchman at Mewburn Park, whose name was 'Franco'. Norman Nicholson claimed he 'heard Mr. McMillan say when Orton first came to Boisdale that there was a Baronet in Mr. Foster's employ as a stockman'.[5] Angus McMillan's wife recalled they used to entertain an aristocratic Frenchman at home. McMillan met him at Dargo; he said he was going under a false name after a family quarrel. She identified a photograph as 'the French Lord'. As Tichborne was educated in France and was equally fluent in French and English, these stories naturally later gave rise to the possibility that the Frenchman was the missing Sir Roger Tichborne.

One Frenchman can, however, be identified there with some certainty. Alex Nielsen said there was a man at Mewburn Park called Michie or 'Micky the Frenchman'. This man also appeared in Arthur Orton's deposition on the Ballarat Harry murder. He was known to Thomas Toke, who used him in an alibi in the case of Ballarat Harry's disappearance. At the inquest on Ballarat Harry, a storekeeper, James Davis, said the ramrod and moulds belonging to Toke's pistol had been taken to Micky the Frenchman at Bruthen. When a bushranger shot Constable Black in 1857 the fugitive hid from police at 'Micky the Frenchmen's' hut on the Glenmaggie run. Micky the Frenchman mixed with a gang of dubious characters who moved from Mewburn Park via the Nicholson River to Omeo.

Interestingly enough, there was a character around Sale at the time who fitted some of these characteristics. William Dexter, an English painter who had spent a considerable time in France, came to live with his wife at Stratford in early 1856. He could have been the Frenchman or the 'foreigner' people remembered. He too brought horses off Whitburn, the person who worked with Orton. Dexter lived in a house on McMillan's run, and, as we have already seen, Mrs Millan remembered them entertaining an aristocratic Frenchman, whom McMillan also met at Dargo. Dexter frequented the Royal Exchange Hotel in Sale, singing to and entertaining the crowd. This was a haunt of Orton when he was groom there. Dexter sketched a Dargo Aboriginal woman, so he had a connection with that remote place, as Orton did. Dexter lived for a time in 1858 in a hut on the morasses near Sale, where Orton worked as a charcoal burner. Both were indulging in low life at the time. Dexter employed a person who had lived in South America, called John Heurtley, to shoot game for him so he could sketch it. Could this have been Arthur Orton, with a South American period of residency in his background and a known good shot, under another alias? Despite these intriguing parallels, there is no known link between Orton and Dexter.

The lawlessness which had characterized Van Diemen's Land and Port Albert earlier on had by the mid 1850s moved to Sale and surrounding areas. In particular Stratford, close to the Mewburn Park and Boisdale runs, became a centre of rowdy activity and a trouble spot for police. Stratford had two hotels, the Shakespeare Hotel and the Bridge Inn, one of which, the police reported, was a disorderly house with constant assaults and violence. Inebriated bullock drivers gave the place a bad atmosphere. Police at Sale had to send out daily patrols to supervise the town. Cattle-duffing and horse-stealing were rife in the district. In late 1855 the police department decided to move the policeman stationed at Yanakie to Stratford as 'it is improbable that any escaped prisoners from Tasmania would attempt to land on that coast during such as tempestuous winter as this'.[6] In July, 1856, the Rev. P.K. Simmons complained to police of constant outbreaks of lawlessness at Stratford. In February, 1857, a man named Jack Ratcliffe was robbed of a watch and a cheque at Stratford after a night's drinking. Although he reported this to police in order to have the cheque cancelled, he wouldn't dob in to the police the names of his mates, who were a gang of old hands.[7]

On 15 May, 1857, a victim of cattleduffing, calling himself 'Sufferer', wrote a letter called 'Wholesale Cattle Stealing' to the *Gippsland Guardian* claiming 'cattle-slaughtering prevails to a great extent, and losses both of horses and cattle have been suffered by many possessing stock of this kind in Sale and its neighbourhood'. He noted that 'a charge of the above very serious nature has been preferred against one who has long since had the name of a cattle stealer, a Vandemonian expiree'. After getting off through lack of evidence, this man was soon seen after driving fourteen cattle into his own stockyards. The letter-writer then lists some other cases of horse stealing, many of which he attributes to 'a well-known organized band of horse stealers residing about Stratford'. He laments that although the guilty parties are well-known, difficulty of detection, a reluctance to prosecute and insufficient police mean the problem continues without resolution.

These cattle and horse thieves are similar to Arthur Orton's ex-Van Diemen's Land buddies at Mewburn Park, and those he mixed with around Sale. This Stratford gang may have been a forerunner of the Bogong Jack gang at Omeo, since we know that some of the latter's members were on the central plain around Sale and Stratford at the time, for example Thomas Toke, William 'the Groom' Robertson, William Armstrong and John Paine/Paynter. Orton was dealing with horses at the time, he was charged with horse stealing at Sale, as we shall see, he mixed with suspected horse-thieves like Harry Pearson, so it is likely he was associated in some way with the horse-stealing fraternity of the central plain. The police were aware of far-flung cattle and horse stealing operations. Inspector Slade reported in June, 1855, that 'a system of horse stealing may be going on from "Maneroo" and Gipps' Land, which can only be stopped by the police at the "Moe".' [8] Two months later he reported that 'a warrant is now out against William Armstrong charged with stealing a horse in the upper district'. Armstrong was a few years later a member of the gang connected with Bogong Jack Paynter gang at Omeo.

One outbreak of cattle and horse rustling occurred at Stratford in mid 1855. The culprit was 'Hopping Andy' Hickson, who had previously been charged with horse-stealing in Melbourne. While he was living in the Stratford area, the police noted that he had the 'worst name in this district as being a noted horse and cattle stealer'. He was seen acting suspiciously at Isaac Buchanan's property at Roseneath and around the lakes in general. Buchanan complained to the police that four of his working horses were missing. The police, who had set up a system of patrolling the main road between Stratford and Delvine, and between Delvine and Bairnsdale, put Hickson, who was observed with a well-packed swag, under surveillance when they learned that he was planning to take a group of stolen horses and cattle to sell at Melbourne, with the intention of then absconding to England. 'Hopping Andy' was seen at Delvine and in the Stratford yards with horses and cattle, and the police took copies of the brands of the cattle without Hickson's knowledge. Two constables were quickly despatched to the Moe River to trap him there, as it was on the only track through to Melbourne. But 'Hopping Andy' got wind of the police plans, and turned the animals adrift; the horses went back to their previous runs. Hickson returned to live and settle down at Stratford unscathed by this episode.[9]

'Sufferer's' letter of May, 1857, was occasioned by the worst outbreak of crime in central Gippsland, during which the whole district was terrorized. (This was at the time Orton was going to Dargo to manage the property there). A man from near Stratford who was splitting and fencing with his mate 'Hopping Andy' Hickson, and was known locally as 'Jack the Fencer', went on a rampage. After being seen at Bennison's Hotel, Sale, he first robbed a house at Stratford, then hired a horse by paying the owner him with the proceeds of the robbery. Pursued to a hotel on the Bairnsdale road twelve miles east of Stratford, he was caught but escaped. Later he returned to Sale and stole horses and saddles from a builder, Mr. Williams, then held up his mate, the sawyer 'Hopping Andy' Hickson, at Nuntin near Stratford, unsuccessfully demanding money but stealing a horse from him. Constable Black, the lone policeman stationed at Stratford, and another policeman pursued him as far as Marshall's Captain Cook Inn near Bruthen (a favourite haunt of horse-stealers), where he was found in the company of two other men with pack horses. Black fired at him to arrest him but the bushranger returned the fire, shooting the policeman in the face, and then beating him severely about the face and head. The bullet lodged in Constable Black's head, rendering him unconscious. (The ball was later extracted from Black's head, but he took a long time to recover.) The bushranger then robbed his companions and Constable Black, from whom he took a saddle, pistol, handcuffs and watch, and escaped.

The police were soon in pursuit. After the affray 'Jack the Fencer' stole a horse at Bairnsdale, and was sighted around Sale and at properties in the vicinity over the next two months. The three police officers located at Sale were exhausted by the pursuit, and as a result local citizens, organized by Commissioner Tyers, were forced to take up contributions to pay two locals to hunt for him. However none of the citizens of Sale were willing to be enrolled as voluntary constables to try to arrest him, so intimidated were they by the violence and lawlessness. The fugitive stopped for a night with the shepherd 'Micky the Frenchman' at MacFarlane's Glenmaggie run, and took rations and a revolver from him.

Police files reveal that 'Jack the Fencer' was previously known to them. He had been a prisoner at Melbourne gaoled for horse-stealing, and had committed the same offence at Ballarat. Known as Jemmy and Johnny Boy, he had been taken into custody at Bunyip River at Western Port and charged with horse stealing on 4 February that year but had escaped. He was next known to have worked in charge of mail horses at Blind Joe's Hut on the Snake Ridge run at Rosedale, but had absconded from that job.[10] In his retirement a former Premier of Victoria, Alan McLean, gave his version of events:

> There were two men employed on his father's station [at Glenaladale], an old and young man. The elder drew the money of both, and would not give up the young man's share. The latter procured a carbine, stuck up the old chap, took all his money, his horse and saddle, and cleared out for the ranges. The one trooper named Black who had lately arrived at the settlement chased him, came up to his camp, fired and missed. The other returned the fire, shot the trooper in the mouth and left him for dead. After taking his money and arms the young bushranger got clean away and was never again heard of.[11]

The details here are clearly a version of the incident described above, with the bushranger being the younger mate of Andy Hickson.

The bushranger probably left the district forever and changed his name.

The theft problem in central Gippsland did not abate. In June, 1858, a meeting at Sale was called over the number of horses and cattle stolen in the region. There were still insufficient police. Duncan Clark of the Royal Exchange Hotel decided to start up a society for the prevention of horse and cattle stealing, as had been done in other areas. But the rustling continued. In April of next year, 1859, Edward Saunders and Daniel Scott were taken to the Sale Court by Simon Gillies and Charles McLean, Alan McLean's father, of Glenaladale run, charged with having taken cattle off the run without the owners' permission. The Police Magistrate, Captain Carey, found them guilty, and fined them £20 each. Gillies remarked in court that he had brought on the case to stop a series of annoyances which he and his partner had been the victim of for some years.

The notorious bushrangers Dan Morgan and John Piesley had possible connections with Gippsland and with Orton. According to Harry Peck in his *Memoirs of a Stockman*, Morgan was working on Black's Tarwin Meadow station around 1850. A man who claimed to have been known Orton at this stage, J. Le Sage, later said that Orton, who sometimes went under the name of Morgan, was in fact the bushranger Dan Morgan who was eventually shot at Peechelba.[12] This story is not true, but hints at some connection during Orton's Gippsland days. Orton was certainly fascinated by Morgan and his career, and later claimed he knew both Morgan and Piesley.

Piesley's history is so confusing that historians of bushranging have speculated that there were two John Piesleys. The bushranger of that name who was hanged in 1862 is thought to have been born in NSW in 1834. But Tasmanian convict records record a John Paisley transported in 1823 with a 14 year sentence, and given a conditional pardon in 1834. Castro 'mentioned Gippsland in conversation about Piesly', implying that he knew him there.[13] In his *Confession*, the claimant wrote about 'Johnny Paisley, the celebrated bushranger at that time. I knew Johnny for years. He was a native, and came from Stratford-on-Avon in Gippsland'.[14] A John Peisley is listed in the Gippsland Electoral Roll of 1856 living at Stratford. The local Piesley may have been part of the Stratford gang. The *Gippsland Guardian* of 18 September, 1857, reported that thieves had broken into the premises of Mr. Leeson, watchmaker and jeweller of Sale, but had missed a nugget of gold belonging to a Mr. Paisly of Stratford. Paisley was involved in another unusual episode at Stratford. In June 1855 John Brown, John Paisley and John Dargan, all of Stratford, went to the pound to release Brown's horse. Though Brown was very drunk and could hardly stay on the horse, the other two let him pursue other horses, but he did not return. He was later found dead with a broken neck; given the records of Piesley and Dargan, foul play could be suspected. The John Dargan in this story abducted the daughter of the manager of Bolden's run and was caught by police on the way to the Monaro. Dargan later appears at Omeo with associates of Bogong Jack Paynter.

By the middle of 1859 a host of familiar legal and financial problems beset Orton. He owed money to a saddler, Daniel Sayer, and to Douglas Manson of Sale. At the same time he was still under some suspicion in relation to the murder of Ballarat Harry. In addition in June he and a man named Aleck (probably his friend from the Mewburn Park escapade, Aleck Nielsen) were charged by police warrant with stealing a mare belonging to a Thomas Blacker. The warrant read:

> ARTHUR ORTON is charged, on warrant issued at Sale, with stealing, on the 22nd ultimo, from there, a chestnut mare...the property of one Thomas Blacker. Description of the offender: About 5ft. 9 or 10 in high, stout built, pale complexion, fair hair, fair whiskers, one front tooth wanting in upper jaw, by trade a butcher, and is a good jockey and horse-breaker. He is supposed to have proceeded to Melbourne, per the steamer Shannon on the 26th ultimo.-29th May, 1859.[15]

The prospect of being brought to court on the Blacker case may have focussed attention on Orton and resurrected other cases. This threat would have worried Orton, so he characteristically disappeared from Gippsland for good; this meant the warrant for his arrest over Blacker's horse could not be executed. In his *Confession* the claimant omits the existence of the warrant; he writes that because of the failure of his venture with the stallion at Duncan Clark's: 'I left Flooding Creek and went to Port Albert and took the steamer for Melbourne.'[16] Police files show that Sergeant Coleman of Sale Police Station reported on 9 June, 1859, that the chestnut mare 'stolen from "Thomas Blacker" by one "Arthur Ortin" has been recovered. The animal in question has been found at Mr. Taylors Station in the lower District of Gipps Land and it appears to have been turned loose by "Ortin" after riding it to Port Albert'.[17] Orton's pattern of evading reality by moving on was repeated. This move ended the rather inglorious Gippsland career of a man who was later destined for international fame. His two long trials in England brought Gippsland, its large properties and its low life, to wider attention,

When Arthur Orton left Sale under a cloud in May, 1859, he went to Melbourne by steamer, as the police suspected. He was seen at Erinvale on the way to Port Albert. After staying in Melbourne a few days, he took a coach to Kilmore and then went to look for work at Reedy Creek, a goldmining community in the hills east of Kilmore and north of Yea. Reedy Creek had its own dubious element. Just as Orton arrived there in late May, three men were apprehended on its diggings for holding up and robbing the Beechworth mail-coach between Broadford and Seymour on the Melbourne road. The Reedy Creek diggings, being near Kilmore, had a heavy Irish population. Orton took employment from June till November, 1859, with the Irish storekeepers and butchers McManus and Soraghan; he was known there as 'Arthur the Slaughterman'. He told Patrick McManus of his troubles with horses in Sale, but on meeting his old friend Norman Gillespie there, warned him not to tell anyone of his Gippsland past. After leaving his job with McManus, Orton spent a few weeks in December, 1859, driving horses and carting.

Orton got into familiar trouble at Reedy Creek. The horses of a man named Phillips went missing, and Phillips offered a reward for them; Orton offered to go and find them, claiming he knew where they were. This was a common ruse of those who had stolen horses, since if they found them, they could get a reward, yet not be prosecuted for stealing. But Orton never returned, which threw suspicion on him. In his *Confession*, the claimant said he 'borrowed – or rather – stole' McManus's horse to leave the Reedy Creek diggings. At any event he cleared out from Reedy Creek in the same way as he had left so many other localities in which he had lived. Reedy Creek in December, 1859, was one of the last places he used the name Arthur Orton; his name changed with the decade. He never used the name in his subsequent Riverina career. As the 1860s broke, he became Tom Castro. He seems to have changed his name, not as the first step in wiping out his past to prepare himself to become Sir Roger Tichborne, but simply to avoid a few local horse-stealing charges. In the Tichborne case, the prosecution described 1859 as the missing year in Castro's life. The claimant could not account for it since it was the time he changed his name. He had to put some distance between the two identities of Orton and Castro.

NOTES

1   See Letter by Henry Pearson, 6 April, 1854, PROV, Police Correspondence, VPRS 937, Unit 226, Bundle 1.

2   Ibid., Bundle 3.

3   This quotation comes from an entry in the so-called Stewart Diary, compiled by someone, perhaps a policemen, who attended sittings of the Australian Commission in Gippsland; a copy is in the National Library of Australia, NLA MS 1816.

4   *The Trial at Bar of Sir Roger Tichborne*, Vol. I, p. 255.

5   Stewart Diary, op. cit.

6   Police Correspondence, VPRS 937, Unit 226, Bundle 3.

7   Police Correspondence, VPRS 937, Unit 227, Bundle 4, File C 281.

8   Police Correspondence, VPRS 937, Unit 226, Bundle 3.

9   Details of the Hickson episode can be found in Police Correspondence, VPRS 937, Unit 226, Bundle 2.

10 Details of the outrage on Constable Black can be found in Police Correspondence, VPRS 937, Unit 227, Bundle 4, File E 1792, as well as in the extensive newspaper coverage of the incident in the *Gippsland Guardian*.

11 Talk given by McLean at Nyerimilang, copy at the Centre for Gippsland Studies, Churchill.

12 *Gippsland Mercury,* 30 July, 1874.

13 *The Australian Commission*, op. cit., p. 73.

14 *The Confession*, op. cit., p. 30.

15 *Police Gazette*, 2 June, 1859, p. 217.

16 *The Confession*, op. cit., p. 6.

17 Police Correspondence, VPRS 937, Unit 227, Bundle 5, File 50/59.

5

DELUSIONS OF GRANDEUR

By this juncture the Orton personality is becoming clearer. In many ways he was a normal, itinerant Australian bush worker of the 19th century, who took up a variety of jobs. Feckless, improvident, and not caring for the morrow, he didn't settle down but in his own way enjoyed his rough life. The drinking, pub brawling and constant debts may be characteristic of the times. More out of the ordinary was the predilection for court cases, both ones initiated by himself, and ones initiated by others because of his own misdeeds. His continuing fantasies of a great past suggest some kind of personality deformation, an attenuation of reality akin to mania. The characteristics of mania include improvident spending, inappropriate sexual behaviour and grandiose plans for the future. Orton/Castro displayed all three traits. Two famous literary personalities who suffered from mania were the biographer James Boswell and the *Bulletin* editor J. F. Archibald. It's an affliction particularly of those who live in their imagination as much as in day-to-day reality.

Evidence given by witnesses at the Australian Commission in 1869 showed, if reliable, that Orton/Castro made repeated claims of having a wealthy background, and of believing he would come into a title and estates. During his youthful stay in South America Orton was known to brag about his supposed superior connections back home, a fantasy habit begun in his teens which was to become a routine. Once after a drinking session in Hobart Orton told his mate Tom Hales: 'Tom, I shall be better off some day', continuing his South American claim of a family fortune. In Hobart he also told Alex McDonald he was a peer of the realm. At Dargo in Gippsland he informed Norman Gillespie his father was rich and would leave him money, and he told Norman Nicholson his father was a nobleman with whom he had quarrelled. He would be heir to some large estate, but was passing under an assumed name. But when he also said he had been an officer in the cavalry in Ireland, Nicholson, who observed he did not ride with a military seat, doubted this statement. William Parker, painter and glazier of Sale, recalled: 'Once when in a great passion, he threw a meat pie into the chimney with a remarkable expression; he said he had given better meat to his father's dogs; his conversation was mysterious; he said once we would hear something of him some day'.[1]

Later around 1859 at Myers Flat near Bendigo he mentioned Lord Seymour, a Tichborne relative, to McDonald, saying he came from a respectable family, adding: 'If I'd go and eat humble pie, I would be right'. All these claims by Orton, if remembered correctly by witnesses, occurred well before Lady Tichborne's first advertisement for her missing son and heir in the London *Times* in 1863, and doubtless contributed to a growing fantasy. Orton exhibited what appears a strange combination of extremes: on the one hand debts, and on the other aristocratic claims. But they may be connected, since instant wealth would relive him of all present difficulties. Depression and mania are interconnected.

Did Orton/Castro have any grounds or knowledge on which to base his famous claim *before* Lady Tichborne's advertisements for her son appeared in the English papers in 1863 and in the Australian papers in 1865, which would have given him an inkling of the case? Orton liked reading novels, and kept a diary, but had a bad writing hand, having neglected his studies in early life. While on the Boisdale run, he read novels provided by the owners. Mrs. Foster kept a good library there. She said most of the men borrowed books; Arthur Orton did not get more than the rest, but was a frequent reader, preferring light novels. He returned these very dirty and with scribbling all over them, which no one else did. He was also fond of writing. She said: 'I read all he wrote; it was worth reading', but we know no more on this intriguing question.[2]

Castro copied into his notebook a quote on social advancement from Mary Braddon novel's *Aurora Floyd* (1863): 'Some men has plenty money and no brains, and some men has plenty brains and

THE TICHBORNE CASE—THE CLAIMANT.

no money. Surely men with plenty money and no brains were made for men with plenty brains and no money'. The actual quotation from Braddon finished with the phrase: 'and that is how we contrive to keep our equilibrium in the universal see-saw'. The quote from Braddon's *Aurora Floyd* naturally caused him trouble at his trial, as it suggested he was a conscious money-seeker. We know Orton/Castro was fond of works by popular Romantic novelists like Gerald Griffin, Mary Braddon and Captain Marryat. He kept notes of his reading; this shows he learnt from novels; he considered himself smart in the sense of being cunning in obtaining money from those above himself. Mary Braddon's sensational novel *Lady Audley's Secret* (1862), immensely popular at the time, has an intriguing plot. An Englishman, George Talboys, goes without any leave-taking to Australia, and is lost to sight on the goldfields. Advertisements seeking news of his whereabouts are published in the Australian papers. (The novel was published a year before Lady Tichborne's first advertisement for her son.) Talboys returns a rich man after his goldfield's success. In the meantime his wife Helen changes her name and marries Lord Audley in order to become an aristocrat. Lord Audley, like Lady Tichborne, is easily deceived because he wants to be. The novel has some echoes of the forthcoming Tichborne case, with Lady Audley playing the claimant's role as intriguer and imposter. Henry Kingsley's novel *Ravenshoe*, published in the same year as *Lady Audley's Secret*, has a plot similar to it and to Griffen's *The Rivals*.

It was on a copy of this Griffen novel that Orton wrote a strange oath swearing to revenge himself on the person who broke the seal on a letter to him. The novel *The Rivals* is interesting in itself, as it is about two men who are both similar and opposite to each other. Richard Lacy, a Protestant landowner and magistrate in Ireland, and Francis Riordan, a populist Catholic leader, are rivals in politics, but both are in love with the same girl. Riordan has to flee Ireland after political agitation and moves to South America, where he is given up for dead. He unexpectedly reappears in Ireland after a four year absence. The analogy to the later Tichborne case is striking, though the novel was published 25 years before the case. In the novel ordinary English settlers displace the old Irish aristocracy:

> "Who is the owner of this house?" "A Mr. Johnson, I think; some fellow of low English extraction, I suspect. A fellow of no family. And yet 'tis such fellows that live in such little elysiums as this, while...all the cream and top of the old Irish nobility are scattered over the country, hedging and ditching and tilling as hired labourers the lawns which their ancestors won...But so it is:
>
>> Since every Jack became a gentleman
>> There's many a gentle person made a jack.[3]

This was a time of rapid social change, including the overthrowing of the normal order. Orton/Castro was a jack who aspired to become a gentleman. The novel's plot was a common one at the time. Reading it and others like it may have lit a small spark in his mind which led, among other things, to the claim. He read the novel seven years before his claim, which was made in 1865. Orton/Castro was a person whose character was partly formed by reading literature, as well as later featuring as a character in literature himself.

The basic structure of exile, descent, rise and return, evident in many novels of the Romantic period, often mirrored actual experience. To this fact-based structure novelists often added the imaginative overlay of the double, or *doppelganger*, theme. Like many novels of the time, *The Rivals* is structured around the idea of the double, two men who are alike in many ways, but also opposites. This theme is not accidental – it structures the story in a neat way. We have witnessed a similar thing in the Tichborne case, where memories of two similar men traveling together were produced. The strange unexplained Orton/Castro duality was a source of public fascination. The device of the double, common in fiction and folklore, can be deployed for multiple purposes. On the level of personality, two apparently similar characters can display contrasting traits – masculine versus feminine, extravert versus introvert, and so on. The device accommodates the possibility of sliding or fluid personalities, who may begin at the centre and move to opposite extremes. One character can throw off social conventions, whereas the other can become an exemplar of them. One can go down in the world in a financial and moral sense, while the other can rise. The idea of the double neatly accommodates the possibility of mistaken identity, both central to the two suggested solutions of the Tichborne riddle – that the claimant was an illegitimate member of the family, or that he had been killed in Australia after which his assailant had assumed his identity.

In addition this structure often incorporates into itself a love triangle. In *The Rivals* the two protagonists are in love with the same woman. In many Victorian novels, including those of Kingsley, Clarke and Boldrewood, a similar love triangle is prominent. The love affair is always thwarted and postponed until the end, when one of the rivals wins out. The loved one plays the role of muse for the hero; she exists on a higher plane, unsullied by the debasing events which the exiled hero must endure. It is the memory of her which keeps the hero going during his long absence and travail. In real life Sir Roger Tichborne was in love with his cousin Katherine Doughty, but left to go abroad when his suit was not successful.

Novels which focused on a hero who gained (or regained) a title were in vogue at the time. R.D Blackmore's *Lorna Doone* (1869), which continues to be popular, is a good example of the genre. In this novel John Kidd from a rural gentry background is in love with an orphan Lorna, who is captured on dark and gloomy Exmoor. He rescues her from the outlaw Doones. Kidd is a witness in battles in court. Lorna is eventually revealed as an heiress with a title, and is able to marry Kidd, who has inherited an ancient estate. Some of the characters in the novel are based on real historical people.

Orton/Castro was typical of many people of the time in being a reader of romantic novels, and this, combined with a natural preference for daydreaming over reality, may have excited a wish-fulfilment strain in his imagination. With the vast majority of readers of romantic novels the fantasies their reading stimulated remained in their minds. What made the Tichborne claimant exceptional was that he tried to transfer his dream into reality by making a claim to a title (an example of literature affecting the course of events rather than merely reflecting them), and then persisting with his attempt for more than eight years.

Lost heir novels were popular in England and Australian before the Tichborne saga; the case itself stimulated even more. In addition claims of an exalted background became more common in Australia. This was a circular or self-reinforcing trend. In a reminiscence, *A Chequered Career* (1887), an Englishman on a 15 year sojourn in Australia tells how he often met people in the bush who claimed aristocratic connections. The landlord of the pub at Glen Innes whispered in his ear: 'I am Count de le Rothe! Our old family Chateau of La Rothe is situated on the coast of Normandy. The ancient archives are yet in my possession. And when the case is settled by the peers of France, before whom I have brought it, I have no doubt but that I shall once more enter upon those dormant titles and confiscated estates.' Another old gentleman told him he was really Sir Henry H----- and was shortly going to England to claim his large estates. George Dunderdale recalls in *The Book of the Bush* a prisoner at Port Albert who claimed: 'I am the lawful heir to the titles and estates of a Scottish dukedom, and am deprived of the possession and enjoyment of my rightful station and wealth by a band of conspirators'. The author of *A Chequered Career* goes on to explain:

> Ever since the Tichborne trial, there has been a mania on the increase in Australia, which takes the form of making the unfortunate victim believe that he is a nobleman in difficulties, or at least an expatriated scion of a lordly house. I have met dozens of such men, who no doubt have seen 'better days', but who on the strength of not dropping their *h's*, and the vestige of a once respectable appearance, mysteriously let you into the secret of their true blood.[4]

Lost heir novels pandered to nostalgia for an older form of society based on status, which was passing away during the 19th century and being replaced by a class-based one. Because of England's long history of stability, enormous prestige attached to the old leisured aristocracy and to traditional ways on large country domains, all the more so as this way of life began to fade. Traditionally, status in English society derived from a fairly rigid hierarchical division of the ranks of society into aristocrats, gentry and the common people. High status was conferred by membership of the aristocracy. It was identified to the public by manners, birth, demeanour, landed wealth, inherited means, and the outward appearance of gentility. A person's status was largely fixed by birth. It was immoveable and could survive financial decline – once a gentleman, always a gentleman. One accepted one's pre-ordained place in the system, a role implicitly understood by oneself and by others, which provided a sense of security. The chief means of entry into the upper echelons of this system were by marriage, inheritance, or ennoblement by the king for some outstanding service to the nation.

Australia was founded as the older status system was being replaced by the class one we are familiar with. This evolving class structure, with its three new divisions (upper, middle and lower class) was based on one's occupation, income, and desire for improvement. Class was permeable, not fixed; one could change one's position in society and rise, or fall, to a new level. This new type of society was much more a free-for-all with everyone jostling for position, which meant less security but more opportunity. The change from status to class meant that in the 19th century social mobility – in both directions – was much more apparent. In the new conditions, a person had to be determined to succeed over the long haul. In Australia land, labour and gold were conventional avenues to prosperity, and possible ways of restoring a relinquished gentry status. Fantasies of instant wealth or a lost inheritance raises hopes of bypassing the long haul.

The new situation presented people with the prospect of a dual decline. Social mobility was now not just a case of moving up and down the class structure. Downward social mobility could involve toppling over from a status into a class society – a much more frightening chasm. You were moving *into* a class pecking order as well as down it. This meant a descent into the straightened, depressed world of the 'genteel poor', a group who attempted to keep up the affectations of their former status even when the money was gone. One of the most vivid descriptions of them in Australia comes from Marcus Clarke's journalism:

> A certain air of sordid and grimy penury seems to hang over the houses. There is no longer any bustle and noise indicative of wealth, and the windows of the shops are blind, and patched with boarding. Everything round about breathes of poverty, but of poverty with a certain pretentiousness, the most melancholy of all kinds of poverty. There is something terrible in the bold defiance with which criminal Bohemia meets starvation halfway, and accepts the penalty for leaving the sphinx-riddle of life and usefulness unsolved; but the futile and miserable struggles made by starving honesty are sickening. Criminality dies defiant. Sinks to the bottom of society's pool at once without a murmur, and scarce a ripple; but honesty splashes and fights and gasps like some wretched cur, ditch-drowning with weights all too light. The spectacle of this uneven combat with death is sickening, but the fight is carried on so quietly that many do not hear of it at all. The last scene of the contest – not that which kills, but that which defeats – is the cheap lodging-house. It is here that honesty makes its last desperate stand, and dies grimly.[5]

This dual decline was the greatest shock of all, and avoiding its humiliations the greatest spur to effort. The cultural aspirations which the genteel poor retained were at odds with their economic position, which rendered them confused and vulnerable. Going down in the world was therefore a worse descent than just losing money – it could mean losing one's accustomed rank as well. In real life and in the novels it is this form of decline which people are most anxious to avoid. A regained title was the easiest means by which this fate might be avoided. The Tichborne claimant had many supporters because he was, they believed, carrying out their secret dreams of wealth and status instantly obtained. Australia held out the prospect of reversing the change from a status to a class society which was happening in England. Many squatters set themselves up like squires and landed gentlemen, thus bypassing change occurring at home.

In colonial Australia there existed as yet no clear-cut class society, just messy embryonic groupings in the process of formation. Few internalized sanctions on behaviour operated here. Immigrants quickly adapted to this novel situation. Released from customary social restraints, people developed very fluid personalities. You could easily adopt whatever role you pleased. Cut off from your past and from people who knew your past, you could imagine for yourself many different positions. You could shift through the whole possible range of roles, including ones opposite to your previous station. This suited the new class mobility. An aristocrat could become an ordinary digger, and a rural labourer a patrician. It was these dual personalities, these combinations of opposites, which fascinated the public, and the novelists. It naturally led to great confusion as to just who people actually were, as it lent itself to unconscious shaping of stories to fit into preconceived archetypes. This is known in folklore as shape changing or shape shifting.

Victoria was unusual in that it was founded before gold by a special, socially elevated group – the sons of the minor aristocracy and gentry of England, the 'Port Phillip Gentlemen'. It was this milieu, in which the transported gentry of Victoria cocooned themselves, that the three novelists Rolf Boldrewood, Henry Kingsley and Marcus Clarke experienced in Victoria. Boldrewood was an early member of the Melbourne Club. This atmosphere sharpened their awareness of the previous hierarchical ways, of the gap between them and demotic Australian society, and of the threat – to be avoided if possible – of dropping from one to the other. The three novelists were not exempt from these rapid shifts of social position. They were themselves part of the phenomenon they were writing about; the tremors and exhilarations of their characters were not unknown to them. For all three coming to Australia held out the prospect of permanent exile, and of possible social decline. All three were in danger of relinquishing their gentry backgrounds, and as a result suffered from status anxieties. So their fictions are not just detached observer accounts, but also displaced musings of their own possible predicaments, taken to imagined extremes of wealth or failure.

All three came from reasonably distinguished gentry backgrounds, and were in decline from their former status. Henry

Kingsley came from a well-known family of Anglican divines. He had failed at Oxford, and was the unknown youngest brother, with few prospects, of the famous writer and clergyman Charles Kingsley, chaplain to Queen Victoria. Clarke was descended from a family in the professions; his cousin was a knight. But he was disadvantaged by the financial and personal collapse of his father in Britain, and by his own improvidence in Australia. Boldrewood's father also descended into insanity. Boldrewood's family had claimed for themselves a grand background in Ireland, so they already harboured social climbing ambitions The family had (like the Tichborne claimant) faked a gentry background for their antecedents. Rolf Boldrewood, alias Tom Browne, was the illegitimate grandson of an Irishman named O'Flaherty from Galway. To hide this the family assumed a fluid identity by adopting the surname Browne after a notable English gentry family in the west of Ireland, a real life story just as fanciful as anything in the novels. Just imagine if Boldrewood/Browne had rolled up to the infant Melbourne Club as an O'Flaherty – he might not have got in so easily. Boldrewood thereafter exhibited a marked striving after the status of a leisured gentleman of the old order, in both his own life and in his writings.[6]

Kingsley, Clarke and Boldrewood had a lot in common. All three spent their early adult life in convict-free. gentlemany Victoria among the respectable classes, they wrote on the same folk myths, and they set many of their fictions not in their own state, Victoria, but in NSW and Tasmania. As gentry Victorians they were horrified by the deeds of the VDL ex-convicts, but as imaginative novelists they were fascinated by the social group opposite to their own, the criminal and convict classes, and focussed on them in their novels as much as on their own group. Going down in the world, they felt the mesmeric pull of the life of non-respectability, of throwing away the traces. They reacted to this situation in contrasting ways. Boldrewood hankered after the old status order, as his novels reveal, becoming himself a squatter and clubman. He let himself go once: in *Robbery Under Arms*, he is strangely sympathetic to the bushrangers, even though this flies in the face of the values we know he held most dear. Kingsley took a middle course; he 'went native' in Australia, and exulted in the freedom from convention he found while wandering around the Australian bush, while at the same time mixing with Western District squatters and members of the Melbourne Club. As his own life disintegrated Clarke relinquished status pretensions, moving towards the milieu of the down-and-outs he wrote about so incisively in his journalism. Given their own reduced circumstances, all three novelists understood that rapid social descent was possible. All three tried to reverse the declining family fortunes by income from writing. Kingsley had to bot off wealthy squatters in Australia; he had no prospects here and returned to England after a five year sojourn to make his mark with *Geoffry Hamlyn*. Marcus Clarke sunk slowly into destitution in Melbourne. Boldrewood set himself up as a Melbourne Club gentleman even though he was a twice failed squatter whose later public service positions came from the old patronage system. Only Boldrewood eventually succeeded in leading a relatively prosperous life here.

Most ordinary Australians strove for improvement through hard work and enterprise. Others like Arthur Orton, who had no such drives, fantasized about a dramatic change for the better. From an English point of view one image of Australia was of a country where wealth could be quickly accumulated; in Charles Dickens' *Great Expectations* the convict Magwitch returns from Australia with a fortune. Short-term wealth could be illegally gained here by a various criminal activities – stealing livestock, holding up people for valuables, or selling stolen meat on goldfields. The only way of legitimately joining the aristocracy was by marriage, or by the appearance of a disputed or previously unknown inheritance. Illegitimate ways included forging a will or impersonating a connection with a titled family. These scenarios were the stuff of much 19th century romantic fiction.

The three colonial novelists connived in these common fantasies of success, writing novels which played up to the prospect of sudden rises in both fortune and status. Their major fictions are loosely based on real events, many on the Vandemonian trail, but imaginatively patterned in various ways to accommodate prevailing social aspirations, as well as their own psychological needs. We rightly distinguish between actual events, and folkloric rumour and literary recreations of them – each has a discrete and different status. But we are forced to admit that in this case the novelists themselves, real life characters like Orton/Castro and Bogong Jack, and the characters in the novels all display the same (infuriating) mix of faltering status ambition, personal anxiety and wish-fulfilment shape-changing. Only the folklore, which ironed out the contradictions and rough edges, presented an acceptably sanitized and credible, though untrue, version which accorded with the public's deepest yearnings.

NOTES

1 *The Australian Commission*, op. cit., p. 105.

2 Ibid., p. 94.

3 Gerald Griffin *The Rivals*, Saunders and Otley, London, 1829, pp. 22-3.

4 Anon *A Chequered Career; or Fifteen Years' Experience in Australia & New Zealand*, Richard Bentley & Son, London, 1887, pp. 210-5.

5 Marcus Clarke 'A Cheap Lodging House', *Australasian*, 31 July, 1869, repr. in *A Colonial City: High and Low Life*, ed. L.T. Hergenhan, University of Queensland Press, St. Lucia, 1972, p. 163.

6 Boldrewood's background has recently been revealed in Paul De Serville *Rolf Biography: A Life*, The Miegunyah Press, Carlton South, 2000.

PART TWO: THE HIGH COUNTRY

6

MINERS, TRADERS, STOCKMEN AND SQUATTERS AT OMEO

The Omeo district was founded in the late 1830s by explorers and cattlemen moving south-west from the Monaro in search of grazing land. The first suitable area they settled was at Benambra, a plain in the high country with an expanse of good land surrounded by mountains and watered by Lake Omeo. The cattlemen were Highland Scots such as Livingstone, Macalister and MacFarlane, and Irishmen such as the Buckleys and Pendergasts. A few years later, in 1841, Edward Crooke, from an English trading family with a base in Calcutta, took up the Hinnomungie run, which covered the Livingstone Creek goldfield and the adjacent town of Omeo; Crooke soon occupied the nearby runs of Bindi, Tongiomungie and Benambra. James MacFarlane settled on the Omeo B run adjacent to Hinnomungie. This was the Monaro group.

A second incursion into the Omeo area was from the west, this time from settlers in north-eastern Victoria along the Ovens River. A group organized by the Gray family of Wangaratta in the early 1850s had found a way through the mountains via the Mitta Mitta River to Omeo and Cobungra. There they set up the Cobungra run on a high plain for the Grays. Over the years more direct routes across the mountains into Cobungra and Omeo from the Ovens Valley were discovered. When gold was found in the early 1850s, miners in came from the north-east via these routes. This was the Ovens Valley-Cobungra group.

A third influx was from the south. Many workers on the central Gippsland plain left their jobs and moved to these new northern goldfields. The most favoured route to the Omeo fields from central Gippsland was east to Bairnsdale, where station hands worked en route at Archibald Macleod's station at Bairnsdale. The

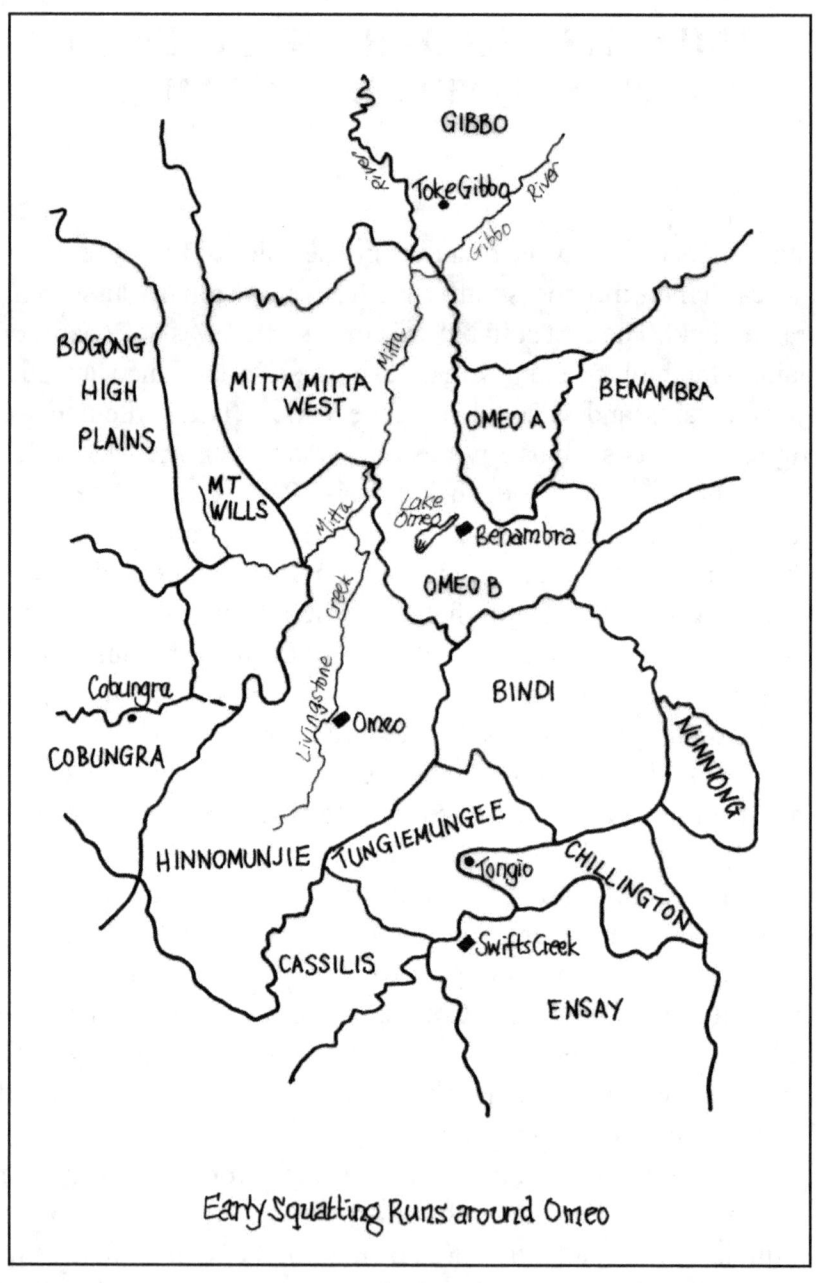

Early Squatting Runs around Omeo

next stopping place was Marshall's notorious Captain Cook Inn on the Nicholson River near Bruthen. Then the diggers took the road north along the Tambo River valley and over the Tongio Gap to the goldfields. Other less direct routes were possible, for instance north from Dargo to Cobungra and then east to Omeo, or through the many small fields in the mountains as miners worked their way north. Workers from Mewburn Park and Boidsale, some of whom were ex-Vandemonians and ex-convicts, were part of this move. This was the central Gippsland group.

Gold was first discovered in the area in 1851 by two stockmen brothers, Joseph and George Day, from Edward Crooke's Hinnomunjie run; Joseph Day was Crooke's superintendent. One of the stockmen from Omeo station, Thomas Sheean, went to the site of Day's discovery and began to pan successfully for gold. Other parties followed. Gold was being found along the Livingstone Creek, and also to the north around the Gibbo River. At the end of the year 1851, the NSW geologist Rev. W.C. Clarke, then visiting the area, confirmed the find. A rush began and soon there were more than a hundred miners on the Livingstone Creek field. In 1853 a party of a dozen Americans from the Californian fields began sluicing successfully; a group of French Canadians also arrived. In late 1854 a movement of people from the Wangaratta region over the Gibbo to Omeo occurred, but hot weather meant many did not survive the journey because of thirst. The English traveller and writer Henry Kingsley, in north-east Victoria at the time, described the scene in his novel *The Hillyars and the Burtons* (1865).

> The news [of gold at Omeo] reached Beechworth, of course, in an exaggerated form, and the consequence was that diggers came flocking over in thousands. The approaches to Lake Omeo are of fearful difficulty. The men came on foot or horseback, but the approach with drays in this burning summer time was exceedingly difficult; the men were there before the provisions, and the consequence was a disastrous retreat, in which the loss of life must have been very great.[1]

The township of Omeo developed out of the miners' tent town along the Livingstone Creek; by 1856 there were about 600 diggers on the field. Omeo was the centre of a number of fields. To the west was the Cobungra field and to the north the Gibbo. To the south Swift's Creek was beginning, and later the fields of Cassilis, Haunted Stream and Tongio grew up. Gold mining spread gradually south through the hills, forests and streams on the west side of the Tambo River, as far down as forty kilometres north of Bairnsdale. Omeo was the first, largest and most central field, on key transport routes, so it developed as the main supply town for the northern goldfields.

Orton/Castro's story was that he had worked his way northeast from Sale to Omeo, as many others did. He claimed to have first gone to the Nicholson River diggings, then to have worked at Macleod's station on the Mitchell River from May to September 1858, and to have moved to the Omeo goldfields until February 1859. This was not true. Macleod denied either an Orton or a Castro had worked for him. Orton was working for Foster at this time, and waiting for the Sale court case over wages in January, 1859. No witness remembered Orton on the Livingstone Creek diggings at Omeo, although many of his Mewburn Park friends were there. In fact because of the charges over the stealing of the Blacker horse, Orton had to leave Gippsland quickly and quietly, so he was not able to travel to the north Gippsland fields with the others.

Particularly strong and noticeable on the Livingstone Creek field from the mid 1850s was a contingent from Mewburn Park, many of whom were former comrades of Arthur Orton, and were likely part of the Stratford gang. Those who came from Mewburn Park to Omeo included Thomas Toke, the most notorious of them all, Alex Nielsen, James Andrews and John Luckman, all Vandemonians, as well as 'Billy the Groom' Robertson. Others often mentioned by later witnesses as forming part of the same central Gippsland group on the Omeo field were Haines, formerly a policeman from Tarraville, and Bennett and Burns. Fred Burrows and Robert Burnett had broken in horses for Macleod at Bairnsdale before both moved to the Omeo goldfields. There many of the central Gippsland group formed claims with each other. The man simply called 'the foreigner' turns up on the Omeo field at this time. He had a foreign accent but spoke good English. Thomas Chapman and the foreigner left central Gippsland and appeared at the Nicholson River together. The foreigner had an iron grey horse which he sold to Toke. Toke, Chapman, 'Billy the Groom' Robertson and the foreigner then left to go to the Nicholson diggings and later to the Omeo ones. The foreigner was described as having a very gentlemanly appearance and quiet demeanour. Naturally the mysterious, gentlemanly foreigner was another person later singled out as a Tichborne possibility.

When the miners arrived at Omeo they found the only inhabitants, apart from a few remaining Aborigines, were squatters and their employees on the squatting runs. The bushmen and stockriders on the stations had the advantage of knowing the lie of the country, so they were essential to miners as guides, and they could organize food and supplies, as they already had their own networks. The first miners had been stockmen. The most active and prominent among the stockmen soon became the storekeepers and traders. We can see this happening in the account given by an ex-Californian miner, John Reid, one of the American group, of his coming to Omeo:

> [We] reached Omeo, East Gippsland, and camped on the swamp on Livingstone Creek, as now known. We went out on the plains...We saw a bullock and killed him, not knowing that there was any settlement near. While killing the bullock, Tom Sheean and Joe Day rode up and informed us that we were at Omeo. This was in 1853. They would not take payment for the bullock, but helped us to skin the beast, and told us to make for their hut and stockyard, up the Morass Creek.[2]

This is how people like Joe Day and Tom Sheean became storekeepers and traders, and later hotelkeepers. Tom and Michael Sheean were brothers from the Monaro. The Sheeans had the Diggers Rest and Squatters Hotel pubs at Omeo, and Joe Day the Diggers Arms. Soon the Golden Age Hotel also began to trade. Thomas Sheean was a prominent Omeo figure, and at one stage a part owner of the Benambra run, till his early death in the 1860s. He was on the side of law and order, helping police and magistrates in difficult cases. (In contrast, another notable Omeo personality with the same surname, Jack Sheean, originally from Hobart, had a more doubtful reputation, as he consorted with those running the rustling gangs.) The trader-publican group was quite powerful, as they acted as gold agents as well. In alliance with local stockriders with their knowledge of bushcraft, they controlled the goldfield in the early days.

OMEO DURING ITS MINING DAYS

Four discernible groups existed in the Omeo district – squatters, stockmen, miners and traders. All groups had different interests, which led to shifting alliances and to conflict. The stockmen-trader alliance was quite powerful. The miners and squatters squabbled over land – could miners freely fossick and stake claims on squatting land? The miners felt the traders took advantage of them. But despite this, the traders and miners often formed an alliance against the squatters. The squatter Edward Crooke, not an impartial witness, wrote that Omeo is 'known as the storekeepers and publicans' diggings, which means that all hands are in their debt and that they are kept so... half of the trade of the country is in their hands, and no one else can deal so cheaply...the diggers are their puppets'.[3]

VDL lawlessness, which had spread through central Gippsland, was soon evident in the Omeo district. Newspapers were constantly reporting disputes over claim-jumping, water races and ditches. Theft, rowdyism and sly-grogging were on the increase. The Omeo correspondent of the *Gippsland Guardian* reported on 15 May, 1857, that 'it seems that there is a class of people in that neighbourhood who carry on an illicit trade, to the serious injury of those who wish to gain a livelihood in an honourable manner, and who have been at the expense of erecting and licensing houses suited for the accommodation of the public. There are others who, instead of contenting themselves with such claims as are lawful, assume to themselves unlimited tracts of land, and even go so far as to defraud others of their rights – by taking their claims from them'. There were few traders willing to buy gold, so diggers were often left with what they could not sell. These happenings were normal in the early stages of a gold rush.

The historian of the Gippsland goldfields, Richard Mackay, commented:

> It would be useless to try to account for the fact that robberies were much more frequent on the southern side of the divide than on the northern, but it was so. Some account for it by alleging that owing to its proximity to Tasmania there was a greater number of Old Hands amongst the Gippsland population, than on the eastern and northern side of the mountains, and this might well be for that period.[4]

As this shows, the VDL contingent were blamed for troubles on the fields.

A dramatic illustration of these trends occurred in February, 1856. An American digger called Henry Bennett was a friend of the central Gippsland group; 'the foreigner' was a mate of his nephew. By mistake Bennett had left a considerable quantity of gold (about 50 oz.) in a jar in his hut when he lent the hut to another digger, Jack the Sawyer, an 'old Derwent-file' (ex-Vandemonian) who had previously been working in central Gippsland. Jack took the gold but was discovered with it tied around his waist while fighting in a pub, and confessed to the robbery. An informal miners' court was quickly convened. Mary Andrews, wife of the digger James Andrews, described what happened next: 'They called a meeting on him and found the gold on him; when they found the gold they blindfolded him first, and were going to hang him; then they were going to cut his ears off; afterwards gave him half an hour start to leave the diggings and put the dogs on him'.[5] Other accounts say he was sentenced to be punished by two lashes from each miner present, then to be off the diggings by noon next day. The miners had taken the law into their own hands, since in the early days of the rush there was no authority – legal, government or police – to resolve disputes. A year later, in 1857, a local squatter, James MacFarlane, acted as magistrate to fill the vacuum. In May 1857 a similar case to the 'Jack the Sawyer' one occurred. A miner named Holland was accused by another miner, Samuel Bladen, of having stolen 7 oz. of his gold and a blanket from his hut. As in the previous case, the accused was later seen drinking at the Squatters Arms hotel. Thomas Sheean, the publican, testified that Holland had gold on him, which was found to be that of Bladen. Holland stood trial at Alberton in August, was found guilty and sentenced to two years' hard labour on the roads.

Miners, a majority of whom were law-abiding, ran their own rough system of justice, and it was lucky that Lynch Law did not prevail. On some occasions locals paid for an escort to take offenders to Sale for trial. Because there was an authority vacuum, the diggers held a large meeting in September, 1857, to formulate rules, to air their grievances and to ask for assistance. Anyone found guilty of theft by the miners' self-government was forced to leave the field within 24 hours. Rules to regulate claims and water races were introduced. A constant complaint was the absence of a legal system; miners asked for a magistrate, police officers, local courts and a gold escort to take the 300 oz. being produced each week to Sale and Port Albert. The Omeo correspondent of the *Ovens and Murray Advertiser* warned constantly about the absence of protection on the fields: 'When blood has been split, or human life destroyed, the gentlemen in Melbourne will be all activity', he wrote in the *Gippsland Guardian* on 17 August, 1857, but the editor of his paper in Port Albert played down the danger: 'We believe from our own advices from Omeo, that the state of things is not so bad as might be inferred from the above account'. The man on the spot was closer to a truth.[6]

The locals could not cope with the rise in serious crime. Cases had to be referred to a warden at Yackandandah in the northern police district, or a police magistrate at Sale, but both were too far away. It was lucky a police magistrate, Mr A. C. Wills, and police were finally appointed in mid 1858, but by then things were getting out of control. The police senior ranks in Melbourne made the mistake of first sending to Omeo a sergeant of police who was from London. As John Sadleir, a policemen stationed at Beechworth in 1856, commented: 'This sergeant had passed all his career in city work, at which he was an expert, but so far as bush lore went he would probably have lost himself in the few acres of ti-tree scrub that then covered Fisherman's Bend.'[7] Sadleir added that the same mistake was later made during the outbreak by the Kelly Gang.

A triangular struggle for power developed between the squatters, miners and stockmen-storekeepers. The local squatter Edward Crooke, who owned Hinnomunjie station, was in a constant war with diggers over trespass, and over the tethering of miners' cows and horses on his runs. Squatters believed they controlled the land, and miners couldn't put their animals on it, even if they had a miner's right. Squatters moreover suspected miners of stealing their stock, especially unbranded ones, for meat, and of stealing horses for their own use. We have seen evidence of this in the early report by the American party of Joe Day and Thomas Sheean helping to cut up a beast. In December, 1858, a showdown occurred between the superintendent of Crooke's Hinnomunjie station, Mr T. Venables, and locals over the grazing of miners' cattle and horses on Crooke's land. Crooke, already plagued by horse thieves, had become highly indignant by this stage. The immediate cause of confrontation was the decision of a man named Thomas Hall ('Tom the Milkman') to set up a dairy herd near Omeo. Crooke, through his agent Venables, threatened to impound his dairy cows. On one occasion in December,

1858, Venables used Crooke's stockmen to try to round up these animals, but the locals warned Hall in time and the dairy stock were hidden.

Police Magistrate and Goldfields Warden Wills decided to intervene and calm things down by acting as an adjudicator. He issued a notice which called on Crooke to prove where the boundaries of his runs were. On the other hand Wills warned the miners and traders that the various licences they had did not entitle them to depasture cattle. Wills then called a meeting of all parties, at which Venables declined to accept Wills' authority to inquire into the location of squatting runs. The following conversation ensued:

> Venables: I shall drive off those cows, Hall.
> Warden Wills: I recommend to you to be careful that the cattle really are on your run, and that you lawfully seize them.
> Venables: Mr. Wills, I never made a mistake in my life.
> Warden Wills: Then you are a lucky man.

An American named Foster, threatened Venables, and had to be calmed down. Another American, Henry Bennett, the man who lost his gold, was in the process of becoming a storekeeper, hotelier and gold dealer. He read out a petition signed by 95 Omeo men, including Mr John Wright, the member of the Mining Board who represented them. The signatories asked for a Grazing Reserve to be gazetted for their cattle and horses. They pointed out that the other local squatter, James MacFarlane, was much more reasonable than Crooke, and that, as the Omeo diggings paid £2000 per annum in gold duty to the government, they were entitled to consideration. Venables was warned by Wills about the consequences of impounding any cattle in the future.

At the time a Bill to amend the Impounding Act was being debated in the Victorian Parliament. Crooke published his response to the petition by Omeo residents against his actions in the *Argus* of the last day of that year, 31 December, 1858. He accused the Police Magistrate and Mining Warden, Mr. Wills, of being an '*ex officio* diggers' advocate'. This was unfair, as Wills had acted impartially and was generally admired for his diplomacy. Crooke denied that he had ever impounded stock that were illegally eating his grass, but complained that the diggers let their stock run over everyone's properties. They felt free to saddle up and use his horses as well: 'Horsestealers and dealers seemed to think that they had a right to 'stick up', as they call it, on my runs because they are near the diggings'. Crooke also objected to 'carriers, and anyone else that would prefer that I should keep their stock for nothing to being at the expense of keeping them elsewhere'. Storekeepers would commandeer his drays while they were on the road. Crooke accused the district of being overwhelmed by drink; storekeepers and publicans made up for their losses in other areas by excessive drink sales. The diggers were the puppets of these traders, who ruled the roost. Only one-half of the people on the field were genuine diggers, Crooke believed; the rest were just hangers-on. Crooke ended his diatribe by complaining about diggers diverting the waters upstream for their races and disadvantaging his cattle in their need for water. Crooke was not the most popular man on the field, but his complaint against the dominance of the storekeeper racketeers had some truth in it. A commonage was proclaimed at Omeo in December 1860.

It was from an element of the former stockman group, not from the miners, that the cattle duffing and bushranging operations based on Omeo developed. In replying to Crooke's outburst, 'An Old Omeo Digger' confirmed this in a letter to the *Gippsland Guardian* in February 1859, stating that criminal behaviour came not from the miners but from 'men whose *stationary* minds and antecedents entirely originate in their experience and associations as stockmen'.[8] The italicizing of the word *stationary* in the original indicates the problem came from stockmen on the stations. John Wright, elected by the diggers to be their representative on the Mining Board, confirmed this:

> I object on my own part, and on the part of every working digger on these diggings to be included among horse dealers and thieves. Such men existed before the diggers and storekeepers, and as numerous as now, and it is well known that, like foals and calves, they did and do generate at such places as are called stations.[9]

On this issue the miners and squatters combined against some station hands who had moved into crime.

NOTES

1 Henry Kingsley *The Hillyars and the Burtons*, 1865, repr. Sydney University Press, Sydney, 1973, p. 384.

2 Quoted in Keith McD. Fairweather *Time To Remember*, Bairnsdale, 1978, pp. 15-16.

3 *The Argus*, 31 December, 1858.

4 Richard Mackay *Recollections of the Early Gippsland Goldfields*, 1916, repr. Graham Publications, Ringwood, 1977, p. 31.

5 *The Australian Commission*, op. cit., p. 155.

6 On this topic see Vic Webber *Taming a Town: Law and Order at Omeo*, Kapana, Press, Bairnsdale, 1993.

7 John Sadleir *The Recollections of a Victorian Police Officer*, 1913, repr. Penguin, Ringwood, 1973, p. 84.

8 *Gippsland Guardian*, 4 February, 1859.

9 *Ovens Constitution*, 28 January, 1859.

7

THE LEGENDS OF BOGONG JACK

A series of legendary tales sprang up about a romantic character called Bogong Jack who led a gang of horse and cattle thieves in the mountains around Omeo. The various tales treat him sympathetically, even as a hero – in one, he tricks a pursuing policeman by crossing a mountain stream and escaping. Did this character exist, and how did stories about him move into the realm of folklore and legend? The evidence suggests there were two Bogong Jacks, the second of whom took over some of the mythic qualities of the first.

The first and main convict trail was north from VDL into Gippsland. But there was also a lesser movement of people, including ex-convicts, south from Sydney. Some former Sydney convicts moved south to places like Campbellfield and Appin, then further south to the Goulburn and Yass areas. From there they travelled across the Limestone Plains into the Monaro and over the alps into north east Victoria. When gold began to peter out on the southern goldfields of New South Wales, diggers also migrated further south to Victoria's Kiewa and Buckland fields. Some station workers, including a few convicts, came down Major Mitchell's line into central Victoria. Convicts were of course a small minority of those moving south from New South Wales into Victoria.

A group of those from NSW reached as far as Omeo, the outer limit of the Sydney push south, where they met and mingled with those from central Gippsland moving north. The graziers who originally came in from the Monaro to the Omeo area (the Monaro group) remained law abiding, even though some had convict origins. John Pendergast, son of a convict from Parramatta, set up Monaro runs before moving to Benambra in 1836. Edmund Buckley was a convict as was his wife, the mother of the squatter Patrick

Coady Buckley. Like the Pendergasts, the Buckleys had moved south from Sydney acquiring properties in the Monaro and then around Omeo. Others from the Monaro moved to the Ovens region of north-east Victoria. The ex-convict George Gray was in charge of a Monaro run before he squatted at Wangaratta. Amos Crisp, son of a convict, held a run on the Snowy River on the Monaro in the 1840s; his son moved to north-east Victoria.

The Monaro squatter, Henry Haygarth, reported that bushranging was rife in the Monaro and Omeo districts in the 1840s, well before the gold-rushes, so the crime gangs of the 1850s were not altogether new.[1] Haygarth was himself held up by the escaped convict bushranger 'Buchan Charley'. The most important early mention of Bogong Jack appears in Henry Kingsley's *The Recollections of Geoffry Hamlyn* (1859), in which the narrator tells the Bogong Jack story as a self-contained folk tale. In this version Bogong Jack was a university educated English gentleman, John Sampson, who was forced to leave England because of a misdemeanour. On his brother-in-law's Ovens River property in the 1840s he continued to live a fast life as a racegoer, brawler and singer of popular songs. A consummate horseman, he resumed his loose ways, and a warrant for horse stealing was issued against him. Compelled to flee, he went into hiding on a hut high up on an out-station in the ranges near the Bogong High Plains ('Bogong' is an Aboriginal term for a mountain), then, after successfully evading a mounted police hunt, was forced to go into the higher, remoter alps where no Europeans had yet been. The Aborigines knew there was fertile country to the east. He disappeared for about four years, living, like William Buckley, with an Aboriginal tribe and discarding his European heritage and tongue. He eventually found a fertile valley with a lake (most likely the Omeo district). But after he reread a letter from his sister, a hankering for his past life returned, and he found his way back to his farm in the Ovens valley, where he married and settled down as a prosperous and respectable farmer.

Kingsley is not sure how authentic the tale, which comes from the old hands, is, but it sounds like an account of an early journey from the Ovens area over the Bogong High Plains towards the

Omeo region. The first reported trip of this kind occurred in 1851 when the Gray brothers and their stockmen, John Wells and James Brown, became the European discoverers of the Bogong High Plains from the Ovens side; they too were led by an Aboriginal guide. They thought someone had been there before them; some accounts say Cobungra was discovered from the north-west in the 1840s. The Grays' expedition of 1851 found its way down the Mitta Mitta River to Omeo and then west to Cobungra, which they set up as a cattle station. Soon they discovered a less circuitous route over the Bogong High Plains. Later, a third, even more direct, route was pioneered over Mt. Feathertop, north of today's Great Alpine Highway. Kingsley's version places Bogong Jack as in all likelihood a member of this Wangaratta-Cobungra connection. The policeman John Sadleir recounts that in the 1860s the Cobungra station was run by cattle rustlers. This connects the Cobungra people with earlier horse and cattle stealing intrigues.

The group from Wangaratta and the Ovens River who founded the Cobungra run was centered on three families of convict origins, the Grays and Crisps (both squatters) and the McKenzies.[2] Old George Gray, sponsor of the Cobungra venture, was an Irishmen convicted for involvement in the political agitation leading to the Irish Rising of 1798. He was sentenced to life imprisonment and transported to Sydney in 1796. His sons were born at Campbelltown and at Camden; in the late 1820s and early 1830s he worked his way down to the Monaro, where he was in charge of the Bungadbo station in 1837. He was the squatter at the Pelican Lagoon run at Wangaratta when he sent an expedition out over the mountains to Cobungra. George Grey married Hannah McKenzie and their daughter married John Crisp. By other links these families became related to two other nearby squatter families in north-east Victoria, the Faithfuls and Gullifers. George Grey's son Ned was later known to police as a horse and cattle thief. The Crisp, Worcester and Rawson families, connected by marriage to the Grays, were also of NSW convict origin. In contrast to the Wangaratta-Cobungra criminal group, those who moved from being employees at Hinnomungie and adjacent stations near Omeo into racketeering mainly came north from Tasmania and Gippsland.

The Cobungra location was not central as Omeo was, but it had its own advantages. It led directly to the Ovens to the northwest, Omeo to the east, and south to Dargo and the Crooked River diggings, which were in full swing in the 1860s, so it sat across some key mountain routes. These routes were remote and less open to police surveillance. Some of the Cobungra group were either thieves themselves or had close associations with known rustlers. The group soon expanded by marriage into a close-knit network of at least a dozen families. Ned Gray married Ellen Meighan, whose sisters married into the Gullifer, Crisp and Parslow squatter families. James Parslow became an owner of Cobungra station with John Meighan, the father of the Meighan sisters, from 1859 to 1868. Ned and Ellen Gray's daughter Hannah married into the well-known MacNamara family. Ned's sister Mary Gray married Tom Worcester from a convict family, and their children in turn married into the Cook and Rawson families. Joseph Rawson, from a NSW convict family, took over Cobungra with Parslow in 1868, replacing Meighan. They divided the property between themselves in 1871. The McKenzie branch of the clan produced a Faithful child, who married James Brown, the original stockman on Cobungra with the Wells brothers. On 8 March 1859, Inspector Hill of Omeo wrote about a stolen horse: 'A person of the name of "Brown" who has got a station on the "Buffalo River", left this [word obscure] with a mob of horses for his station about a week after these horses were missed – He is intimately connected with the "Greys", notorious horse stealers, he is therefore strongly suspected of taking them.'[3]

No known historical personage precisely fits Kingsley's Bogong Jack, John Sampson. Though the Cobungra venture in outline fits Kingsley' story, these families were not educated Englishmen, as John Sampson was. The best possible candidate is John Andrews, described in the *Ovens Constitution* in November 1857 as 'a well-known character, an elderly criminal known by the sobriquet of "Bogong Jack". This delinquent on Monday evening last, at Wangaratta, was detected in the act of horse-stealing.' This is the first mention of the name Bogong Jack in print, two years' before

Kingsley's. Andrews was described in the *Ovens and Murray Advertiser* in its account of his trail before Judge Barry on November 5th 1857 as 'being a ticket of leave holder illegally out of his district, when he was remanded in Melbourne'. The Government Gazette notified that 'the prisoner, a native of New South Wales, had been convicted twice of horse stealing at Melbourne in 1853, and had received in July last a ticket of leave for the Wangaratta district'. Andrews had stolen a horse and when its owner tried to repossess it Andrews struggled with him and tried to drown him in the Ovens River. Judge Barry sentenced him to nine years on the roads. Andrews is a good fit in many ways for Kingsley's Bogong Jack: he is the only person living at the time known to have been called 'Bogong Jack', he was an habitual horse-stealer operating on the Wangaratta/Ovens side of the mountains, and being 'elderly', was old enough to have been operating back in the1840s, but he was born in NSW, not England, and was not an educated gentleman.[4] Sub Inspector John Sadleir was present that day at the Wangaratta court proceedings.

Another possible identification can be made with members of the Simpson family. John, James and Robert were sons of John and Sarah Simpson. The family was settled around Tarrawingee in the Ovens valley near Wangaratta. In March 1858 at Beechworth James Simpson was tried for horse stealing but acquitted. He was involved in another horse-stealing case which went to court in June 1861. His brother John Simpson was named as a butcher at Dargo in 1861 in connection with some cattle-stealing carried out by the cattle-rustler Bentley and his mates, who were connected with the Cobungra mob. Some members of the Simpson family moved to the Omeo region. Robert Simpson together with Jack Sheean, who had a dubious record since his Hobart days, put up bail for Bentley in the case. Robert Simpson was a hotel licensee at Omeo and Swift's Creek and storekeeper at Snowy Creek. James Simpson was a miner at Saltpetre Creek north of Omeo. This family comes from the right area, the father's name John Simpson is almost identical to the John Sampson name provided by Kingsley, is involved in stealing rackets, and continues to live in the region. The father was old enough to have been operating as early as the 1840s, as in the Kingsley story.

The second Bogong Jack is thought to have been an Omeo cattle and horse thief of the late 1850s. He was been identified as John Payne or Paynter, an Omeo stockman and later butcher, who appears in newspaper accounts of the area in the late 1850s. In the 1960s Eric Harding identified Bogong Jack with John Payne/Paynter in his book *Bogong Jack: The Gentleman Bushranger* (1967). Without disclosing his sources, Harding claimed that he was the son of Captain John Payne from a middle class family from Leicestershire, but Harding's account of his origins is implausible.[5] John Paynter was in fact the son of William Paynter, butcher, and Elizabeth Paynter (nee Jenkins) of Hobart, born in 1830. William Paynter was one of the butchers Arthur Orton, later the Tichborne claimant, worked for in Hobart. This Orton-Paynter link provides an explicit connection between Orton and the later events in Gippsland, like the Ballarat Harry murder. John Paynter may be the John Paine who appears in the records of Boisdale station as a storekeeper; this would be in keeping with the documented movement of Hobart people through central Gippsland and then north to Omeo. John Paynter married Ann Cook at Omeo on 18 October, 1858, in one of the first marriages on the Omeo goldfields and a son, Edward, was born to them on 4 August, 1859. John Paynter slaughtered cattle at Omeo for the goldfield's market. A police description of him in 1859 reads: 'Age about 30 years, 6 ft, high, fresh complexion, dark hair, rather thin on top, a large aquiline nose, stoops slightly but is otherwise a well made man and a butcher by trade'.[6] The age given by the police fits in with the 1830 birthdate in Hobart.

THE MARRIAGE CERTIFICATE OF JOHN & ANN PAYNTER

These facts seem to suggest that there are two distinct Bogong Jacks – Sampson and Paynter – the early one from the north-west connected with the Wangaratta-Cobungra group, which arose out of a NSW convict milieu, and then John Paynter, connected with the Omeo group, which had VDL convict origins. Paynter later assumed the 'Bogong Jack' sobriquet. Kingsley's story, which he picked up in the mid 1850s, relates to events in the 1840s, when Paynter was in his teens, so he could not be the original Bogong Jack. Paynter came in much later from the south, from central Gippsland. Folk legends, as they often do, seem to have telescoped the two Bogong Jacks into one.

One mystery is when, if at all, John Paynter got the nickname of 'Bogong Jack'? The connection was first made known only as recently as the 1960s. Jane Vince (Mrs. W. A) Pendergast disclosed that two old Omeo identities, Michael McNamara and

James Madden, had told her that in their family memories Bogong Jack had been known as John Payne or Paynter, an Omeo butcher. McNamara came from one of the families connected by marriage to the Cobungra group. The linking of Bogong Jack and Paynter first appeared in print, to my knowledge, in the *Age* of 8 September, 1962, in a letter by Eric Harding, later in his book in 1967, and then in Jane Vince Pendergast's *Pioneers of the Omeo District* in 1968.

We have no earlier linking of the surname Paynter and the nickname. The nickname is much scarcer than its later proliferation in folk tales suggests. The name 'Bogong Jack' was rare at the time of bushranging outbreaks – as far as I can discover, it occurs on only three occasions in print in the 19th century. The first mention was at the trial of John Andrews in Wangaratta in 1857. The next mention of a Bogong Jack is by Henry Kingsley in his 1859 novel. But Kingsley does not link his Bogong Jack with the VDL convict-bushranger Touan and his Bogong Jack-like gang in his novel *The Recollections of Geoffry Hamlyn*. To my knowledge no newspaper account of the time (the later 1850s and early 1860s) uses the name 'Bogong Jack' in connection with events centred on Omeo, though they do mention John Paynter a number of times in recounting court cases and other matters. The lack of a connection is surprising, and raises the possibility that Paynter was not called Bogong Jack during his lifetime. The only other mention of the nickname in print in the 19th century is in the *Ovens and Murray Advertiser* of 11 April, 1865, in its report on the death of the bushranger Morgan at Peechelba. Alex Tone, a Wangaratta pound-keeper, asked the dying Morgan, among other questions, if he knew Bogong Jack, and Morgan answered 'Yes'. As well as establishing a link between two famous bushrangers, Morgan and Bogong Jack, this passage confirms that the nickname Bogong Jack was known at the time, at least on the Ovens side, for Tone to ask the question. All three early mentions of the name are on the Ovens, not on the Omeo side, and do not link Bogong Jack with the Omeo-based John Paynter.

Rolf Boldrewood was based at Albury when he wrote his novel *Nevermore* (1892), which describes in great detail the rackets later associated with Bogong Jack. Boldrewood describes the leader of the gang, Thomas Toke (whom he calls Caleb Coke), as well as Ballarat Harry and Cornelius Green, two victims of the gang. But he never uses the names John Paynter or Bogong Jack, though he knew Kingsley's novel well. This strengthens the view that Toke was better known at the time than Bogong Jack. The retired police inspector John Sadleir, who had also read Kingsley's novel, gave descriptions of Bogong Jack's gang (the fourth appearance of the name in print) in his *Recollections of a Police Officer in Victoria* in 1913. Sadleir's evidence is important, as he was a police officer in the area during and after these events. Sadleir's account fits in with what we know of Paynter's activities, but, though Sadleir described Bogong Jack as well-known, he did not name him. Sadleir's account suggests the name Bogong Jack was current around 1860. It may have been a transferable nickname given to a number of thieves who operated in the alps. Bogong's Jack's hut was known in the mountains by cattlemen and bushwalkers sometime in the 20th century, but from when precisely isn't clear. The hut is near Mt Fainter, which people surmise may have been named after Paynter, but this is most likely a later convenient folk accretion. With stories kept in families and among small, isolated groups, it is very hard to tell when such names and connections first arose. As a result they may have been projected back to an earlier period than is warranted.

Another conundrum is the changing reputations of the two alleged leaders of the Bogong Jack rustling gang, John Paynter and Thomas Toke. Toke was a former VDL convict with a horrific record. At the time (the late 1850s), Toke, short and unprepossessing in appearance, was the leader of the gang and the one much in the public eye, notorious and feared, the subject of editorial denunciation, and in contrast Paynter was a minor figure who attracted relatively little attention. There was no Bogong Jack gang, but there was a Thomas Toke one. In our time the roles have been reversed. Toke is known only to historians, and has no folkloric cachet, but the tall, handsome John Paynter is now a well-known romantic folk-hero, wrongly considered the leader of the Bogong Jack gang. Similarly in the early Robin Hood legends, Little

John was often the main character and Robin Hood his offsider, but later on Robin Hood came to the fore as the leader of the band. [7]

There are further parallels between the Robin Hood and Bogong Jack legends. It is common in folklore for a series of disparate events to coalesce over time into a neat, unifying pattern. There were originally at least two Robin Hoods, the first an outlaw from Yorkshire known as Robert Hood or 'Hobbehod', and a later one from Nottingham, in some versions a nobleman deprived of his lands. They eventually became amalgamated in the public mind. Bogong Jack similarly was in one version a gentleman and in another a low grade thief, but the folk imagination was able to bridge this gulf and include the more grandiose background in its retelling. The short, physically unprepossessing Toke was unpromising folk hero material. As a result the later Omeo Bogong Jack, tall, dark, and well made, seems to have taken on something of the respectable aura of his earlier Ovens Valley double. Eric Harding calls him a 'gentleman bushranger'. Captain Melville and Boldrewood's Captain Starlight in *Robbery Under Arms* are examples of dashing bushrangers looked upon sympathetically by the public, as Bogong Jack was. But the activities of the real John Paynter, who was a criminal and an accomplice in murder, were anything but romantic.

Both Robin Hood and Bogong Jack are admired as anti-authority figures, both were outlaws banished from civilization who set up a mini-community in defiance of accepted order. Jack Paynter was part of a gang, just as Robin Hood had his 'merrie men', but the first Bogong Jack figure on the Ovens side was a lone operator. Both the Robin Hood and Bogong Jack legends are protean and elastic, able to accommodate a range of variations connected to a common thread. For the sake of historical clarity John Paynter will be referred to from now on in this study under his own name, not that of Bogong Jack, which he may never have been called in his lifetime, and the gang in which he and Toke participated will be called the Toke-Paynter gang, not the Bogong Jack gang, as Toke not Paynter was its mastermind. (Interestingly, the name John Paynter can arise as a pseudonym, 'Jack the Painter' being an Australian slang phrase for strong bush tea, and by extension for murky business. Catherine

Spence quotes a goldfield's letter which uses the phrase 'Jack the Painter's mob' in her novel *Clara Morison* (1854), published five years before Kingsley's novel.[8])

John Paynter lived on Livingstone Creek about a mile north of the town in the Benambra direction. He had a partner in butchering called David Jones. On 6 April, 1858, Jones was found dead in a gully near Omeo. Jones often stood near a mine shaft taking to the miners, but on this occasion, perhaps due to drink – he had been drinking in an Omeo hotel with John Dargon – he had fallen to this death. John Dargan, a member of a Stratford horse thieving gang, has been previously mentioned in a similar incident when a colleague John Brown got drunk and was later found dead with a broken neck. The historian of the Tambo River goldfields Keith Fairweather had his suspicions about David Jones' death: 'The nature of his injuries are not in the report, but the name of Jack Paynter gives rise to some conjecture...considering these things [his stealing rackets and involvement in the Cornelius Green murder] one must wonder just how butcher Davis happened to fall into an adjoining claim'.[9] Police records show his partner John Paynter later turned up, requested and was given Jones' account books.

Thomas Toke connected the central Gippsland mob to the Toke-Paynter gang, whose members were drawn from the more unreliable elements on the stations. Toke was described as dealing in horses on the Omeo in the late 1850s. Paynter and Thomas Toke had worked for a time as stockmen on Edward Crooke's property at Hinnomungie. Paynter drove cattle to Port Albert (as Arthur Orton did from Boisdale). Paynter and Toke caused Crooke great trouble, as one would expect with such people working on his property. The men later implicated in the Cornelius Green affair, William Armstrong, George Chamberlain and Sydney Penny, and some others who gave evidence over Ballarat Harry's disappearance, were members of the gang. The gang gradually moved from legitimate butchering operations into branding cleanskins and rebranding cattle, which were resold or butchered for local miners to eat. They also stole horses, which were much more valuable than cattle. Paynter was reputed to be able to alter the appearance of a horse completely by the use of bleaches and dyes. He was adept at changing brands – Crooke's brands of EC and FJ could easily be altered to Paynter's own brands of EB and PJ. Jane Vince Pendergast reports in the reminiscences of Omeo old timers that these were common activities around Omeo at the time. The best contemporary evidence of John Paynter participating in a criminal gang is a statement by the Omeo correspondent of the *Gippsland Guardian* on 11 March, 1859, in relation to suspects in the murder of Cornelius Green: 'It is known that an organized band of horse-stealers exists in the colony, and that two of the prisoners (if not more) were connected with it'. As Paynter was among those charged, and Toke gave evidence, this is the clearest evidence at the time confirming the existence of the Toke-Paynter gang.

Omeo in the late 1850s was described in the *Ovens and Murray Advertiser* of 21 March, 1863, as a 'metropolis of crime'. A number of gangs, including the Toke-Paynter and Cobungra ones, widened their area of operations. The retired policeman John Sadleir wrote that the gang 'collected the best of the studs of such breeders as Edward Crooke, Robert Firebrace, and William Pearson of Gippsland, drove the horses across the mountains into North-eastern Victoria and Riverina, and, having disposed of them, returned, not empty by any means, but with the best mob of horses they could collect in these districts'.[10] The larger scheme which developed has best been described by the novelist Rolf Boldrewood:

> Strayed cattle and ownerless horses accumulated in the virgin mountain passes. These were at first driven to the nearest market by tracks only known to the outlaws of the waste, or their confederates the stock-riders in charge of rarely visited cattle-stations. Suddenly the trade developed, owing to the higher prices ruling since the gold eruption. An organized system of horse and cattle stealing arose. Outlying lots of fat cattle were 'cut out' or separated from the border herds of Monaro or Gippsland, and crossed into opposite colonies. Detection in such cases was well-nigh impossible. Much of the illegal work was done by night. If pursued, the tracks were purposely blinded by station cattle driven across the trail, while, from the rugged character of the country, strangers were at a special disadvantage.[11]

From Omeo there were a number of routes over the mountains. One went across the Bogong High Plains via Tawonga and along the Kiewa valley to Albury. Another was through Cobungra, Mt. Hotham and Harrietville to Bright, Beechworth and Wangaratta. A third took a more westerly direction to the Buckland River and Mt. Howitt. There was one north through Glen Wills and the Mitta Mitta to the Murray River. Another went via the Gibbo River to Corryong, and another north-east through Mt. Leinster to the Monaro. The miners on the Beechworth and Buckland fields were an obvious target for selling cheap meat. So were those on the Crooked River fields, reached by the track leading south from Cobungra. Bogong Jack's hut was near Mt. Fainter on the headquarters of the Kiewa River near the Bogong High Plains. It was a strategic spot where brands could be changed in secrecy. Bogong Jack's stockyards were said to be in the hills north-east of Omeo near Limestone Creek. Thomas Toke's hut was north of Omeo on the Gibbo, another remote area. These routes extended the convict trail into northern Victoria.

The *Gippsland Guardian* of 18 September, 1857, reported: 'During the last few days the miners and residents of (Livingstone) Creek have been in a state of excitement and uneasiness, owing to the disappearance of a number of their horses. Suspicion attaches to two men, apparently father and son, supposed to have come here from Beechworth. They left last night or early this morning, ostensibly for the purpose of spending a few weeks in the bush and will probably pay Gipps Land or Maneroo a visit next to ascertain the value of horse flesh there.' On 23 October, 1857, the *Ovens Constitution* reported, perhaps describing the same gang: 'Some ten days or a fortnight ago a gang of horse-stealers made off with a number of horses from different parts of the Omeo, and were tracked into Beechworth. One of the horses was sold in this township, and the purchaser was nearly getting into trouble in consequence of being found with it. He however produced the auctioneer's sale-note, which cleared him, and he was set at liberty. Since then further information has been received of the whereabouts of some portion of the gang.'

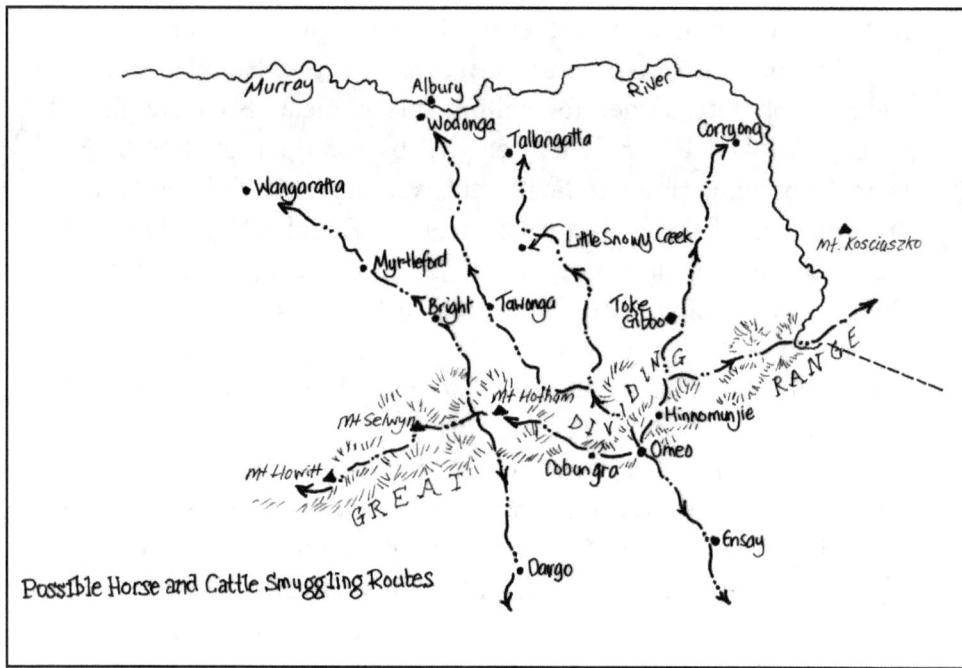

Possible Horse and Cattle Smuggling Routes

As a result of repeated public protests the authorities made an attempt in the late 1850s to stamp out these rackets. But the police were handicapped in their efforts by not knowing the mountain routes and passes as well as the locals. In June, 1858, the police reported: 'the crime of horsestealing is greatly on the increase, and very few offenders are brought to justice, principally because the general police are not in a position to ferret out the haunts of horsestealers, or the localities where they plant the stolen cattle.'[12] In October, 1858, a horse stealer from the Omeo station took a well-known horse, Cantab, and another horse, owned by Thomas Sheean and one of the Pendergasts. Thomas Sheean and Constable Fane pursued the man suspected of horse stealing, named as John Parker in police records and likely to be John Paynter, through the Gibbo to the Murray River, Albury and as far as Wagga Wagga, then back via the Mitta Mitta, but was unable to pin anything on him. On this journey Constable Fane had great difficulty crossing the Murray River; this incident is probably the basis for the folkloric story about Bogong Jack evading a policemen in a river. This pursuit extended the convict trail into the Riverina, as happened commonly in the 1860s. Often these journeys by lone members of the gang were feints to put police on the wrong track, while others carried on their criminal activities unhindered. It was just after this fruitless chase that John Paynter was married in Omeo; the conjunction of these two events may account for the comment made by the Omeo correspondent in the *Gippsland Guardian* on 29 October, 1858. Paynter was married at a dual marriage, the first on the Livingstone field. The correspondent wrote:

> The less said about these melancholy and unfortunate affairs the better, suffice it that as the bridegroom did not "shout" for the miners on the occasion, the miners shouted for themselves and passed a first rate, pleasant night dancing at Tom Sheean's, bowling in Jones' American Saloon, or in lively fun and sparkling wit at courteous Johnny Hewitt's Hotel.

Thomas Sheean, who had chased the thief, was now one of those hosting the wedding celebrations.

In the later 1850s police made a concerted effort to rid the district of these desperadoes. John Sadleir records that: 'A smart sergeant of police named Reid, stationed at Omeo, managed to get a knowledge of the plans of "Bogong" Jack and his friends and broke up the combine.'[13] When things got too hot for them in Omeo, the bushrangers fled to remote huts in the mountains to the north. The correspondent of the *Ovens and Murray Advertiser* was relieved to write on 23 March, 1863: 'Through the exertions of the Police officers, especially those of Sergeant King, even the 'horse stealing society' at Omeo is now virtually and morally defunct'.

NOTES

1   Henry Haygarth *Recollections of Bush Life in Australia*, John Murray, London, 1848, p. 140.

2   For these family interconnections see John R. Grenville *Sedition, Treason & Other Pastoral Pursuits*, High Country Publishing, Dargo, 1997, and 'Cobungra Station' in Harry Stephenson *Cattlemen & Huts of the High Plain*, Graphic Workshop, Armadale, 1980, pp. 288-293.

3   PROV, Police Correspondence, VPRS 937, Unit 409, Bundle 3.

4   Details of Andrews' trial can be found in the *Ovens and Murray Advertiser* of 5 November, 1857, and in *The Argus* of 13 November, 1857.

5   Eric Harding claimed in the *Age* of 24 July, 1962, that Bogong Jack, whom Kingsley had named as John Sampson, was an uncle of the then Prime Minister, Robert Menzies, whose mother was a Sampson, and whose uncle and grandfather were both called John Sampson. A cousin, Frank Menzies, writing on behalf of the Menzies family, and indignant that the Menzies family had been named as having a bushranger background, denied the identification by pointing out that these two John Sampsons lived in the western part of Victoria.

6   *Police Gazette*, November 3, 1859, p. 420.

7   See Stephen Knight *Robin Hood: A Complete Study of the English Outlaw*, Blackwell, Oxford, 1994, p. 83.

8   William Howitt wrote of: 'Jack-the painter tea, a green preparation of leaves of some kind, which taste like a mixture of copperas and verdigris, and leave a green scum on the infusion', *Land, Labour and Gold*, op. cit., p. 132. Catherine Spence quotes a letter from the Forest Creek, Castlemaine, goldfields: 'The dirtiness of the work has earned for it the sobriquet of Jack the Painter; and for the last three weeks we have given up the more aristocratic employment of sinking, for the certain though small

gains of Jack the Painter's mob'. Catherine Spence *Clara Morison*, 1854, repr. Rigby, Adelaide, 1971, p. 240.

9   Keith McD. Fairweather *Brajerack: Mining at Omeo and Glen Wills*, Bairnsdale, 1983, p.14.

10 John Sadleir, op. cit., p. 72.

11 Rolf Boldrewood *Nevermore*, Macmillan, London, 1892, pp. 227-8.

12 PROV, Police Correspondence VPRS 937, Unit 227, Bundle 1.

13 John Sadleir, op. cit., p.72.

8

THE DISAPPEARANCE OF BALLARAT HARRY

The most mysterious criminal act connected with the Omeo goldfields was the disappearance and suspected murder of the miner Ballarat Harry in early 1858, a deed associated with members of the Toke-Paynter gang. Ballarat Harry was an Englishman, Walter or William Clare, originally from Kent. After spending some time in Adelaide and Gawler, South Australia, he moved to the Ballarat goldfields. On the Wardy Yallock (Smythesdale) field near Ballarat, where he mined with 'Jack the Sailor' Taylor, he found a large, eagle-shaped nugget which he kept with him.

Ballarat Harry arrived at Omeo in early 1855; he had been there over two years and was well known before this incident happened. He has some similarities to the person known as 'the foreigner' on the Omeo fields – both Harry and 'the foreigner' had an iron grey horse, shared a lease with Toke and fell out with him, but Clare's English origins makes the appellation 'the foreigner' unlikely. In personality he was different from the rough, run-of-the-mill Omeo miners, being steady, cautious and keeping his own counsel. He was averse to drinking, and seemed a cut above his companions on the goldfield. He kept papers, such as details of the ownership of his horses, and was careful about them. Another distinguishing feature was his relative wealth. Though somewhat of a loner, he foolishly let others see how much money he carried around. Friends said he possessed 30 to 50 gold sovereigns, a quantity of gold dust, some pound notes, a gold and a silver watch, and nuggets, including an eagle-shaped one from Wardy Yallock which he was so attached to he wouldn't part with. Estimates of the worth of the valuables he carried around with him varied from £300 to £600. He had a mare, a foal, and a dog, a Newfoundland, which followed him faithfully everywhere. Local opinion had it that he was a poor horseman and a poor bushman, another unusual feature. He brought to Omeo his brother, James Clare, who survived him by many decades.

Thomas Toke, the central figure in the Ballarat Harry incident, had a grim previous history. After his release in Tasmania, he travelled north to Gippsland, where he was employed as a stockrider on the Mewburn Park run and then at Hinnomungie. He subsequently moved to the Livingstone Creek goldfield where he mixed with other miners, many of whom, as part of the fringe criminal group, had dubious reputations. At the Omeo diggings Jack Taylor, Ballarat Harry, 'Tom the Milkman' and Robert Whittaker had a mining claim together at one stage; then Toke replaced Whittaker, Ballarat Harry paying Toke's share, and William Robertson replaced 'Tom the Milkman'. Eventually Toke and Ballarat Harry had a row when Toke borrowed money from Harry for a claim. A witness to this row, the butcher Edward Crane, has Toke saying: 'He [Ballarat Harry] robbed me of five ounces of gold the other night; when we washed down the boxes I am sure there was ten ounces; I went to the hut and left him to pan it off and when we weighed it there was only five ounces.'[1] Crane was a local butcher with an ambiguous record, sometimes fraternizing with the criminal element and sometimes working with the police, as later incidents reveal. It was strange that Ballarat Harry, who had a very different personality from the others, was caught up with such characters.

Gippsland had three main goldfields. In the east, the fields lay down the Tambo River, from Omeo in the north to Deptford in the south. Well to the west lay the Goulburn-Thomson fields, from Jameson to Walhalla. In the middle of the two was the Crooked River field, with Dargo as its suply town. Dargo was the pivot of the mountain goldfields tracks. One track led west from Dargo to the Thomson fields. Another track led north to Cobungra and then east to Omeo. Another went south-east through the Nicholson fields to Bruthen. The Ballarat Harry story connected all three goldfields.

A little before Christmas 1857, Toke encouraged a party of diggers from Omeo, which included Whittaker, Crane and 'Lanky Tom' Grice, to go on a long trip to Malcolm Macfarlane's run on the Macalister River in the Glenmaggie region south of the Goulburn-Thomson fields. This was because, in Crane's account, Toke said he had heard Macfarlane had found gold there: 'Malcolm Macfarlane picked up a two ounce nugget of gold in the stream and it is a mountain out there, the blacks call it brassy mountain and it is a mountain of gold, and when we work out this claim we will go out there.' This was strange, as Glenmaggie was never a gold field. Toke claimed to have marked a line from Dargo station to the Livingstone, implying he had pioneered that route. On the way the party called in at the Dargo station. Glenmaggie was near the most western of the Gippsland fields, and a long way from Omeo. In Edward Crane's version of the incident, when they went to the Glemaggie area Macfarlane said there was no gold there, and as a result Whittaker accused Toke of being a liar. Their search for gold was naturally unsuccessful, and the party got lost on the way home, having to eat a horse for rations. They eventually emerged via Shady Creek at the Tambo River, ending up at Marshall's Inn at Bruthen, a criminal haunt. There is a suspicion they were involved in horse stealing on this trip. After it was over, the others wondered why Toke had suggested the trip. Armstrong said later that Toke planned to get rid of Ballarat Harry on the trip, but Harry did not come.

This first trip was a rehearsal for the second. Toke now persuaded Ballarat Harry the two of them should go to Glenmaggie to look for the gold themselves. This was strange, seeing that they had already had a row, and there was no gold there on the first trip. Lanky Tom and others had meanwhile moved to prospect at Shady Creek. In the middle of March 1858 Toke and Ballarat Harry set out, apparently without telling people they were going. Harry's dog was later seen back at the Omeo diggings, which people thought unusual. The two were seen at the Dargo outstation, where they stayed for the last two weeks of March 1858, playing cards in the hut there with Arthur Orton and others. The last time Ballarat Harry was seen alive was by a shepherd on the Dargo run. It was clear from Arthur Orton's hurried departure from Dargo soon after that something terrible had happened to Harry Clare.

Edward Watson was a Sale contractor, bridge builder and borough councillor, who had close relations with the police – he built the police stable and forage store at Sale. Watson wrote in 1859 that 'the universal opinion is, that Clare has met with his death by some unfair means'. Thomas Toke then returned to Omeo by himself more than two weeks after leaving Dargo. He said he had left Ballarat Harry on good terms in the bush and understood Harry was going to Boggy Creek or Adelaide or elsewhere. Toke claimed he picked up Harry's horse 25 miles from McMillan's Dargo outstation. Toke, Orton and Armstrong gave different versions of events later on. In a statement on the matter Arthur Orton deposed:

> I remember Thomas Tooke and Ballarat Harry coming to Dargo on the 16th or 17th of March. Tooke inquired whether Michie the Frenchman was there – I said no. They remained until the second of April. In conversation with Clare, he told me that Tooke had informed him that Michie had shown him (Tooke) a nugget of gold weighing 13 (half) ozs. and that Michie had promised to meet Tooke with his mate. When I asked Tooke why they were to meet at Dargo, he said that Michie had found gold at Glenmaggie, and that J Johnstone, Esq. had given Michie the Bruthen station for three years – to keep it secret – and that they were going to cross the mountains that nobody should see them.[2]

This complicated story from Toke is most likely a pack of lies, just as his earlier story about Glenmaggie was dubious; its object was to convince Harry to come on the trip. Edward Watson later met Michie (Micky the Frenchman) and asked him what stopped him from coming. Michie seemed quite surprised at the whole suggestion, saying he hadn't found a nugget and hadn't promised to meet them. Orton also stated that he knew Ballarat Harry had money and gold on him while at Dargo, as Harry had shown him a nugget. In addition Orton said that while Toke was at Dargo, he told Orton that he had no money, but that as soon as he got some, he would return to Omeo, as he had debts to pay there.

It took some time for it to sink in at Omeo that Harry was missing. Toke returned about 20 April, with Harry's mare and saddle in his possession. The miners began to notice that many of Harry's possessions, such as the gold watch, the nugget and the horses, were now seen with Toke, who had suddenly become very prosperous. The publican Thomas Sheean received £120 off Toke for goods Toke needed to set up his own store on the Gibbo. Others were involved in complicated deals with Toke buying or swapping horses, gold nuggets and watches previously associated with Ballarat Harry. The policeman John Sadleir at Beechworth reported on 30 June, 1858: 'Two watches of the following description were forwarded to Beechworth for repairs by a woman living with Toke as his wife: Gold hunting Geneva watch   Silver hunting lever watch'.[3] Sgt Manson reported: 'The animal [Harry's dog] returned; it was therefore remarked by some of the remaining miners that "Clare" was done for, else the dog would not have returned without his master'. The Toke-Paynter gang were implicated. John Paynter himself had purchased one of Ballarat Harry's horses, a foal, via Toke. 'Bill the Ostler' Armstrong, another member of the gang, said Toke had about £600 or £700 on him. The evidence Armstrong gave damaging to Toke was to have severe repercussions in the future for Armstrong.

By mid June 1858 diggers had reported their anxieties about Harry's disappearance to the authorities. Harry was first publicly noticed as missing by a notice in the newspapers of 25 June. Dr Fisher, after seeing Toke with suspicious goods in Thomas Sheean's pub, made a formal complaint. Sheean took Magistrate Wills to interview Toke at the Gibbo. At this stage Charles McDonald, who was looking after Toke's store on the Gibbo, noticed that Toke took many possessions in a bag with him, saying that he was in trouble. Constable Fane next appeared at Toke's with a search warrant to look for items such as watches and receipts of horse ownership, some of which he found, though many of the stolen articles had been removed. Although no body was ever found, Toke was now indicted on suspicion of the murder of Ballarat Harry, with a bail of £100, given the accumulation of circumstantial evidence and the fact that he was known to have had a falling out with Ballarat Harry.

The Omeo correspondent of the *Gippsland Guardian* pointed out on 9 July that rumour on the Livingstone Creek goldfield had already convicted Toke, which was dangerous, and warned against premature judgment:

> It was really laughable to observe what acute physiognomists the Livingstone possessed, on a sudden there could not be the slightest doubt of his guilt, murder was indelibly stamped upon his face, and the fact of the man being an old hand, also tended to confirm the suspicion in some of the shallow-pated fools.

The Police Magistrate, Mr. Wills, began the hearing at Omeo on Thursday, 17 June, 1858.[4] Witnesses who knew both Toke and Ballarat Harry well said they had seen Harry's goods in Toke's possession after his return, and gave details of Toke's buying and selling since. A witness, Fred Bird, subsequently involved in murky business, identified Toke's nuggets as being originally Ballarat Harry's. Charles Gadd saw Toke with a gold watch, sovereigns, nuggets and dust. And other witnesses, including Thomas Sheean and Richard Whittaker, had seen horses with Toke which may have been Harry's. Toke in defence asked questions of the witnesses in order to confuse the issues by getting them to agree that Toke habitually traded in such goods. The inquest continued on the Friday and was adjourned to Monday, 28 June. At the end of the hearing on Monday, the Magistrate adjourned proceedings for eight days in order that a summons be served on 'Jack the Sailor' Taylor, who, as a mate of Ballarat Harry's from a long way back, was a key witness. But Taylor and others were reluctant witnesses. Police had been sent to bring Taylor in on three occasions, but informers had misled the police, sending them on wild goose chases in which the police had had their clothes stolen and a horse lost. Such diversionary tactics were typical of the Toke-Paynter gang, and one Bogong Jack legend about misleading police has close parallels with this incident. Some locals were obstructing the inquiry, and some witnesses clearly did not want to appear and speak. Many of those called as witnesses were friends of Toke, and may therefore have been associates of the Toke-Paynter gang.

The inquest resumed on July 5 and 7. 'Jack the Sailor' Taylor, now found and brought to the inquest, was first to appear. He said he had been Ballarat Harry's mate at Wardy Yallock near Ballarat, and had been in a claim with him at Omeo. Taylor said that the horses Toke had were Harry's, as were receipts for horses he had seen in Harry's possession. Further evidence covered the same ground as in earlier days. Then Toke was given an opportunity to make a statement in his defence. Toke smartly covered all his weak points. He gave his version of how he had left Harry in the bush. He explained how the dog had never left Omeo. He had, he claimed, exchanged or bought the goods of Harry's he possessed, as he commonly dealt in this way. After further witnesses were heard on these matters, the Magistrate gave his decision, dismissing the case against Toke. He said that he had not received full support; some witnesses were reluctant to appear and give evidence on what they knew. People should keep proper receipts of horses and other goods traded. He requested that missing miners be reported more quickly, as it was hard to investigate after such a lapse in time. These caveats imply that Wills had misgivings, and may have come to a different finding had more evidence had been produced. Arthur Orton, still working at this time at Boisdale, was surprisingly not called, though he was one of the last to see Harry alive. Another reason for witnesses being reluctant to appear emerged later: the trader Joseph Day sued two of the witnesses, Whittaker and Hamilton, when they came to town, for money he claimed they owed him.

At a later inquest into the murder of Cornelius Green, William Armstrong, a suspect in that case, claimed that the following had happened in relation to Ballarat Harry's disappearance. Toke had suggested that Armstrong go to Glenmaggie with Toke and Harry, and then said he would let Armstrong into a secret: 'If we could get Harry down there we will settle him'. Armstrong said he would have nothing to do with this. Toke then pointed out that both he and Armstrong were short of money and that Harry had about £400 on him. Armstrong still refused and Toke then said he would give Armstrong £100 the next time they met to say nothing more of the matter. When Armstrong next saw Toke six months later at Sheean's hotel, Toke said: 'You see, I settled him...down on a river the other side of Dargo'. Toke described to him how he had tomahawked Ballarat Harry to death while he slept, stolen £400 from him, cut up the body in small pieces, ground up the bones and burnt the whole lot in the bush. Armstrong thought it was foolish for Toke to have had Harry's things with him, but Toke said he had got rid of most of them. For going quiet on the matter, Toke offered Armstrong a saddle and a double-barrelled revolver he had at the Gibbo. This account has some credibility, though Armstrong would have been bitter with Toke, who had implicated him in the Cornelius Green murder.

Later stories said the Haunted Stream, a gold prospecting area on the Tambo fields, was named after the terrible event of Ballarat Harry's murder, which had been carried out there; others said the stream's name came from the blood-curdling cries of the barking owl. Toke and Ballarat Harry may have called in at Shady Creek, near Haunted Stream, to see Lanky Tom and others on the way back from Dargo, and the murder may have taken place there. Constable Barham reported on 28 June, 1862, finding a white man's skull with a fracture at Shady Creek. Edward Watson suggested that the murder may have happened on Iguana Creek.

Later on people speculated that Ballarat Harry was the missing Sir Roger Tichborne. Both were said to have been on the Ballarat goldfields; both were respectable, wealthy and quiet, and therefore different in style from the ordinary digger. Ballarat Harry's disappearance also fitted the theory that Tichborne had been murdered in the bush by his mates, one of whom, Arthur Orton, then assumed his identity. Ballarat Harry's penchant for keeping personal papers with him could have led his murderers, it was assumed, to have gathered information on his background; this would explain Orton/Castro's knowledge of the Tichborne family. This is the plot of Rolf Boldrewood's novel *Nevermore*, where Ballarat Harry, the heir, is murdered and his identity assumed by one of his assailants. Much was made of Ballarat Harry's disappearance in the two Tichborne trials in England, but the claimant Orton/Castro refused to be drawn on the matter on the grounds that it might incriminate him. There is of course no real evidence linking Ballarat Harry and the missing aristocrat.

NOTES

1 Edward Crane 'How Ballarat Harry met his death', repr. *Gippsland Heritage Journal*, No. 15, December, 1993.

2 Orton's statement, which could be a court deposition or a private statement Watson obtained from Orton, is contained in Edward Watson's letter to the *Gippsland Guardian*, 15 April, 1859.

3 PROV, VPRS 937 Unit 227, Bundle 1, File 172/58. All police records cited in this chapter are from this file.

4 Reports of the inquest can be found in the *Gippsland Guardian* of 9 and 23 July, 1858.

9

THE MURDER OF CORNELIUS GREEN

Gold smuggling was a much more lucrative operation than cattle stealing, and easier to conceal. A further escalation of criminal activity was into armed robbery, where crimes of violence against humans were involved. By the late 1850s lawlessness was increasing in the Omeo area but so also were the risks. The climax came when the Toke-Paynter gang seriously overplayed its hand with the murder of Cornelius Green in early 1859.[1] Thomas Toke, John Paynter, William Armstrong, 'George the Butcher' Chamberlain, and a young man called George 'Sydney' Penny (a brother-in-law of Michael Sheean, Omeo storekeeper and publican), all members of the gang, were involved in this outrage.

Cornelius Green, originally from Suffolk, England, had arrived in Omeo in the mid 1850s, setting himself up as a gold and commission agent, in addition to being a storekeeper at the Gibbo. He was therefore a rival to Thomas Toke, as well as to other storekeepers and agents in the district. Early in his stay he had been living at Joseph Day's hotel and acting as a commission agent for Day. On 16 July, 1858, Green published a letter on lowering gold prices and related matters in the *Gippsland Guardian*. There were significant price differentials for gold within Victoria. Green stated that assays showed the value of gold increased the nearer the coast it was found. Omeo dealers had previously paid 75 shillings per ounce as they could sell the gold on the Ovens market, but as this was closed because of transport problems, the price would be 68 shillings from now on, though the old price would be paid for gold from nearer the coast, such as at Boggy Creek. Omeo gold was of poorer quality, Green claimed, so attempts were made to sell it at places like Yackandandah as local gold, which commanded a higher price.

Remoteness and difficult transport were also problems for Omeo gold, as was the reluctance of Gippsland traders to buy gold themselves, preferring cash. At Omeo almost nobody traded gold for cash, Green claimed; the storekeepers took it in exchange for goods. As about 250 ounces a week was being produced on local fields, 'the establishment of an escort service is a very material matter', wrote Green. A monthly police escort from Livingstone Creek to Port Albert had, he announced, been promised by the government. He looked optimistically to the future, never dreaming that he himself would be a victim of such arrangements.

As in the Ballarat Harry case, a lot of circumstantial evidence exists to implicate Toke as a factor in the subsequent criminal activity, which went horribly wrong. The two main actors were William Armstrong and George Chamberlain, both only 23 years old. Chamberlain, known as 'George the Butcher', was from Richmond near Sydney, one of those who had moved south. He had worked for and lived with Paynter; both had been involved in deals over horses. Armstrong was an Irish Protestant who had arrived in the Port Phillip district in 1851, and was said to be a deserter from the 40th Regiment in Australia. He is listed on the electoral role of 1856 as a worker at the Hazelwood run near Morwell in central Gippsland. At Omeo he worked as a horse-breaker, and had been in service to Green and to Henry Dickens, a Swift's Creek storekeeper and friend of Green's. Both Chamberlain and Armstrong were boarding at the time at Joseph Day's hotel. They were described in a *Weekly Herald* article of July 8, 1859, as 'gaining their livelihood by occasionally trafficking in horses, at other times acting as stockmen for the butchers who supplied the miners'. This reveals they were involved in shady deals, and were dependent on the local butcher-tradesmen. Sydney Penny, who had worked for Green and lived at Michael Sheean's hotel, may be the same person as 'a Sydney native, named Halfpenny, who was a good deal in Gippsland', mentioned in the Australian Commission on the Tichborne case.[2]

On 5 January, 1859, Cornelius Green left Omeo to take between 1,000 and 1,500 ounces of gold, worth some thousands of pounds, for delivery in Melbourne. On the night before he left, he spoke to Chamberlain and Armstrong at Joseph Day's Limerick Castle

Hotel, where all had been staying. It was probably here that the two bushrangers learnt that Green had a valuable cargo. Armstrong, with military training in the care of arms, cleaned the gun of his employer Green; it was subsequently found that he had removed a screw and disabled it. Green left Omeo with the police escort he had campaigned for, because of his worry about armed hold-ups on the long journey through mountain and bush tracks. The escort was Constable Greene. Like Armstrong, Greene was an Irishman who had served in the military there. Also in the party was a Miss Eliza Mutter, said by some to be a fianceé of Green's. During the first day's travel, as they were passing through a wooded gully, they met up with Armstrong, Chamberlain and Penny, and exchanged greetings. An unidentified man was seen nearby. Later it transpired that this was an aborted hold-up attempt, called off because 'Sydney' Penny had welshed on the deal. Later on they came across John Paynter. The party then stayed the night at Burns' Hotel at Tongiomungy, where, according to some accounts, they discovered the gun had been nobbled.

Next day the party, joined by another storekeeper, 'Harry the Snob' Dickens, continued its journey south. Just north of Swift's Creek, as they were moving along a narrow path with good timber cover, they were bailed up by a posse of armed bushrangers, some wearing flourbags or white handkerchiefs as masks. Shots fired from close range wounded Cornelius Green, Dickens and Constable Greene. The latter's account of the incident describes what happened:

> Immediately after I heard a shot, and, thinking it must have been Mr. Green's revolver that went off, I looked and saw Mr. Green leaning forward in the saddle. I also saw a man on my right hand armed with a gun. I drew a holster pistol and fired at him, and he either fell or got behind a tree. I was then fired at from a tree on the left side, and was shot through both arms.[3]

Constable Greene soon became unconscious. Miss Mutter saw two men hacking at Cornelius Green with a weapon. In the confusion that followed, the storekeeper Dickens, Miss Mutter

CORNELIUS GREEN AND HIS GRAVE AT SWIFT'S CREEK

and Constable Greene escaped, as did the horse carrying the gold. Cornelius Green, who had probably recognized his assailants, was brutally attacked with a tomahawk. John Paynter and 'Sydney' Penny were observed during the incident nearby holding horses. Dickens too thought he had recognized the assailants. When Constable Greene recovered and reached Swift's Creek, he raised the alarm. An old soldier, Harry Cross, went back with Greene to the scene. On 22 January, 1859, the *Melbourne Leader* quoted a private letter from Omeo which said in part 'when [Cornelius Green's] body was found it was positively most awful to look upon...His right hand was nearly cut off, and his nose right below the arch of the eyebrows. On the left temple there was also a frightful looking gash. His death must have been instantaneous'. Armstrong and Chamberlain arrived back at Day's Hotel at 10 pm that night, claiming they had been out catching cattle on the Omeo plain during the day. As the Magistrate and local JP were both away, Mr Venables conducted the funeral service. All stories and public houses were closed as a mark of respect for Green. A few days before, Cornelius Green had himself conducted a service for a miner who had drowned.

Saddle straps found at the scene were soon identified as having been sold to Armstrong by Joseph Day, publican and storekeeper. The Omeo Police Magistrate, Mr Wills, then issued a warrant for the arrest of Armstrong and Chamberlain, who had been recognized as the principal attackers, on murder charges. They meanwhile had stolen horses from Soames Davis, another Omeo storekeeper. Joseph Day later gave evidence that on 7 January he had traced horses' tracks 'very close to John Paynter's house, which was north-east of the town on the Benambra road, and from there away into the bush again, as if making for the plain, in a north-easterly direction. That direction, if followed, would take them to the Gibbo'. The two had gone into hiding at Toke's hut on the Gibbo, where they asked Toke for help. Armstrong explained that Green had to be killed since 'a dead cock will never crow'. Chamberlain here wrote a letter to John Paynter, asking for help, and establishing alibis for the murder for Paynter and Penny, and for the horses stolen for their getaway. It concluded: 'If we ever get nabbed, I want you to stick to this story; so you will have to learn this by heart: but for God's sake don't let anyone see this paper – not even your wife ... Make that bloody Sidney understand what he will have to pitch; don't tell him too long a story. I don't think there is any danger of the snavolers [snafflers, i.e. police] copping us'. This letter was so obviously incriminating that counsel for the defence at the trial suggested that it hadn't been written by Chamberlain. Then, refreshed and supplied by Toke, the two rode north to effect their escape. Toke rode into Omeo to give the letter to Paynter, who rejected it, saying it had nothing to do with him. Toke returned to his store, and then turned Queen's Evidence by handing the letter over to the police via John Wright, the member of the Mining Board, and divulging the route of the escapees.

A police party consisting of Inspector Hill, mounted troopers Reid and White, a blacktracker and three local citizens, including the publican Thomas Sheean and the squatter Matthew Macalister, proceeded to the Gibbo, where Toke's assistant, James McMahon, gave them information. The escapees by this time were heading north across wild mountain country towards Wheelers Crossing, halfway to Corryong. The police party caught up with them near there. On being challenged, the two escaped on foot after their horses were bogged in a swamp, but some distance further on, an Aboriginal blacktracker, Tommy, spotted them hiding up a tree. Inspector Hill ordered them down, and they were arrested without resisting. They were then charged with horse stealing. Two-thirds of the town of Omeo turned out in joy to witness the return of the prisoners.

A public contretemps arose over who had effected the capture. An article on the chase in the *Gippsland Guardian* of January 28, 1859, praised the civilians for the successful apprehension:

> The gentlemen who thus voluntarily assisted the police at this important time, are certainly deserving of our hearty thanks: without their assistance it is very doubtful whether the capture would have been effected at all, for our small company of police were by no means equal to the task.

This supports Sadleir's later claim that the police were

inexperienced in the bush. A letter by 'Observer' on 18 February supported these sentiments, giving great praise to Macalister. Inspector Hill took this as an insult, saying Macalister was spreading the word that he (Macalister) had led the chase, at the expense of the reputation of the police. Things boiled over when the two met and confronted each other at Bruthen, where Macalister horsewhipped Inspector Hill for his claim that Macalister was involved in self-praise. Macalister was subsequently charged with assault and fined £12 at the Omeo court.

A separate dispute erupted over the letter Edward Crooke had written to the *Argus*, which appeared just before the Green murder. The letter was republished in the *Weekly Argus*, where Omeo residents would have read it two days after the murder. This was the letter in which Crooke damned the Omeo area as ridden with drunkards, horse-stealers, thieves and murderers. Crooke, as a resident squatter, had had a lot of trouble, and the Green murder seemed to confirm his picture of problems in the district. But 'An Old Omeo Digger' replied in the *Gippsland Guardian* on 4 February, 1859, disputing Crooke's claim by arguing that the diggers were not to blame, it was the people who originally worked as stockmen on cattle stations who caused the trouble. This was true in that it was people like Toke and Paynter, and Chamberlain and Armstrong, not the ordinary diggers, who were the villains. The Omeo correspondent of the paper confirmed this impression.

Although the events surrounding the Green murder were relatively straightforward, the aftermath was quite complex. There were five legal proceedings in all. The first was the inquest, beginning on 25 January, 1859, at Omeo, and conducted by Police Magistrate Wills. Armstrong and Chamberlain were charged with murder, and Paynter and Penny with being accessories to the crime. It was at this stage that Armstrong, realizing that Toke had been the cause of his capture, revealed Toke's account of how Toke had killed Ballarat Harry and burned his body. The evidence on the Green murder was detailed and damning, and the two were committed for trial on the murder charge. The prisoners could not be taken to Beechworth, the normal place for a trial, for fear they would escape on the mountain tracks across the ranges they knew so well, so the trials were set down for Melbourne at a later date. The Omeo correspondent of the *Gippsland Guardian* was worried that a rescue attempt would be made as the prisoners were being conveyed to Melbourne. As the prisoners were about to leave in a bullock dray, guarded by six policemen, Chamberlain stood and said to the crowd in attendance: 'Let this be a warning to all you young men: remember it as long as you live'. This sounded a bit like an admission of guilt. No escape attempt was made, but on one of the sidings south of Omeo, the dray tipped over, and deposited the prisoners in the Tambo River. But they were not injured, nor did they escape.

The first trial, in Melbourne on 15 March, 1859, was of Armstrong and Chamberlain for stealing the horses they had used in the getaway. On this charge they both sentenced to five years' imprisonment. Later that month they faced murder charges. The prosecution, which should have had an easy case, faced many difficulties, some of its own making. The chief prosecutor, the Solicitor General, Richard Ireland, was not present for much of the trial, allegedly taking the case lightly. Many key witnesses from the Omeo district, who had vital evidence and who had appeared at the inquest, were not brought to Melbourne for the trial. Toke, who was the key Crown witness, was evasive and unsatisfactory, as he had been in the Ballarat Harry case. The prosecution had no positive identification of the culprits at the scene. The defence counsel pointed the finger at Toke as the most likely culprit, given his sinister past. Judge Molesworth in summing up cast doubt on Toke's veracity, and on whether Chamberlain had written the incriminating letter. As a result of all these factors the jury returned a verdict of 'not guilty'. Given the evidence at the Omeo inquest, this was a remarkable verdict. Next Paynter and Penny appeared on the 'accessory to a crime' charges. But as the others had been found not guilty and many witnesses had left to go home, the two were released from these charges.

These verdicts caused a great outcry – public indignation was high. It seemed people could openly get away with brutal murder on the roads. The most damning legal indictment of the prosecution appeared in a letter to the *Age* signed by 'Justitia' and reproduced in the *Ovens Constitution* of 8 April, 1859. 'Justitia' argued that

> The public mind is not satisfied with the result of the trial...in every place where men commonly assemble together, there is but one unanimous expression of opinion that the Crown, through its law officers, failed to perform its duty, in placing the case for the prosecution before the jury in such a manner as to enable them to decide fairly between the accused and the contrary.

'Justitia' then analysed Omeo evidence which had not been presented at the trial, and listed other defects to prove his case. For example, at the Omeo inquest, Armstrong had questioned a witness Eliza Mutter, asking her what he had worn on his head at the murder scene. Armstrong disagreed with her answer, but as 'Justitia' pointed out, the question amounted to an admission that he was present. Sydney Penny's confession was not used at the trial. The slugs found in Green's body and at the scene were not compared with those from the rifles of Armstrong and Chamberlain, which were in the police's possession. For these reasons and others 'Justitia' concluded with an attack on the Solicitor General, Mr. Ireland. In addition the O'Shanassy government, whose hold on power was weak and which was being assailed on other issues, like land reform, was vulnerable to the charge that it was not upholding public law and order.

An Indignation Meeting at Omeo was held in early April. Mr William Jack, cousin of the late Mr Green, complained that parts of the Crown evidence were left untouched, and that the 'billiard loving' Solicitor General had absented himself from the case. The meeting called on the government in the strongest terms to act, otherwise citizens would not feel themselves safe. A resolution was passed:

> That until the criminal business of the country is more efficiently conducted than it has been in the case of Regina v. Chamberlain and Armstrong this meeting does not consider either life or property safe in this colony.

Editorials in papers in the surrounding districts contained similar sentiments. The *Ovens Constitution* on 23 April commented:

> Who will venture to condemn men, residing in regions like the Omeo, if they take the law into their own hands, since they find that those who are sworn and paid to assist its administration, so foully and wilfully neglect their duty?

As a result, the Crown, under pressure, charged Armstrong and Chamberlain with the attempted murder of Constable Greene, to avoid the double jeopardy provisions – after an initial acquittal, a person cannot be charged again for the same act. The final trial took place in Melbourne from 30 June. Six witnesses not at the first trial gave evidence, and the damning letter was shown to have been written by Chamberlain. Toke refused to say in how many prisons he had been incarcerated in England and Australia. The two were speedily found guilty of the attempted murder and sentenced to death. The verdict met with general approval in the Omeo area. But nonetheless it was a strange legal outcome. As Mr A. Metelot, writing four decades later on the case in the *Bairnsdale Advertiser* of 19 October, 1897, put it, Armstrong and Chamberlain were acquitted for what they did do, and then tried and hanged for what they failed to do. Before their execution both produced confessions. In his Armstrong directly implicated Toke in the act for which he, Armstrong, had been sent to death. This may have been a ploy to gain a remission from execution while this charge was being investigated, as just prior to their death both said that their former confessions were false. They were executed on 12 July, 1858.

To many people it seemed likely that the hold-up of the Cornelius Green party was masterminded by the experienced and older Thomas Toke and perhaps John Paynter, but carried out by the younger and more naive Armstrong and Chamberlain. Paynter and Toke got away scot free. Some believed Toke was the unidentified person seen at the scene, and that it was he who tomahawked Green to death, just as he was alleged to have done to Ballarat Harry. Two bizarre incidents occurred in the aftermath of the case. The storekeeper and gold-trader Soames Davis disappeared a few months later in suspicious circumstances, and there was widespread feeling that he, like Ballarat Harry and Cornelius Green, had been done away with. And a decomposed body was found near the murder scene, perhaps one of the bushrangers shot during the affray.

Why was Green shot, apart from the motive of gold stealing? The horse with the gold escaped, which may suggest that the prime target was Green, not the gold. Was he got rid of because he lowered the price of gold to ordinary diggers? Perhaps some Omeo traders wanted rivals like him and Davis out of the way, and used the services of the Toke-Paynter gang. Chamberlain and Armstrong worked for the Omeo trader-butchers and were dependent on them. We don't know the answers to these questions.

The police pursued Paynter, Toke, Penny and other members of the gang in an effort to stamp out horse-stealing operations. On 26 July,1859, Inspector Hill wrote about two men under police observation:

> The individuals herein described have long been suspected of being connected with a horse stealing gang operating here. It is conjectured that they anticipate revelations being made by Chamberlain & Armstrong which would implicate them, & hence their anxiety to leave this part of the country, where they are so well known. I think it is probable they will all make for N.S.Wales…Two of these men were met by a Frenchman about 50 miles from this proceeding in the direction of Beechworth & the Murray…they had in their possession some horses closely resembling some of those missing – these mens names are "Sheean & Clarke".

NOTES

1 Reports of the murder and the subsequent inquest and trials are extensively recorded in the Gippsland and Melbourne press in the first six months of 1859. The police file on the case can be found at PROV, VPRS, Unit 227, Bundle 5, File 79/59.

2 *The Australian Commission*, op. cit., p. 137.

3 'Bushranging, Omeo Road', *Every Week*, Bairnsdale, 5 March, 1919.

10

HENRY KINGSLEY ON THE TRAIL

Events on the Vandemonian trail featured in imaginative literature for the first time when Henry Kingsley appeared on the Australian scene. His four and a half years' Australian sojourn turned him into a novelist. *The Recollections of Geoffry Hamlyn* was published in 1859, a year after he returned to England. Just after Kingsley landed in Melbourne in late 1853, the VDL escapees O'Connor and Bradley terrorized the Barker's Cape Schanck run before running amuck in the environs of Melbourne. As a result Melbourne public opinion was up in arms about the fear of a mass outbreak of Vandemonian bushrangers on the mainland. Kingsley must have been deeply affected by this outcry, his first experience of Australia, because he used it as a key element in his writing. In both his Australian novels, *The Recollections of Geoffry Hamlyn* (1859) and *The Hillyars and the Burtons* (1865), escaped VDL convicts land at Barker's run near Cape Schanck. The latter novel opens with a police group led by Lieutenant Hillyar capturing escaped convicts there. In the novel Kingsley comments on the outbreak:

> His Excellency's speech at the opening of the Houses contained – nay, mainly consisted of – a somewhat offensive comparison between Cooksland [Victoria] and the other five colonies of the Australian group; in which the perfect security of life and property at home was contrasted with the fearful bush-ranger-outrages in New South Wales. And now their turn had come – Cooksland's turn.[1]

Victoria had been up till this time an almost convict-free haven where respectable families could flourish. The main events in volume three of *Geoffry Hamlyn* are based on these fears. Kingsley mentions in a later novella, 'The Two Cadets', a rumour circulating in Victoria at the time:

> There was a great gang of bushrangers abroad; by rumour more numerous, more bold, more cunning, and more cruel than any which had appeared on the continent. One had to go to the legends of the neighbouring island of Van Diemen's Land to match them for strength and ferocity. There was little doubt about their leader: he had been seen many times, and could be sworn to by a hundred mouths – no less a person than Mike Howe, the baby-killer of Van Diemen's Land. This was not true: Howe never went into the bush on the mainland, as far as I can gather. But that awful name was sufficient to cause a panic among the outlying settlers.[2]

This was the fear caused by the Bradley-O'Connor and similar outrages. A large VDL gang didn't appear around Melbourne in the early 1850s. But it did in the mountains around Omeo in the later 1850s, and Kingsley used such an outbreak as the main story line in the third volume of *Geoffry Hamlyn*.

Most of Kingsley's years in Australia were spent in the Western District and in Melbourne. However in late 1855 he left Melbourne for Sydney, hearing on the way the story of the disastrous mining rush to Omeo from Beechworth the year before. In north-east Victoria he picked up some folk stories from local families, including the first known version of the Bogong Jack story. In early 1856 he travelled, mostly on foot, from Sydney back to Melbourne via the Monaro and Gippsland. Kingsley walked down the Vandemonian trail, and grasped something of the distinctive pattern of events associated with it. On the Monaro he stayed with local squatters, one of whom he had known in England. One important source of information for Kingsley was Henry Haygarth's *Recollections of Bush Life in Australia* (1848). Haygarth had been a Monaro squatter but had returned to England before Kingsley's visit. Haygarth's book has many similarities with Kingsley's novel. Both are recollections of life in the same area, both describe new settlers moving south into the Monaro around 1840, and both include bushranging outbreaks in the region.

Kingsley arrived in Gippsland a short time after the Tichborne claimant Arthur Orton, who came in November 1855, but Kingsley stayed there only a few months. He entered Gippsland from the Monaro most likely via Omeo, or perhaps down the Snowy River – both locations are mentioned in the novel, which gives extensive descriptions of the landscape of the southern Monaro, the Australian Alps and the border area of north-east Gippsland.[3] In the novel the Inspector of Police who pursues the gang, Capt. Desborough, is modelled on the Dana brothers, senior police who led bushranger hunts on the Mornington Peninsula and other places, just as Lieutenant Hillyar does in *The Hillyars and the Burtons*. Kingsley coupled his 1853 memory of the VDL escapees crossing the strait with his 1855-6 experience of north-east Gippsland to form the outline of his plot. The activities of the VDL-led Toke-Paynter gang came to a climax in 1859. After that the gang, chased by police, fled north of Omeo to the mountains. In the third part of *Geoffry Hamlyn* a gang of convicts escape from Van Diemen's Land, land on the Victorian coast, form a bushranger outfit, move north into the Gippsland mountains and, after some mayhem and murder, flee further north of Omeo when pursued by mounted police:

> Across the mountains, north of lake Omeo, not far from the mighty cleft in which the infant Murray spends his youth, were two huts, erected years before by some settler, and abandoned. They had been used by a gang of bushrangers, who had been attacked by the police, and dispersed. Nevertheless, they had been since inhabited by the men we know of, who landed in the boat from Van Diemen's Land, in consequence of Hawker having found himself a pass through the ranges, open for nine months of the year...In these huts Hawker intended to lie by for a short time, living on such provisions as were left, until he could make his way northward on the outskirts of the settlements, and escape.[4]

This is the historical pattern of events already described. The remarkable thing is that this was written before the Omeo outbreak happened. The climactic events of Cornelius Green's murder and the subsequent police chase of the gang into the mountains happened in 1859, the year of the novel's publication. The mastermind of the events which culminated in the murders of Ballarat Harry and Cornelius Green was the notorious ex-Van Diemen's Land convict named Toke. In the novel the mastermind is a notorious ex-Van Diemen's Land convict named Touan. The most plausible explanation of Kingsley's eerie premonition of events is that he was sensitive to the general pattern of activity taking place while he was in Gippsland, activities with which Orton was also connected. There is, intriguingly, a much later connection between the two – Kingsley visited the claimant in London at Newgate Prison in March, 1874, after Orton's conviction. We don't know why, but possibly to compare notes on their simultaneous Gippsland experiences.

There are other similarities with actual events. In the novel the gang is led by the bushranger Hawker and his son. This parallels the correspondent's report from Omeo in the *Gippsland Guardian* of 18 September, 1857, in which a father and son, suspected of being horse-stealers, are reported to have come to Omeo from Beechworth. In addition the scenes in the novel in which ex-convicts act as hutkeepers on remote outstations are very close to actual events – the murder of a hutkeeper in Chapter 37 of the novel has close resemblances to the actual murder of Ballarat Harry after he stayed at the Dargo station hut in March, 1858. By this stage Kingsley had just left Victoria (in February, 1858) to return to England to complete his novel.

In Kingsley's version of the Bogong Jack story, two details have migrated from another captivity narrative, the William Buckley saga. Buckley had lost his use of English after 32 years in isolation from Europeans. Bogong Jack is said in Kingsley's account to have similarly lost his English after living with an Aboriginal tribe in the Alps. But this is highly unlikely as he was away for only four years; this detail has been taken over from earlier captivity narratives. Like Buckley, Bogong Jack is seen by the Aborigines as 'one of their own tribe, dead long ago, who had come back to them, renovated and beautiful, from the other world.'[5] Aborigines, having observed their dead turned white, thought Europeans were returned ancestor spirits.

Kingsley frames his telling of the Bogong Jack story in ways which reflect on its possible authenticity. Characters in *Geoffry Hamlyn* admit they love hearing Captain Desborough's yarns: 'Desborough delighted in making them up, he often confessed, as he went along'.[6] This hint that the tales are not wholly factual is confirmed when the narrator Hamlyn, in introducing the Bogong Jack yarn, says: 'I don't think that it has so much foundation in fact as Captain Desborough's. But there must be some sort of truth in it, for it comes from the old hands, and shows a little more sign of imagination than you would expect from them'. This suggests the tale is a subtle blend of fact and fantasy. After it is told, another character in the novel, Dr Mulhaus, reflects: 'I hope you won't pass it off as authentic, you know, because if we once begin to entertain these sort of legends as meaning anything, the whole history of the country becomes one great fog-bank, through which the devil himself could not find his way'.[7] Kingsley shows here he understands how folk stories can seriously distort reality. Kingsley was interested in finding his own way through the fog-bank in order to discern any underlying patterns. These were stories whose basic structure was retained even as they were turning into legends. In *The Hillyars and the Burtons* Kingsley noted: 'New stories require frequent repetition to give them the stamp of authenticity'.[8] The *Sydney Morning Herald* review of *Geoffry Hamlyn* on 20 October, 1859, thought the novel consisted of 'old stories...so altered and so vividly described as to possess all the charm of a real narrative'.

In a footnote to the Bogong Jack tale Kingsley notes: 'This legend is said to be among the "Archives" of one of our best North Border families. It is but little altered, since the author heard it narrated at a camp fire, one night, in the western Port Phillip country'. The families referred to may be those of the squatters Faithful or Reid, from Wangaratta and Yackandandah, both mentioned in the text. Kingsley heard the story either around Western Port or in the Western District of Victoria; this shows the story had travelled quickly, and had perhaps been altered in transmission.

Geoffry Hamlyn (1859) is a long novel with a complex plot. Nonetheless many of the structures common in Victorian fiction can be found in it. The novel begins with a group of respectable families in rural Devon in the early 19th century, whose way of life contrasts with scenes of low-life skulduggery, in which the villainous George Hawker meets William Lee, a convict returned from Australia, on bleak Dartmoor. Two years later Charles Dickens' *Great Expectations* (1861) opens with a similar scene on the marches where the hero, young Pip, meets Abel Magwitch, also a convict returned from Australia. Pip and his rival Bentley Drummle both fall in love with a beautiful young girl Estella. The fortune Magwitch has made in Australia helps Pip in the end to achieve his ambition of becoming a gentleman.

Kingsley contrasts two originally similar Devon men, James Stockridge and George Hawker, who are rivals for the love of their childhood friend, Mary Thornton, the same pattern as in *The Rivals* and in *Great Expectations*. In *Geoffry Hamlyn* one family, the Buckleys, moves to Australia because they have sold their family seat, George Hawker because he is convicted of forgery and deported. The novel is structured around rises and declines in fortune in Australia. George Hawker goes to the bad, but the other Devon men redeem their fortunes in Australia, which is depicted as a place where the old leisured ways of the English rural gentry can be replicated, at a time when that was less and less possible in England itself. The novel opens with James Buckley and fellow squatters leisurely sitting on a verandah looking out on the rolling plains of a prosperous Australian station. This is contrasted with the declining squire class in Devon they have come from. The ancestral Buckley property Clere House, which dates from Elizabethan times, is described as 'this useless tumble-down old palace, without money enough to keep up your position in the country.' James Buckley's aging father says to him: 'Don't hang on here in the false position of an old country family without money, living in a ruined hall, with a miserable overcropped farm, a corner of the old deer park, under their drawing room window'.[9] This is a classic account of the situation of the depressed squirearchy. The gentry can improve their position here in Australia, but the freedom Australia offers is dangerous for the lower classes. One character exclaims: 'What a happy exchange an English peasant makes when he leaves an old, well-ordered society, the ordinances of religion, the various give-and-take relations between rank an rank, which make up the sum of English life, for independence, godlessness and rum!...My friend the labourer has got his farm, and is prospering, after a sort. He has turned to be a drunken, godless, impudent fellow, and his wife little better than himself; his daughters dowdy hussies; his sons, lanky, lean, pasty-faced, blaspheming blackguards, drinking rum before breakfast, and living by cheating one another out of horses.'[10] Kingsley novel's revolves around a contrast between the resurgent Buckley and degenerate Hawker milieus.

Three characters regain their gentry or aristocratic rank at the conclusion of the novel. The Buckleys improve themselves financially by becoming successful squatters; as a result they are able to satisfy their gentry pretensions by regaining their ancestral Devon seat. Some characters benefit from a hidden or acquired title. The German Dr. Mulhaus has been hiding his aristocratic status; he is really Baron von Landstein and is restored to his proper place in Germany. The Hawker gang is pursued by police led by Captain Desborough, who in the end succeeds to an Irish title as Lord Covetown.

In *Geoffry Hamyln* Kingsley predicted the Omeo VLD-led bushranger outbreak of the late 1850s. Another remarkable prediction occurs in his second novel, *Ravenshoe*. The historian Paul de Serville has pointed to an article by 'Aegles' in the *Australasian* of 15 July, 1871, which shows that *Ravenshoe*, published in serial form in 1861 and in book form in 1862, was in many ways a premonition of the Tichborne saga.[11] The Tichborne case became known to the world only when Lady Tichborne first advertised for her son in the *Times* in May, 1863. But *Ravenshoe*, published before this, is a rehearsal of the case. The novel concerns an old established English West Country Catholic family like the Tichbornes. In the novel two boys, an heir and a servant's son, Charles and William, are brought up together. They are interchangeable, partly alike and partly opposite. There is a lost heir, who is a groom called Horton. (The Tichborne claimant was a groom called Orton.) He is thought by his family to have gone to America or Australia, whereas he is working in a lowly occupation in London. Advertisements are put out about him in the newspapers, as in the Tichborne case. In both cases, real and fictional, the central figure falls in love with his cousin, but the match is thwarted before his disappearance. The heir disappears and goes underground, leading a low life and then reappears to claim his rightful aristocratic position. The solution is connected with a past illegitimacy in the family, one of the proposed solutions to the Tichborne conundrum.

How can we explain *Ravenshoe* as a prelude to the Tichborne case? One likely possibility is sheer coincidence. Another possibility is that Kingsley, living and writing after his Australian years at his brother's place in Hampshire, where the Tichborne family seat was located, had heard about the Tichborne story. But this does not explain the Orton/Horton naming. Another possibility, suggested by de Serville, is that Orton might have read *Ravenshoe* in a Mechanics Institute library in the Riverina from 1862 to 1865 (either before or after the Tichborne advertisement in the newspapers), and carried out the deception based on his reading of the novel. (Orton's reading habits and claims of exalted ancestry will be further examined when we consider his sojourn in the Riverina.) Or Orton may have been told the Tichborne story by the Hampshire man Slade in Wagga Wagga. All these explanations are based on the supposition that Arthur Orton learnt from Henry Kingsley's novel.

Another, more general, explanation is the prevalence of the lost heir theme, which was in the air at the time. There are a number of overlays here, both in fiction and real life. One is the idea of going down in the world, of voluntarily discarding one's status in England. In *Ravenshoe* Charles Ravenshoe wishes to undergo a change of identity, or to lose his identity, and changes his name to Horton. Tichborne and the first Bogong Jack (and Kingsley himself) in real life, and Ravenshoe in fiction, do this. They leave England, and enjoy the freedom conferred by mixing with the lower classes.

They don't write to their English families while away, cutting themselves off completely. When the claimant appeared, he was so different from Sir Roger that the mother, Lady Tichborne, famously said: 'They [Australians] must be savages to have made him so rough'.[12] Within Australia itself, the equivalent to the story of the declining aristocrat was leaving European society and mixing with wild Aboriginal tribes, as in the Bogong Jack, lost white woman and William Buckley captivity narratives. All have the same basic pattern, which Kingsley was alive to.

Henry Kingsley's other novel to have substantial Australian content is *The Hillyars and the Burtons*, serialized from 1863 to 1865, and published in book form in the latter year. As the title indicates, it is a comparison of two families, the gentry Hillyars and the artisan Burtons. Of the two Hillyar brothers, George is the strong, masculine villain and Erne, the more passive and sensitive figure who is admired by the author, partly because he has Henry Kingsley's own qualities. George, the grandson of an aristocrat and a reprobate, travels to Australia where he redeems himself as a police Lieutenant who captures escaped convicts at Barker's station in Victoria. By a secret earlier marriage he has a son Reuben, who thinks he is the son of a convicted servant, Samuel Burton, a vengeful man who keeps the family will to himself. George returns to England and the family inheritance, but after his death Reuben, the lost heir figure, eventually succeeds to the title. The aristocratic Hillyar family are in decline, whereas the hard-working Burton family succeed in Australia in business and politics. Once again the novel is a study of how quickly one's fortunes can change in Australia, which, Kingsley believed:

> opened, in the first place a career for young gentlemen possessed of every virtue, save those of continence, sobriety, and industry – a sort of way of escaping cheaply from the consequence of debauchery for a time…But [Australia] gave an opening also for really honest, upright fellows.[13]

Some Australian novels before and after *Geoffry Hamlyn* have traces of the familiar fable of the lost heir. 'The gentleman with a past' (implying a hidden past) is a standard figure in colonial fiction. The phrase contains a number of possibilities – that a disreputable past is being overcome, or that an aristocrat one is being concealed, or both. The visiting writer William Howitt, in Victoria from 1852 to 1854, published his novel *Tallangetta* in 1857 after returning to England. The novel is set mainly in central Victoria, with a section on the Ovens goldfields. It is a squatting saga, in the mould of *Geoffry Hamlyn* (published two years later), with bushrangers, convicts, bushfires, a love story and so on. The Fitzgerald family are squatters who return to England at the end. Sir Thomas Fitzgerald, dissipated in his youth by a passion for the turf, has been deprived of his title and estates in England by his cousin Patrick Fitzgerald, who claims to have proof that Thomas' parents were not properly married. In the end it transpires that a neighbouring squatter in Australia, calling himself Dr. Spencer Grayson, is in fact a convicted forger, George Hersant, acting as a spy for Patrick Fitzpatrick. The hero, Peter Martin, another cousin, exposes this trickery and produces a sealed packet from Thomas' mother, which contains the true certificate of the parents' marriage. Thomas Fitzgerald and his family then return to England with their title and estates restored. (A sealed packet left by Roger Tichborne was an important element in the Tichborne case.)

Charles De Boos's novel, *The Stockman's Daughter*, was published as a serial in the *People's Advocate*, a Sydney weekly, in 1856. The action is set near Bungendore and the Lake George area before the gold-rushes of the 1850s. Captain Huntley is a prosperous squatter with a son, Frank, who is in love with Helen, the daughter of 'Big Jack' Evans, a stockman on the run. This is a mismatch in social terms, but people notice that Evans seems to have come down in the world from a higher position. He is a natural gentlemen, but taciturn and secretive about his past. A bushranging gang, comprising the villain Roger, Opposum Jack, Williams and others, attacks the run, during which raid Evans is stabbed and dies in the ensuing melee. He leaves a sealed letter, to be opened after his death, which reveals that he is really Ernest Wyvil, the heir to one of the oldest baronetcies in England. In Australia as an officer he had led a dissipated life. He was blackmailed over a cheque he wrote out in his colonel's name as a joke, which ruined him. He staged a disappearance, and fled upcountry incognito with his daughter Helen, after his wife died of a broken heart. After this information has been revealed, the squatting group chases the bushrangers. Roger, who has Wyvil's papers on him, captures Helen, but she is rescued and Roger killed by an Aboriginal helper, all in melodramatic style. The papers are reclaimed, and Frank and Helen go off to live as aristocrats in England, the daughter having inherited from her father.

One of the first pieces of literature to emerge from eastern Victoria was 'A Gippsland Romance: a True Tale', which appeared anonymously in the *Gippsland Guardian* in two instalments on 24 and 31 May, 1861. The hero, named only as C----, arrives at Port Albert in the early days looking forlorn and seeking work. He has the dress and appearance of a British dandy who has seen better days, but still looks a cut above the rest. It is clear he is from the leisured classes, though he is now a servant. A squatter employs him. Eventually he tells his own past history to the narrator, a local inhabitant. He came from Cheshire, where his father was a landed proprietor, and led a dissolute early life, gambling, wasting the family money and incurring debts. On a trip looking after his father's investments, he falls in love with a curate's daughter, Lucy, but his suit is rejected by the curate because of suspicions of his dissolute ways (similar to the rejection of Tichborne's suit by his cousin's parents). Under the weight of this double disaster he goes to Sydney, and there he tells nobody where he is and, like Henry Kingsley, does not write to his family when in Australia. When he hears Gippsland is being opened up, he moves there to lose himself in its vast, untouched forests.

Life in Gippsland restores his physical health and disposition. He is a steady and trusted worker on the run, soon an overseer, and takes cattle to market for his boss (like Orton and John Paynter). In 1851 his father dies and advertisements are put in the papers to try to find the heir, who is supposed missing or dead (this is identical to the Tichborne case a few years later). The narrator tells C--- about the advertisements and acts as a go-between with the family estate's lawyers in England, negotiating the ending of his debts and eventually allowing him to return to England and take over his proper inheritance. He meets his old mother who is ill with worry and is reunited with Lucy, whom he soon marries. Both are then restored to the paternal estate. He calls their son 'Gipp' after the region 'which served to make him a happier and a better man'. As with *Ravenshoe*, this tale appeared before the advertisements for the Tichborne heir.

The Berresfords of Ellalong is an anonymous and unfinished novel published in Melbourne in 1866. In it a settler family moves south from the Monaro into north Gippsland near Omeo in the early days. The hero, Charles Berresford, is expected to inherit a large sum of money from his father, but the will surprisingly leaves most to this cousin George, a lawyer, who is disliked. The suspicion is that the will has been forged. As the novel is unfinished, we don't know how this works out, but it looks like the 'lost inheritance regained' theme. At one stage some characters come across a deserted hut in the mountains:

> The only solution he had to suggest was, that the man in charge of the hut had deserted his service, and, perhaps, stolen some of his master's property, which was a very common method, in those early days, of returning evil for good, and was chiefly practised by old convicts from Tasmania and New South Wales. The man who was in charge of the place had been a ticket-of-leave holder, and had escaped over the border into Victoria, or Port Phillip, as it was then called. It was no unusual thing for men of this class, to take an uncontrollable longing to return to their old haunts in the settled districts. Sometimes a quarrel with their fellow servants, or employers, was made the pretext for running away. Sometimes they were guilty of cowardly atrocities, often cold-blooded murder, and then they took to the bush with whatever provisions, firearms and property they could lay their hands on.[14]

NOTES

1. Henry Kingsley *The Hillyars and the Burtons*, op. cit., p. 35.

2. Henry Kingsley, 'The Two Cadets', op. cit., p. 349.

3. On Kingsley's Australian travels, see J.S.D. Mellick *The Passing Guest: A Life of Henry Kingsley*, University of Queensland Press, St. Lucia, 1983, especially Chapter 9 'The Monaro and Gippsland'.

4. Henry Kingsley *The Recollections of Geoffry Hamlyn*, 1859, repr. Ward, Lock & Bowden, London, 1894, p. 416.

5. Ibid., p. 386.

6. Ibid., p. 383.

7. Ibid., p. 387.

8. Henry Kingsley *The Hillyars and the Burtons*, op. cit., p. 383.

9. Henry Kingsley *The Recollections of Geoffry Hamlyn*, op. cit., p. 12. *Arcady in Australia* (1970), written by Coral Lansbury (Malcolm Turnbull's mother) covers the idea of Australia's broad acres as a new arena for English rural gentry ambitions.

10. Ibid., pp. 223-4.

11. Paul de Serville *Pounds and Pedigrees: The Upper Class in Victoria 1850-1880*, Oxford University Press, South Melbourne, 1991, pp. 219 & 536-8.

12. *The Australian Commission*, op. cit., p. 47.

13. Henry Kingsley *The Hillyars and the Burtons*, op. cit., p. 239.

14. *The Berresfords of Ellalong*, F.F. Baillière, Melbourne, 1866, pp. 42-3.

PART THREE: NORTH OF THE DIVIDE

11

CATTLE RUSTLING IN THE RANGES

The murders of Ballarat Harry and Cornelius Green caused the police to make a concerted, and eventually successful, effort to wipe out illegal operations based on Omeo, especially those of the Toke-Paynter gang, which had been involved in both incidents. In November, 1862, the head of the Victoria Police, Commissioner Standish, deplored:

> the prevalence of the crime of cattle stealing in Gipps Land, arising principally from the great influx of people to the new diggings. I should wish Mr [Assistant Superintendent] Palmer to direct the special attention of the Police to this matter. For I have no doubt if they would succeed in getting up two or three good cases of the kind, they would [do] much to check the prevailing crime. The utmost efforts of the police must be directed to this object.[1]

John Paynter, Sydney Penny and Thomas Toke, the best known living suspects connected with past events, who had escaped convictions over the Green murder, were kept under observation, and all three were eventually arrested.

This was the end of the turbulent decade of the 1850s. The police finally nailed a charge on John Paynter. In November 1859 they announced a 'warrant for the arrest of John Payne, alias Paynter, has been issued at Beechworth in which he is charged with stealing a brown filly, the property of Robert Gregory, Allen's Flat, Yackandandah, on 15th September last'. Inspector Hill reported: 'Stolen horse has not been recovered and has probably been disposed of by him at Snowy Creek or some other place on the Omeo route as he did not make his appearance here with the animal'. Paynter faced the Beechworth Court in December 1859, but as the prosecution was not able to produce the horse nor witnesses, the charge was dismissed and once again John Paynter escaped the law. Just as Arthur Orton was slipping away from Reedy Creek in December 1859 to dodge horse-stealing charges, both Toke and Paynter were laying low. From this time onwards local folklore, and accounts by Eric Harding and others, have it that 'Bogong Jack' Paynter retired to his mountain lair and was never heard of again.

This however is not true. Paynter does turn up in court on two more charges. In September, 1861, he was arrested for stealing a horse belonging to Alexander Fraser of Doctor's Flat. In January 1862 he was bound over to appear on the charge at Bairnsdale in February. In addition he was reported for being drunk while in charge of despatches.[2] This is the last record we have of Paynter. If he subsequently left the Omeo area, his most likely move would have been over the border into southern New South Wales, where he could have resumed his career under a new name. Interestingly a John Payne was gaoled at Deniliquin for bushranging in 1867, but he was probably too young to be 'Bogong Jack' Paynter. Old timers reported that he was once met in a hut on the high country. A skeleton was found and some said it was his murdered body, which later led of course to wild stories that he was the missing Sir Roger Tichborne.

The gang member Sydney Penny was mentioned in connection with a horse stealing charge against Thomas Martin at Crooked River in November, 1861. Penny was arrested next month for stealing a horse belonging to Richard Smyth. The *Gippsland Guardian* of 9 December 1861 commented: 'The notorious Sydney Penny has just been brought down in charge of the police who have long been looking after him...It is not well to prejudge any man, but the bad character which this one bears is enough to cause all respectable persons to rejoice that an opportunity is now afforded for investigating his career'. At the trial at Sale on April 12, 1862, a witness testified he had brought the horse off Penny, not knowing it was stolen. Penny's counsel, Mr. Frederick Webb, who had appeared for Orton in his wages case in Sale in 1858, asked the jury 'to dismiss from their minds any prejudice they might have received through hearing of other charges which had previously been brought against the prisoner', a clear reference to Penny's involvement in the Cornelius Green case. But Penny was found guilty and sentenced to two years' imprisonment with hard labour.

In 1863 Toke was, like his two former partners, arrested for horse-stealing. His accomplice was a young man named Adam Lynn, who had previously been employed by 'Mitta Mitta Jack' Ahern. Both at first denied the charge, but Lynn eventually made a statement of confession, which accused Toke of being the mastermind of the event. Fourteen horses had been taken from the Omeo plains with the connivance of John Jones, a farmer at the Water Holes near Omeo, and briefly yarded at Jack Sheean's yards. (Jack Sheean and John Jones had previously appeared together in a Hobart court case in 1855.) The horses were then driven to the Gibbo and later to the Mitta Mitta River. Next day Toke sent Lynn to retrieve one of the horses at Italian Point, a miner's camp nearby. John Jones gave evidence in support of Lynn, but police were suspicious Jones was himself involved in the heist. Police Sgt King eventually questioned Toke and Lynn, who denied everything. Sgt King then retrieved two horses from Italian Point and arrested the two men on suspicion.

At the Omeo Police Court on 2 April, 1863, the magistrates 'discharged Toke with a plain intimation that it did not arise from any doubt of his guilt, but because his accomplices' confession could not legally be used in evidence against him'. He has escaped in the same way from previous charges. Lynn was committed for trial, but later discharged because of lack of evidence against him. However police later found independent witnesses to confirm Lynn's confession, and Toke was rearrested in the same month. He was found guilty at the Beechworth court and sentenced to seven years' imprisonment in the Beechworth gaol. After his release, he led a quiet life at his place on the Gibbo, subsequently named after him as Toake's Gibbo, dying in July 1887 at the age of seventy, the last known survivor of the events of the 1850s.

With the belated arrests of Toke, Paynter and Penny, crime around Omeo diminished. An article on Omeo in the *Ovens and Murray Advertiser* of 21 March, 1863, commented: 'The first sweep made at [Omeo's] Thugs, was the arrest of the (since then) notorious Toke for the murder of Ballarat Harry...Several horse stealers were captured at Omeo, and convictions effected'. In August, 1863, Sgt King wrote of 'the suppression of crime (particularly horse stealing) in this wild district, and [it] has been the means of eradicating a gang of horse stealers that have hitherto been a complete curse to the neighbourhood'.[3] Sadleir later gave a similar account, but attributed the police success to Sergeant Reid.

Different states had different rates for gold. The price was higher in New South Wales than in Victoria; customs houses were situated on borders like the Murray River. As a result tracks though the mountains were used to whisk gold out of Victoria to NSW. A centre of this operation was Omeo, through the storekeepers there, who acted as gold merchants. Soames Davis was an Omeo storekeeper and gold agent, the same occupation as Cornelius Green. It was his horses which had been stolen by Armstrong and Chamberlain during their attempt escape after Green's murder. In August, 1862, Davis took a consignment of gold north from Omeo through Snowy Creek towards Yackandandah, perhaps to get a better price there, or perhaps to take it over the border to the north. As often happened, Davis took quantities of gold from other dealers with him, so that he had about a thousand pounds worth of gold with him at the time. No escort was provided. North of Snowy Creek he disappeared; evidence at the scene suggested he had been stripped by assailants and led away. All the gold and cash were gone, but his horses, the ones stolen by Armstrong and Chamberlain, were found near the scene. His clothing had been concealed along the route but his body was never found. Rumours circulated that Davis was in financial trouble and was to be sued by Omeo traders, and that as a result he had absconded, faking his disappearance. But most thought that his previous character and financial probity made this unlikely, and that he had been done away with for his gold. Was this a case of another rival storekeeper and gold agent being eliminated? Soames Davis, David Jones (Paynter's partner), Cornelius Green and Ballarat Harry, all of whom had close relations with the Toke-Paynter gang, were either murdered or died in mysterious circumstances.

With the police putting pressure on the Omeo area, cattle duffing moved to two north-south routes on either side. To the east was the old Snowy River road from Wulgulmerang via Butcher's Ridge to Buchan. Assistant Superintendent Palmer called in November 1862 for a police station at Buchan since 'horse stealers and other offenders will doubtless flood in to Gipps Land [to the new gold rushes] from the NSW side'.[4] To the west of Omeo was the Cobungra-Dargo connection. Cattle-rustling and lawlessness were now evident around Dargo and the Crooked River goldfields, which were beginning in the early 1860s, and along the road from Dargo to Cobungra, and then over the divide to the Ovens. The Cobungra mob and its associates were now more active than the Toke-Paynter Omeo gang. Close-knit networks, even if they did not amount to gangs, still obviously existed, as many names from the past reappear, and new ones come to light as the police net tightened. The Gray, Simpson and Brown families, connected with the Cobungra mob, remained prominent.

The leading group in the Buchan area after the demise of the Toke-Paynter gang was John Bentley and his network of accomplices. Bentley had a farm east of Doctor's Flat in the Nunniong area, later named Bentley's Plain, supposedly after him. A road linked Ensay to Butcher's Ridge (the name suggested a remote mountain butchery), and then to Black Mountain and over the mountains to the Monaro. Like the Toke-Paynter gang, Bentley had a set of yards in the mountains, where he altered brands and other means of identifying cattle stolen from the Omeo plains. Later they were sold on the Monaro. Bentley had connections with the Cobungra mob.

In March, 1861, Bentley was charged at the Omeo Police Court with stealing a horse belonging to a French Canadian, Charles Le Blanc. John Jones, the Omeo carrier who was involved in the Toke horse-stealing case, warned Le Blanc that he had seen his horse and another belonging to a second Frenchman in Bentley's possession about ten miles towards Omeo from the diggings. Jones said Bentley had ridden up with three horses asking about the whereabouts of Thomas Worcester, a nephew of the Grays of the Cobungra mob. Bentley claimed that he was told by the butcher Edward Crane to take two of Crane's horses, that there had been a misunderstanding, and that he would return the horses. Crane was one of the witnesses who had given evidence about Ballarat Harry. Previously from Swift's Creek, he was now butchering at Crooked River, in partnership with John Simpson (from the Ovens area, who may have been the son of the original Ovens-side Bogong Jack) and Mat Taylor. Crane backed up Bentley's story. Crane said he sent his own horses to Squirrel Forest in the company of Fred Bird, another one of the witnesses at the Ballarat Harry case. Alexander Fraser, who had appeared in the last Paynter case, testified to the respectability of Bentley. These convoluted accounts had an air of implausibility about them.

Magistrate Wills ordered Bentley to stand trial. Jack Sheean and Robert Simpson, two men implicated in other horse-stealing cases, put up Bentley's bail. At the Sale Police Court on April 12, John Bentley was discharged on the same count, since it was clear after examination of witnesses that the evidence could not hold water. Why soon became clear – the butcher Crane was charged with perjury at Omeo Police Court on May 2 for saying that he sent his horses to Squirrel Forest with Fred Bird. Bird said he was not requested to take the horses by Crane. He added damagingly that Bentley had subsequently approached him at Crooked River asking him to confirm what Crane had stated in evidence. Bird also alleged that Crane had sent him a letter, since destroyed, by Bentley giving him minute instructions as to the evidence he was to give in support of Crane. At a later hearing a witness Denis Connolly was 'afflicted with a most defective memory'. Magistrate Wills committed Crane for trial at the next Circuit Court at Beechworth.

In the spring of 1865 Bentley and James Neville stole about 50 head of cattle from Hinnomunjie station. In December Sgt Reid heard that some had been driven to the Mt. Hotham area. Soon after this Senior Constable Harkin of the Bright Police found some of the cattle at Brandy Creek near Cobungra. Harkin also discovered that Bentley and Neville had sold fifteen head to the butcher Joseph Brown of Bright. Brown had already sold some to 'Neddy' Gray, the Wangaratta butcher operating from Dargo, whom police believed was a well-known horse and cattle thief. Constable Baird found Gray at Dargo in possession of some of the stolen bullocks. Warrants for issued at Bright for the arrest of Bentley and Neville, and around Christmas time Sgt. Reid arrested the two at Omeo. At the Beechworth Court on 13 January, 1866, each received two years' imprisonment with hard labour.

As these cases show, Bentley and his confreres, though based to the east of Omeo, had connections with the Cobungra mob. The policeman Sadleir recounts traversing the Crooked River to Cobungra track during a sortie as officer in charge in Gippsland from 1867 to 1871. The Crooked River-Cobungra track had, Sadleir states, been used by Bogong Jack and his confreres in earlier years. Sadleir's guide was a man who previously had, like Bogong Jack, made visits to Wangaratta as a decoy when major stealing raids were on. This guide could have been one of the Simpson, Wells or Gray brothers. Sadleir adds: 'Our host at Cobungra was a fellow-student in the same School of Art'. The residents at Cobungra at this time were Parslow and Rawson, both married into the Cobungra mob.

Police pressure meant that from the early 1860s, criminal activity was increasingly located over the ranges and to the north towards the Murray River border, rather than in the Omeo area. At the time of Toke's indictment, in early 1863, 'Mitta Mitta Jack' Ahern, another involved in these rackets, was charged with cattle-stealing at Snowy Creek. He had previously been gaoled on a similar charge. James Kelly, uncle of Ned Kelly, was sentenced to 14 years' imprisonment at Beechworth in 1863 on cattle stealing and arson charges. 'Gipsy' Smith of Yackandandah, 'Billy the Puntman' John Hyde of Wangaratta, and Black Douglas, who ranged over a wide area, were prominent in illegal activities in this period. 'Gypsy' Smith was a Vandemonian convict who had escaped to Victoria in a whaleboat. The criminals were confined to this area by pressure from the north, in the shape of the New South Wales Felons' Apprehension Act of 1865, which allowed bushrangers to be shot on sight in NSW. In April, 1867, an alarm was raised on the Yackandandah-to-Omeo road that the notorious Clarke gang of bushrangers from Braidwood were in the area, but they were captured by police in southern New South Wales in the same month.[5]

The bushranger Dan Morgan was active in this area and in southern New South Wales until his death at Peechelba in 1865. John Le Sage said Morgan was in Gippsland in the 1850s under the name of Horton. Margaret Carnegie in her biography of Morgan believes he was released as 'John Smith' to report to police in the Yackandandah and Ovens area in January 1860, but failed to do so. He worked intermittently as a horse-breaker on properties in the King and Ovens Rivers areas in this period, being known as 'Down the River' Jack or 'Bill the Native', and suspected of horse-stealing. The squatters Bond and Evans found him in the bush in late 1860 after pursuing him and stolen horses, but he managed to escape. He was then seen in the Upper Murray region and over the border in New South Wales.

Another cattleduffer filled the vacuum along the Mitta Mitta River left by 'Mitta Mitta Jack'. He was Jimmy Lee, the subject of a number of legends.[6] Lee, born in Sydney in 1844, moved with his family south to the Monaro. As a young man he worked as a stockman there, but when the Mitta Mitta goldfields developed in the later 1860s, he set himself up at the town of Wombat Creek as a butcher and rival to Edward Crane, formerly of Omeo and the Crooked River. Lee's sources of cattle were suspect; he was thought to be involved in 'gully raking', and then cutting up and selling meat to the diggers. His operated from north-east Victoria to the Monaro.

In 1868 Lee undertook his most daring enterprise. With a few helpers he rode across the mountains to the Towong-Tintaldra bend of the Murray River near Mt Kosciusko and stole cattle from the Monaro graziers Charles Douglas and Cyrus Smith. The cattle were then driven to a hidden gully near Wombat Creek to be used as supply for Jimmy Lee's business. However the graziers noticed some of their sliprails were loose and their cattle missing, and followed the trail to Jimmy's lair on the Mitta Mitta, notifying the police there of their suspicions. Police Sergeant Hall used Crane, who seems to have gone clean by this stage, to set up Jimmy Lee, by inducing him to sell some of the suspect cattle to Crane. Lee was arrested and taken in handcuffs on horse towards the nearest lockup.

But in thick bush near the Mitta Mitta River he slipped off his horse and escaped into the bush. The handcuffs were filed off by a friend, and from then on he was on the run. Lee's young helper, Michael Daley, found with the stolen cattle, was charged, but later acquitted. Next Sgt Reid came across Jimmy Lee and his mate Lucy Williams on the Omeo-Dargo Road, but the cattle-duffers escaped after exchanging shots with the police. John Sadleir was Inspector of Police at Sale at the time, and had to explain these escapes and poor police communication to the Melbourne authorities. Later the policemen Reid and Walsh came across Lee and his helpers as they were depositing a bullock's head in the Mitta Mitta River at Williams' Crossing, but Lee escaped, and like John Paynter, was never heard of again. A legend about Jimmy Lee, which telescoped some of these incidents into one, grew up that he had slipped off his horse while handcuffed crossing the Mitta Mitta stream, and had floated downstream to escape police detection, and then hid under the cover of a large wattle tree near the bank. Some of the Bogong Jack legends record a similar escape.

A connecting link between earlier and later events was the career of the bushranger 'Old Harry' Power. Power had a much longer career of crime than any other bushranger. He was originally convicted in his home country, Ireland, of robbing a bank, and was sentenced to seven years' transportation in 1840, served in Van Diemen's Land. After his term he spent two years in the bush there and then escaped from The Island to Twofold Bay and thence to Sydney. An alternative account has him arriving in Port Albert in 1848. He was next suspected of shady dealing involving horses in the Geelong area and then went to the Ballarat diggings. In 1855 he fired at troopers attempting to arrest him and was sentenced to 14 years' imprisonment, the first part of which he served at the notorious Williamstown hulks. In 1856 he was charged with others with the murder of a prison guard, Owen Owens, but was found not guilty. In 1869, near the end of his sentence, he escaped from Pentridge and began the last part of his career of crime as a bushranger in north-eastern Victoria.

He held up travellers as he ranged in his activities over a wide area including Porepunkah, Mansfield, Greta, Benalla, Beechworth and the Ovens, and was said to operate as far afield as Bairnsdale in Gippsland, and Adelong in New South Wales. An expert bushman, he was a friend of the Kelly and Quinn families, who admired his exploits. Young Ned Kelly was at one stage charged with having assisted him. In 1869 he narrowly avoided capture in Benalla. In 1870 he robbed the magistrate Robert McBean, an enemy of the Kellys, of a watch and was betrayed by a member of the Lloyd family, who led police to his bush hideaway. He was sentenced to 15 years gaol at Beechworth, and was finally released in 1885 after having served three long terms in his lifetime. Power's activities led on the Kelly gang, and completed the connection back to earlier events.

The story of the Kelly family and its tragic history holds a central position in Australian mythology. The Kellys have been seen by the public and by commentators as *sui generis*, and therefore without a detailed prehistory. But they didn't come out of the blue – they fit into the pattern of the Vandemonian convict trail, and are as much the climax of an older narrative as the beginning of a new one. The old bushranger Henry Power befriended the Kellys. Boldrewood imaginatively made the connection between the Kellys and earlier events around Omeo in his novel *Nevermore*. Ned Kelly's father Red was a convict who had served his time in Van Diemen's Land. The inter-connected Kelly, Quinn and Lloyd families had convictions for horse and cattle-stealing in the 1860s. At one stage the Kellys had horse stealing connections with the Baumgartners over the Murray River, on the pattern of previous rackets.

The first big VDL outbreak, long feared by Victorians, was the Toke-Paynter gang outrages around Omeo in the late 1850s, a significant event in its time. But it was also a preliminary to the outbreak which occurred two decades later in north-eastern

Victoria, the Kelly Gang saga, the last big explosion. Cross-mountain stealing rackets may have continued after the Kellys. One explanation of the Wonnangatta murders of 1917 was that the two murdered men had stumbled on cattle duffers who were rebranding stolen beasts before moving them over the mountains to be sold.

Police Inspector Sadleir noted that Bogong Jack and his confreres used a pass between the King and Ovens Rivers in the north and the Wonnangatta River in the south to get from northern Victoria in Gippsland.[7] Henry Power also used this pass, and during the Kelly outbreak the police were worried that the gang might use this route to escape into Gippsland. Gippslanders feared the outbreak might touch them, as Jessie Harrison, living in central Gippsland, recorded in her diary:

> The Kelly gang was much nearer, and rumours of the bushrangers here, there and everywhere were prevalent...the Kellys we almost expected to see at any moment, such tales of their sudden appearances and ruthless doings were circulated everywhere...From their seclusion in the Glenrowan ranges, they might force their way southward through uninhabited parts and appear among us.[8]

Mary Fullerton of Glenmaggie recalled 'the game of 'playing Kellys' as a bush pastime at school: 'Two sections of us – one the police, the other the gang – would go into the bush, and desperate things would follow. The real bushrangers were then at large and what more natural than that we should do honour to the Robin Hoods and Dick Turpins that a kind, if melodramatic, fate had brought, as it were, to our door'.[9] The Kellys divided Victorian almost equally into supporters and opponents. That split in 1880 reflects the marked division of Victorian society in the 1850s between the respectable original settlers and the more demotic element which entered the colony during the goldrushes.

NOTES

1. PROV, Police Correspondence, VPRS 937, Unit 228, Bundle 2.

2. *Gippsland Guardian*, 7 February, 1862.

3. PROV, Police Correspondence, VPRS 937, Unit 228, Bundle 2.

4. PROV, Police Correspondence, VPRS 937, Unit 228, Bundle 3.

5. For these activities see Graham Jones *Bushrangers of the North East*, Charquin Hill Publications, Wangaratta, 1991.

6. Max Dyer & John Murphy *The Tale of Jimmy Lee*, Bairnsdale, 1994.

7. John Sadleir, op. cit., p. 146.

8. John Leslie and Helen Cowie, op. cit., pp. 62-3.

9. Mary Fullerton *Bark House Days*, 1921, repr. Melbourne University Press, Parkville, 1964, p. 64.

12

WANDERING IN THE RIVERINA

The next move was north over the Murray River, either to the Riverina or the Monaro. The Riverina, whose principal town was Wagga Wagga, was a wedge between New South Wales proper and Victoria. Here people moving south from Sydney met those moving up from Van Diemen's Land and Victoria. Dan Morgan, John Paynter and Ned Kelly made this move north at various times during their careers. In many ways the colonies were like two separate countries, with customs barriers between them. Once in New South Wales criminals faced a different police force, which did not co-ordinate effectively with their Victorian counterparts, so there was less chance of being recognized.

Orton/Castro arrived in the Riverina by a more circuitous route than normal. He appeared in a number of places in northern Victoria on his way to crossing the border. In 1859 he found his way from Reedy Creek to central Victoria. Castro admitted in his *Confession* that he had sold at Castlemaine a horse stolen from McManus at Reedy Creek, while going under the name John Paisley, the celebrated bushranger. Witnesses at the Australian Commission testified to having seen him at Myers Flat near Eaglehawk on the Bendigo diggings. Castro at his trial also said he and Orton were tried for horse stealing there in 1859. Witnesses remembered him at Myers Flat with Henry Pearson (the former pound-keeper at Sale) trading in horses and hanging around pubs. One witness, Bernard McGawran, said of Pearson, who dealt in horses: 'Pearson went frequently to the Gipps Land side, and to the Murray side to buy horses'.[1] This sounds as if Pearson and Castro may have been involved in selling on the goldfields horses stolen elsewhere.

Castro then lived for a time in the Wimmera on his way to the Riverina. He applied for a situation as a bullock driver on the property of a Scots farmer called Campbell on the Campaspe

River under the name of Tomas Castro, the first time he is known to have used this name. Then he moved further north through the Wimmera. In the second Tichborne trial, a Mr Richard Redman, who had returned from Australia, told of an experience he had at a station called Nowhere Else eighty miles north-east of Glenorchy in the Mallee. It was called Nowhere Else because it was the last station; this is most likely the station called Ultima (which has a similar meaning to Nowhere Else), south of Swan Hill. It was controlled at this time by George Curlewis, a Sale squatter whom Orton may have known during his Gippsland days. Redman was working as a sheep-dipper on the property, and the cook in the hut they stayed in was a character called Arthur, who styled himself 'the Doctor'. Redman identified the claimant in court as the person he knew there. Presumably Castro had here reverted to using the Arthur Orton name by which Curlewis would have known him in Gippsland.

One day a strange incident happened. On returning to the hut the workers found two policemen there, and no Orton. The police had been looking for an Aborigine, but on their approach Orton had cleared out with his horse. So the workers went without dinner that day. When Orton returned he offered no explanation for his disappearance, but it was assumed he had no receipt for his horse, which meant it was a stolen one. When Redman left the job, 'the Doctor' told his fellow workers: 'Do not say that you have seen me up here'.[2] This man talked of Wapping, and of Valparaiso and Melipilla in Chile, which sounds like Orton. Redman said: 'He was continually talking of prizefighters, and bushrangers', and claimed acquaintance with Broome, a well known English boxer, and Morgan, the Australian bushranger, and their various deeds. Orton may have wished to identify with famous people like the boxer and the bushrangers in order to vicariously become famous himself, as he later achieved when he took on the Tichborne role.

After his time at Nowhere Else Castro (as he was now calling himself) wandered in his usual desultory style around the Riverina for four years before his Wagga Wagga period, taking a number of jobs (carter, butcher, horse breaker, mail driver) at different places, but always moving on. His first stop was at Deniliquin, which was on the major stock-routes supplying the Ballarat and Bendigo goldfields at the time. Here he first worked for the butcher Charles Lucas in early 1860. Then he worked for the brothers John Burrows, butcher and racehorse owner, and Fred Burrows, horsedealer and hotelier, as a journeyman butcher for about eighteen months from mid 1860 to late 1861. Fred Burrows, who had previously been in Gippsland, at Bairnsdale and Omeo, had known Orton there, so he must have noticed the name change. In Deniliquin Castro read borrowed copies of the *Times* and the *London Illustrated News*, which kept him posted on English affairs.

But once again there was trouble with a horse, which led to court cases. Castro brought a mare off William Gibson with a promissory note for £14 drawn on John Burrows, for whom he was working (a stratagem he had used in Hobart). Castro took the horse to a Deniliquin racetrack. But Burrows refused to honour the promissory note when it was presented to him by William Gibson, as there were not sufficient funds in Castro's account to meet it. John Gibson, brother of William, then repossessed the horse. This sequence of events led to two court cases. John Gibson was charged by Castro with illegally taking his horse, and William Gibson charged Castro with not having the funds to meet the payment under the Statute of Frauds. Castro represented himself in both cases, which were heard at Deniliquin in late November, 1861. In the first case Castro claimed the mare was his, but Gibson's solicitor argued there was no case, as the owner was allowed to lend the horse to his brother. The magistrate agreed with this and dismissed the case. In the counter charge Castro maintained that he had been loaned the horse in the meantime. The Magistrate found that although Castro's actions had been reprehensible, there was a total absence of false pretences on his part, and dismissed the charge. Had he been aware of Orton/Castro's previous court record in Hobart and Sale, he might have been less trusting in his judgement. But Castro had performed well in his own defence. A solicitor at the court was impressed with the way Castro cross-examined the witnesses against him.[3]

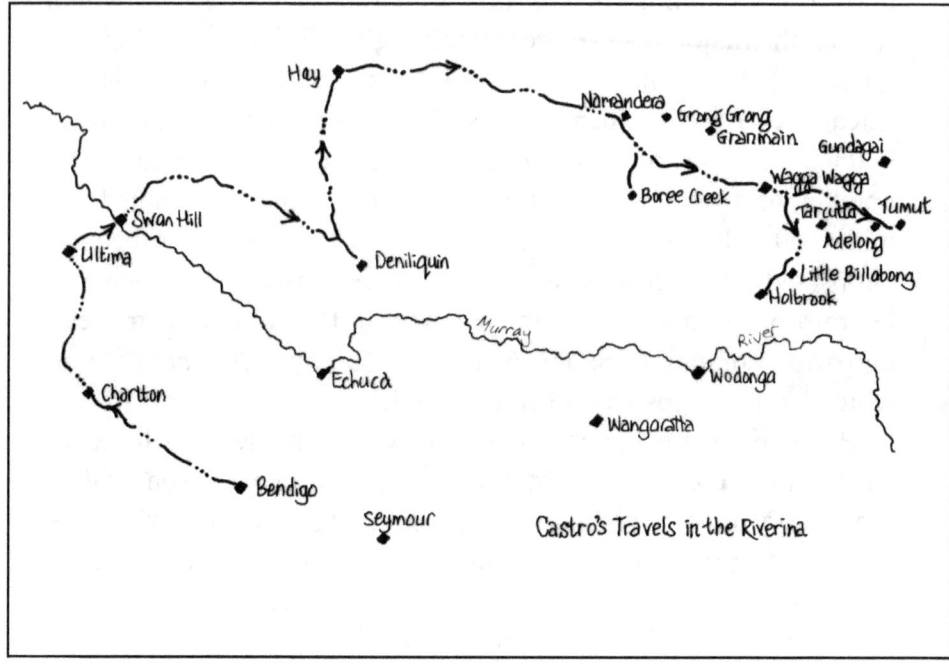

Castro's Travels in the Riverina

Castro then characteristically decided to move on. He travelled to the next major town to the north, Hay, where he worked as a slaughterman and horse-breaker for the butcher John Lee Ward, popularly known as 'Parramatta Jack', from late 1861 to mid 1862. In Hay he met an old Hobart friend, Alexander MacDonald, who noticed he was going by the name Tom Castro. Castro told him: 'Mac, don't say anything about it, I have changed my name, call me Tom, Tom Castro'.[4] James Gormly, a prominent Riverina identity of the time, has left an account of Castro's buckjumping prowess at Hay: 'Castro professed to be a horse-breaker, and to be able to ride buckjumpers. But he was not proficient at that work, and would be frequently bucked off. But he showed a large amount of determination and would mount again, often to be pitched off a second time. It used to be considered a good joke at Hay to see Tom Castro attempting to ride a wild horse, but through his determination, he usually succeeded in taming the horse'.[5] This is an example of his part-fantasy belief that he could do anything, though he does emerge reasonably well from this account.

Castro applied to Gormly, a contractor, for employment driving coaches on Riverina routes, though he had no experience of driving. This was in late 1862 or 1863. During the winter it was so wet that coaches couldn't run, so Castro delivered the mails on horseback between Wagga Wagga, Hay and Narrandera. But he was too heavy for the horses, and was given a job as groom at Boree. In mid 1863 he was at Grong Grong on the Narrandera road, minding mail horses. Around the same time he was seen on the Murrumbidgee River between Narrandera and Hay. Gormly wrote of him: 'Castro during the time I had known him was always sober, he could quote passages in English and Latin from the Catholic prayer books, and could repeat the responses to the priest when serving mass.' This knowledge came from his South American days.

In mid 1863 Castro moved along the Tarcutta Creek to Adelong near Tumut, east of the Melbourne-Sydney road and south of Gundagai. He worked for the brothers John and Phil Davis, but was not a success. Here Castro was remembered by Edward Stidworthy, a blacksmith who later lived in Wagga Wagga.[6] Castro wanted to enter a weedy little mare of his called 'Goldfinder' in a race but did not have the money to get her shod. Stidworthy let him get the horse shod at his smithy, to be paid only if 'Goldfinder' won. Stidworthy later bought the mare. Castro was at this stage so poor he did not have enough to eat. He left Adelong owing Stidworthy a pound. Later he worked at 'The London Butchery' (presumably named in remembrance of his father's business) in a cottage in Fitzroy St, Tumut. He kept to himself there, didn't flourish, and soon left.

He told Stidworthy while selling him the mare about the bushranger Piesley: 'He said he and Piesly were mates at one time; he did not say in what way he was a mate, whether it was bushranging or not' and 'he mentioned Gipp's Land in conversation about Piesly'. He said he sometimes went by the name Piesley. The Riverina bushranger John Piesley was born in New South Wales in 1834, and sentenced in Bathurst to gaol for horse-stealing in September 1854. Released on a ticket-of-leave in 1860, he commenced a series of outrages, some with Frank Gardiner, on the western plains of New South Wales from 1860 to 1862. He was captured at Tarcutta near Wagga Wagga in January 1862, tried and executed soon afterwards. Castro 'spoke a great deal about Piesly, and seemed to know all about him'. Was this true or another fantasy of knowing the famous or infamous? Bushrangers were known in the area. Mr Lockhart, the Crown Lands Commissioner on Tumut, had been stuck up in 1857 by bushrangers.

Castro left Tumut some time with some bills not paid, and had to retrospectively honour them before he left for England to claim the Tichborne inheritance. At this later time, 12 July, 1866, the *Tumut and Adelong Times* reported:

> ROMANCE IN REAL LIFE.- It may perhaps be in the recollection of many of our readers that a man calling himself Thomas De Castro...left Tumut and opened a butchering establishment at Wagga Wagga. It now turns out that the said Thomas De Castro is no less a person than Sir Roger Charles Tichbourne, with landed estates bringing in a rental of £9000 per annum, and an accumulated fund of some £50,000 in the bank. De Castro was in possession of his title and property when living in Tumut, but not having been in communication with his family for some years was not aware of his good fortune.

After a short stay in Albury, in late 1863 Castro took employment as a horsebreaker on James McLaurin's large and prosperous 'Yarra Yarra' station on Billabong Creek in central Riverina near Germanton (Holbrook), north of Albury and south of Wagga Wagga. Here he told stories of connections with the notorious bushranger Dan Morgan, just as he had earlier told of connections with Piesley. At this time the depredations of Mad Dan Morgan in the Riverina were at their height, and Morgan operated from the vicinity of the Yarra Yarra station. Castro claimed to have met Morgan on many occasions when the latter was camped there. Castro also used the name Morgan himself at the time. This may have been for the purpose of copy-cat crime, as many bushrangers imitated Morgan. At his trial in England, Castro said Orton was charged with bushranging at this time, but would not answer if he himself was, on the grounds that it might incriminate him.

Morgan's background is obscure. His biographer Margaret Carnegie thinks he was born William Moran in 1833 and grew up in Campbelltown, NSW. He moved south to Victoria and worked for George Black at Tarwin Meadows about 1850, which indicates he had been in Gippsland. Morgan appeared in the Ovens and King Rivers area in June 1860. He was mixed up in horse-stealing and was known as 'Dan the horse-breaker'. He had originally moved south from Sydney, but was now moving north and soon crossed the border. His reign of terror in the Riverina from mid 1860 to mid 1865 occurred at the same time as Tom Castro's arrival and career there, though that infers no necessary connection. Morgan had many aliases such as 'Bill the Native', 'Sydney Native' and 'Bill the Jockey'. In June 1863 with an unknown accomplice Morgan held up four young men. He hid in the Piney Ranges in the vast scrub of the lower Billabong, where Castro was employed.

In August, 1863, Morgan and a mate held up the Police Magistrate Bayliss, who at first escaped but was soon tracked down in the scrub and captured by them. Morgan's companion was short and stout, about 30 years of age and with a light coloured beard. After some unpleasantness, Morgan released Bayliss, saying 'You needn't say anything about this little affair'. But Bayliss and a posse of police went out to track Morgan through the vast scrub and after several days came on Morgan's camp when the bushrangers were away. A shoot-out ensued on their return, in which both Bayliss and Morgan's mate were seriously wounded. Morgan took his companion back into the bush to die; his body was found in the scrub a couple of years later. This means his companion could not have been Orton/Castro. Bayliss recovered in hospital. The novelist Rolf Boldrewood was the owner of 'Bundidjaree' station on the Murrumbidgee River at the time of this incident, and wrote an account of it in a series on Australian bushranging much later in 1905. Boldrewood later became a police magistrate in New South Wales, like Bayliss, whom he knew. His article on the Bayliss-Morgan incident opens with an account of Castro, whom Bayliss knew, and the Tichborne claim. Boldrewood and Bayliss discussed the Tichborne claim at the time; to Boldrewood's belief that Castro was too stupid to have invented such an ingenious plot as the claim, Bayliss replied in conversation: 'Tom Castro is anything but a stupid man. On the contrary, he is a very clever rogue – a gambler, and a schemer; this is just the kind of plot that would commend itself to him'.[7]

At another stage Morgan befriended the cook and shepherd on McLaurin's Billabong run (one of these could have been Castro, who was working on the run). The shepherd led McLaurin and his men to Morgan's camp, while Morgan at the same time arrived at the homestead and got supplies from the cook. Morgan frequented the inn at Ten Mile Creek near Holbrook, where Castro said he lived for a while. When a reward was offered for Morgan's capture after the Round Hill and other murders in 1864, Castro bragged that he would attempt this, as Morgan would have no suspicion of him. The New South Wales Felon's Apprehension Act of March 1865 was one reason why Morgan moved back over the border into Victoria. Morgan's death by shooting at Peechelba in northern Victoria in April 1865 triggered the much publicized letter, so important in the Tichborne trials in England, which Castro sent to the Richardson family of Wapping, asking them to convey to the Orton family the news of Morgan's death, which seemed to have some special importance for Castro. In the letter, dated 13 April, 1865, Castro wrote: 'I beg to say here with pleasure that one of the most notorious of the Bushrangers has fallen by a *Rifle ball* and that on the news of his death and doings being properly chronicled I will send you the paper containing such'.[8] Morgan died on 9 April, 1865, so it is obviously him being referred to here. Why did Castro think Morgan's death was so important? It was shortly after this in late 1865 that Castro, then living in Wagga Wagga as a butcher, made his claims to be Tichborne.

A recurrent folk story later on was that Tichborne and Orton-Castro were bushrangers together in the Riverina during this period, sometimes going under the names of Morgan and Smith. The story went that they stuck up travellers on the road from Wagga Wagga to Melbourne. On one occasion Tichborne was said to have shot a person dead and to have received a severe blow in return. This story has some resemblance to the Bayliss encounter, in which an unidentified accomplice of Morgan was shot and died in the bush later. The implication in all the stories is that Tichborne was either shot by others or murdered in the bush by Orton/Castro, who, after Morgan's death, emerged to assume Tichborne's identity. But all this is surmise, without any real evidence. Much more likely is that Orton/Castro identified with Piesley and Morgan to appropriate their fame (or infamy) to himself.

Thomas Castro arrived in Wagga Wagga in late 1863 or early 1864. Wagga Wagga was the northernmost point that those following the Vandemonian trail could end up at in the Riverina. Once again Castro's pattern of a desultory life, including many short-term jobs, some debts and a few court cases, was repeated. At one stage he dug potatoes for a farmer, then he resumed his old butchering trade. He worked for the butcher Byrnes for a few months, and then after that for Robert Higgins, who took over the business from Byrnes. He was employed by Higgins for about two years, slaughtering cattle and making sausages. Eventually he set up butchering by himself, with a shop or stall in Garwood St. with his name in linen outside it. All this was a repeat of his activities in every place since his Hobart days.

James Gormly, dubbed 'The Father of Wagga' because of his prominence in the early days, employed Castro as a fencer, providing him with a hut to live in. Castro also worked for Gormly as a horsebreaker. Gormly described how Castro had hopes of winning money by racing a horse at Wagga Wagga. He had heard of a race worth £1000 at the coming Champion Race meeting to be held in March, 1864, and told Gormly that he hoped to win with his mare. But she was a small, weedy thing, and Gormly knew he had no hope, especially considering the large size of the jockey. On the last day of the championship races Castro 'began to boast about the speed of his mare and offered to match her for a good stake against any hack for a spin once around the course, he to ride his mare, the other to carry an equal weight'.[9] This challenge again reveals a fantasy about quick money-making – Castro and his horse were in the event beaten by a furlong.

Court cases along the usual lines ensued. One was against a

TOM CASTRO'S HOUSE AT WAGGA

former employer – Castro sued the butcher Eliott, for wages, a rerun of the case against Foster in Sale, but this time Castro won the case against Elliot, who was represented by the solicitor William Gibbes. In another case, in which Gibbes acted for Castro, Castro wanted to secure a certain place to start a butchery. A dispute over a slaughtering yard arose between Castro and the owner Downey, and Orton was able to get an ejectment order against Downey. In another case, a man had a court verdict against Orton and was going to have him imprisoned; in this matter Orton was worried about the legality of making a schedule under an assumed name, so the matter was likely one of debt. Mr. Bayliss was the magistrate in some of these cases. In another incident police found a Ganmain bullock in Castro's yard which he was about to slaughter. He said he had brought it from a selector, who was then put on trial for stealing and convicted on this evidence from Castro. Many thought Castro had made up the story to escape trouble himself. In addition to these court troubles, Castro was as usual in debt to various people.

An acquaintance at this time, the solicitor William Willans, later described the claimant as 'a large lubberly man, with lightish yellow hair, a heavy jaw, tremendous thick legs'.[10] A new element, which was to increase over the years, now revealed itself in the claimant's personality – strong sexual drives. He had been living with a woman called 'Gentle Annie' Hume, but he left her and after proposing to several other women, he settled into a relationship with the working class Mary Ann Bryant, daughter of a bricklayer, who already had a young child. She was of Irish background, illiterate, and there were hints of a dubious past – the claimant's first daughter Teresa later said her mother's people were bushrangers. Tom and Mary were married in the Wesleyan/Baptist chapel in January, 1865. Castro's wife was a hard worker, who did laundering chores to keep the family afloat when Castro was unemployed. In his *Confession*, the claimant wrote: 'I often went into the shanties (unlicensed premises) to have a drink during the day, but I always went with a customer or my master, but never with the assistants in the shop'.[11] Castro led his usual life of drinking, gambling at the races and not paying his debts. He warned old acquaintances from his Hobart and Gippsland days that he had changed his name, and that they should keep quiet about his past.

Castro's claims to an exalted ancestry became more frequent during his Riverina years. In Deniliquin he told a constable, James Fegan, that he was heir to a property and would be able to help his friends. One story to Cornelius Haxall, a boarding-house keeper of Denilquin, was that he was richer than any squatter, and had a secret. He told the photographer William Fearn at Yarra Yarra station that his family had position. But Haxall and others had reason to doubt his stories because of their inconsistencies. Some of the stories were quite unbelievable. The claimant seems to have been a fantasizer who, perhaps by overdosing himself on a diet of romantic novels, developed the fancy common at the time that he had a hidden aristocratic lineage. Orton/Castro seems at this time to have been the victim of a mounting, multiple mania. He was soon to take a giant step forward in this regard.

In Homer's *Odyssey*, Penelope at home in her palace at Ithaca listened eagerly to visiting seafarers who told her of rumours of her husband Odysseus on his wanderings. Similarly Lady Tichborne at home on the Tichborne estate in Hampshire hearkened to various visitors who claimed knowledge of the whereabouts of her missing son. A passage in Homer could be applied to this case:

> Beggars in need of creature comforts find lying easy, and to tell a true tale is the last thing they want to do. Whenever a tramp comes to Ithaca he goes straight to my mistress and tells a pack of lies. She welcomes him graciously and asks him every detail, point by point, while tears of distress stream down her cheeks, as is natural for a woman whose husband has met his end abroad.[12]

Against the advice of her family who feared publicity would attract imposters, Lady Tichborne first advertised for her lost son in the London *Times* on 13 May, 1863.

Castro first made his claim to be Sir Roger Tichborne in September, 1865. The first advertisement for Sir Roger had appeared in English newspapers sixteen months earlier. This did not mention Australia, but simply offered a reward for information. The advertisement in Australian papers in August 1865 mentioned the possibility that Sir Roger may have arrived in Melbourne after being shipwrecked. It is difficult to gauge how much, if any, knowledge Castro had of the Tichborne family prior to his claim. His two major reading sources were newspapers and novels. In his Riverina career Castro widened the reading interests he as Orton had shown in Gippsland. At Deniliquin Mr. William Love, a storekeeper, remembered that when the mails came, Castro would ask to borrow the London *Times* and the *Illustrated London News*.[13] Love considered him well informed on English affairs. Another Deniliquin acquaintance Mr. Haxall remembered him as educated, reading English novels, and saw him carrying copies of the *Illustrated London News*. So it is just possible with his novel-reading habits that he read Kingsley's *Ravenshoe* (first published in book form in 1862) during his Riverina years, and used it as a basis for his claim. It is also possible that he saw the earlier English advertisements for the lost Tichborne heir in May 1863 in the London *Times*, before the Australian ones appeared. With or without the imaginative stimulation of *Ravenshoe*, he would have had a couple of years to devise the details of his impersonation, if he had seen the English advertisement.

A crucial period is between May 1863, when the English advertisement for Tichborne appeared, and August 1865, when the advertisement appeared in Australia. His claims at Wagga Wagga from late 1863 have to be assessed with the knowledge that he could have already read the advertisement in *The Times*, and so he could already have been devising his imposture. He bragged to the butcher Reardon: 'I'll be the owner of this place yet'. To Michael Golden he dropped hints of wealth and position, claiming he was from one of the oldest Catholic families in England. To the butcher Perrin he said he was from a respectable Hampshire family. Patrick Reardon claimed that Castro wrote 'R.C.T., Hampshire, En.' on a piece of paper saying 'That's my name, I leave you to guess it'; this was in April 1865, months before the Australian advertisement appeared, as were the claims to Golden and Perrin.[14] In April, 1865 – before the Australian advertisement in August, 1865 – he wrote the mysterious Richardson letter under his Castro name seeking knowledge of the Orton family in Wapping. He also wrote indirectly to his old Wapping, Van Diemen's Land and Gippsland comrade Schottler, but wouldn't reveal his real name. This may suggest that, before the Australian advertisements, he was already preparing the ground for his imposture by keeping his old Wapping relatives and associates quiet. The letter was written four days after the bushranger Morgan's death, which is alluded to in it. Was the claimant implying in the Richardson letter that Orton was Morgan, so that the death would conveniently explain the disappearance of Orton? If the claimant had not seen the earlier advertisement, the motivation for writing to friends and relatives without revealing himself is puzzling. The Richardson letter is the first clear documentary evidence of a link between Castro and Orton.

NOTES

1. *The Australian Commission*, op. cit., p. 202.

2. Ibid., pp. 175-6.

3. Both cases are reported in the *Pastoral Times*, Deniliquin, 29 November, 1861, p. 2.

4. *The Australian Commission*, op. cit., p. 88.

5. James Gormly 'Tom Castro', *Wagga Express*, 26 August, 1915, repr. in James Gormly *Exploration and Settlement of Australia*, Sydney, 1921, p. 140.

6. *The Australian Commission*, op. cit., pp. 71-3.

7. Rolf Boldrewood 'Wild Deeds of Wild Days in Australia: IV - Face to Face with Dan Morgan - Bushranger', *Life*, March 15, 1905, p. 269.

8. *The Australian Commission*, op. cit., p. 209.

9. James Gormley *Exploration and Settlement in Australia*, op. cit., p. 143.

10. *The Australian Commission*, op. cit., p. 73.

11. *The Confession*, op. cit., p. 6.

12. Homer *The Odyssey*, trans. E.V. Rieu, rev. ed., Penguin, London, 1991, p. 211.

13. *Trial at the Bar of Sir Roger Tichborne*, op. cit., Vol. 2, pp. 199-200.

14. *The Australian Commission*, op. cit., p. 79.

13

BACK TO BRITAIN

In June 1865 Lady Tichborne had contacted Mr Cubitt of the Sydney Missing Friends Agency to advertize for her son in some Australian papers. At the same time Castro had come to see the solicitor Gibbes about his debts, which totalled about £200, a very large amount, about two years' wages for a person in Castro's humble position. Gibbes suggested bankruptcy as a solution, but this worried Castro, who hinted that other property he had in England might have to be included in his statement of assets, or he would be in trouble with the law. A friend of Castro's in Wagga, Richard Slade, was an educated man from Hamsphire, where the Tichbornes had their seat. In the claimant's much later *Confession* of 1895, he explained that after his friend Slade brought him the Australian advertisement for the missing heir, thinking it might be himself, he said for a lark 'I put my hand to my head, and appeared moved to tears'. Gibbes later recalled Castro saying he did it 'for devilry'.[1] When Slade asked him if he knew anything 'I gave him a sort of shake of the head, from which he seemed to think that I knew something more than I choose to say'.[2] (This was the same technique of suggestion he was soon to use with the solicitor Gibbes.) Slade then showed the advertisement to Gibbes, who pursued the matter, because of Castro's previous claims of wealth, and the deception took root. Castro pumped Slade for knowledge of Hampshire and the Tichbornes, in order to imitate the heir.

Castro's mentioning his ownership of property had aroused Gibbes' suspicion that he might be the missing heir mentioned in the advertisements. In early September, 1865, Castro, now furnished with details from the Australian advertisement and Slade's coaching, mentioned a baronet in the family, South America and being shipwrecked – this amounted to leading Gibbes on. When

Gibbes subsequently met Castro, he said that he knew who he was and could tell him his real name, but Castro demurred with mock innocence, saying Gibbes was fishing, but showed him a pipe with RCT recently inscribed on it, which seemed to clinch the case.[3] Both were colluding in the 'discovery', which Castro was cunningly making it look like Gibbes had made. The claimant's posture in his *Confession* that the deception was 'forced on me' is hardly plausible.[4] Both Castro and Gibbes, as well as Cubitt, had a financial interest in making the identification, so its revelation is not surprising. Gibbes wrote to Cubitt in early October suggesting he had found the heir and asking for more information.

In these early stages the Wagga Wagga solicitor Gibbes and the Sydney agent Cubitt were the ones pursuing the matter vigorously. Having made the claim, Castro was at times strangely reluctant and indifferent, as though not wanting to go through with the whole thing, presumably having an inkling of what he was in for. He maintained this pattern of oscillation between interest and indifference to his claim for the next decade. He made a will with totally inaccurate details about the Tichborne family, merely to surmount an immediate hurdle – a will was needed to borrow money. His short-term need for money kept getting him into deeper and deeper strife, an endless nightmare. The will was to cause him great trouble in the future. All three, Cubitt, Gibbes and Castro, applied to Lady Tichborne for funds. She eventually sent £40 to Castro in February 1866, which enabled him to move his family to Sydney. From the time of making the claim, September, 1865, Castro ceased to work for a living; this leisure continued up to the time of his conviction in February, 1874, a period of eight and a half years. Gibbes, who first met Castro in connection with helping to relieve him of debts and thinking that he had struck a bonanza, was eventually left being owed hundreds of pounds by the claimant and with the threat of charges of complicity in a fraud against him. He was not the first victim of the claimant, nor the last.

Castro had begun with fantasies of a wealthy past, and Slade's pushing had acted as a trigger. He had got into the scheme to get out of working and to get out of Wagga. He admitted in his *Confession*:

'Money was what I wanted, and money was my game'.[5] This was a limited goal. But he was getting into something much bigger than his previous debt-avoiding flits. In his buckjumping, he could take on an unruly horse without much skill and perhaps tame it, or come off with nothing worse than a dumping. But now he was mounting something that would control him. Previously by moving on he was able to cut himself off from his past, and move to a new location unimpeded. But now he was embarking on a venture where his past would catch up with him, be ever present and be raked over endlessly for years in pre-trail investigations and in two lengthy trials. The case took on a momentum too great for any one mortal to control, and he eventually became, with many others, its victim. As his *Confession* puts it: 'I found that by listening to others the story really built itself, and in that way it grew so large that I really could not get out of it'.[6] Like Lady Macbeth he had 'stepp'd in so far that, should I wade no more,/ Returning were as tedious as go o'er.'

He was soon faced with an endless series of impostures, like inventing the will, which must have imposed a great strain on him. Something in his personality seemed to have been detached from reality. Gibbes later said of him at this stage: 'He delighted in making secrets and being mysterious...[He] used to tell that which was not true occasionally for fun'.[7] He had engaged in fantasy and deception before, but this was on an unimaginably grander scale. He became steadily stouter from this period. He probably ate and drank to excess because of worry about what lay before him, now he could not back out. The defence later portrayed him as a fortune hunter, brandishing the Mary Braddon quote about men with brains and no money contriving to get on top. That was no doubt true, but only half the psychological story – he was a schemer, but not a consummate one. His own explanation, that he was acting like a novelist inventing a narrative, probably comes closest to the truth of the matter:

> Imagination, as everyone knows, goes a very long way, and from experience I know that if a man sits down quietly for any length of time and dwells upon one subject, he can either

> convince himself that he is not going to be poor all the days of his life, but that some lucky incident will occur which will lift him up from his present impecunious position.[8]

The Castros had a baby daughter in March. His attitude to his family was peculiar. At some stages he spoke as it he would leave the whole family in Australia. His letter to a Wagga Wagga baker named Cater inviting him to Tichborne Hall said: 'on no account allude to me being a Married Man'. In the *Confession* he said: 'I could then go to Sydney and take the steamer to Panama where I could join my brother [in California], and nobody would ever hear more of me' – a typical escape.[9]

To leave Wagga for Sydney, as the Castro family did in June, 1866, seemed to the world simply a first step on the way to a momentous claim. But for Castro it fitted a familiar pattern – the habit of leaving places which got too hot for him. He then married his wife for the second time in a Catholic ceremony in Goulburn, his wife's home town, in July, 1866, as befitted an aspiring Tichborne, who were a Catholic family. In Goulburn he also dipped into *Burke's Peerage* to swot up on his claim. In Sydney he was lucky to be recognized by two former Tichborne retainers and by a family friend. Castro took the Tichborne valet Bogle into his employ, and extracted useful information about the family from him. Time in Sydney was spent living lavishly and raising more money on promises; £20,000 was soon spent or owed. The claimant couldn't pay the bills at the hotel, so he soon found a novel way of avoiding payment by 'buying' the hotel for £10,000, but the bank draft was dishonoured. He left Sydney in September, 1866, to claim the fortune, but also to get away from the new Sydney mess. He took his family and a retinue consisting of Bogle and his son, young Butts from the hotel as secretary, and a nursemaid, Rosina MacArthur. He left Australia for ever, after an eventful sojourn of thirteen years (1853 to 1866) which had included many court cases. On the way to England there were long delays at Panama and New York, where money deficiencies and the claimant's reluctance to proceed were evident. On a number of shipboard occasions and again in New York he tried to seduce the maid Rosina into going to live with him in America, starting up a new life in California and leaving his family. He proposed the same scheme to a stewardess on board. His sexual and eating demands were becoming grandiose like his claim.

The Castro contingent arrived in London at Christmas 1866. He immediately visited Wapping and asked after the Ortons; when subsequently revealed, this visit caused him a lot of trouble. His greatest coup was to be recognized by the mother, Lady Tichborne, who gave him £1000 per year. Thereafter he journeyed to the Tichborne estate and was acknowledged by some locals; he was also recognized by some family friends, employees and locals who had known the young Roger. But no close family members did, except the mother; they were positively hostile to him, branding him an imposter, and raising funds for the defence of the estates. Other things did not go well with him. The Tichborne family sent an agent, Mr John Mackenzie, to Australia to collect information on his Australian background. In his *Confession*, the claimant admitted that Mackenzie's assiduous researches in Australia were damaging to him. A detective in London, Whicher, traced the family of Orton's friend Schottler to Wapping where they knew the Ortons. The suspicion that Castro was an Orton was fed back to Mackenzie, and from mid 1867 stories of a mystery Arthur Orton presence in the story came back from Australia. Castro's claimed past corresponded with Arthur Orton's in many details, but not all. So the claimant had to resort to the explanation that he knew Orton well for long periods in Australia, where he (Castro) was known as Tom, Bob or 'the foreigner'. But Mrs Macalister (the former Mrs Foster of Boisdale) identified Castro as Orton from photographs, which was damaging, and William Hopgood said he knew the man as Orton in Gippsland and Castro in Wagga Wagga. The Australian evidence suggested some definite, though as yet not fully explained, Orton-Castro connection.

The evidence from Australia about Arthur Orton worried the claimant's supporters in England, particularly his solicitor, Mr Holmes. In addition the claimant was in constant financial trouble, with a big household retinue, extravagant tastes and no regular income apart from his 'mother's', who unfortunately for him died in 1868. He moved from Croydon to Hampshire to avoid creditors, following his Australian habit of moving on to avoid debts. Many friends and supporters lent him large sums of money, but he was declared bankrupt in 1869. Commissions were sent to Chile and Australia to gather evidence for the court case, but the claimant appeared at neither of these.

The Australian Commission, set up by the English court, sat from May to November, 1869, in Hobart, Sydney, Wagga Wagga, Deniliquin, Melbourne, Sale, Bairnsdale and Kilmore. The Commission produced contradictory evidence, but mostly unfavourable to the claimant, since the possibility of Orton and Castro being the same person began to look more likely. A crucial fact was that no hard documentary evidence was produced about Castro's existence before 1860, whereas it did exist about Orton in Tasmania and Gippsland. The claimant's witnesses in the main said they remembered two similar men together, who could have been Castro and Orton. As it was already fifteen years after the events, memories were faulty, especially after rival agents had muddied the waters by inducing recollections favourable to their respective cases. Recent publicity on the case affected witnesses, who read back into the past what they wanted to recall. Already folklore and gossip were gaining the upper hand. People were gradually patterning the case to fit their own preconceptions. An aristocrat had turned into a worker, and after this low period had reverted to aristocratic status. Or the scenario was split into two people or doubles, an aristocrat and a worker, who wandered around the Australian bush together. On balance of probabilities the case was against the claimant. No 'Osprey' shipwreck survivors were ever traced. The Wapping visit was inexplicable – why would Sir Roger go to Wapping on his first night back in England? There were many gaps in the claimant's memory of his childhood, especially of his time at Stonyhurst College, and he didn't, like Roger Tichborne, know any French. He did not have Tichborne's tattoos. The Wagga Wagga will was ludicrous.

The first Tichborne trial was a civil action by the claimant to eject Lushington, lessee of the Tichborne estates. It began in London on 11 May, 1871, and lasted till 5 March, 1872, 103 days of hearings, a very long ordeal. It turned on certain key aspects: the sealed packet Tichborne was supposed to have given to his beloved cousin Katherine Doughty, his Paris childhood and Stonyhurst education, his army life, Chile, Orton in Australia, and marks such as tattoos. Castro survived cross-examination by Coleridge, the defence counsel, just enough to make his case possible, but displayed lamentable ignorance in many areas. On 9 September, 1871, the *Gippsland Times* reported that the defence, that is, anti-Castro lawyers, were investigating whether an unexecuted warrant against Orton for horse stealing in Sale in 1859 was still in the hands of the Gippsland police. They were also looking into Castlemaine court records to see if Orton had also been charged with a similar offence there in the same year. It was shown at the trial that Roger had distinctive tattoos, which Castro did not have. This was the final straw. The jury wished to retire, with the clear implication they would find against the claimant, but Ballantyne, Castro's counsel, asked that he be non-suited, that is, withdraw the case. The judge immediately arraigned Castro for perjury, to which the charge of forgery was later added. Castro was kept in Newgate Gaol, until with some difficulty he gained bail. He once again had no money.

At first Castro had been viewed as an aggressive litigant, but attitudes to him changed after the Crown pursued him. Now seen by many as a victim, the claimant received great public support in England and Australia, as a poor, struggling man persecuted by an unrelenting establishment. Mass meetings were held around England to gain public support, and to raise money for his cause. In the second trial his counsel was the Irish Queen's Counsel Edward Kenealy, who injected partisan religious and class arguments into the public discussion. Castro was allegedly a poor Catholic persecuted by a vengeful Protestant upper-class. In the second trail Kenealy used the fact that Castro was half-hearted about his claim as evidence that he was not a cunning, calculated imposter. Castro's reverting to the role of victim was a kind of death-wish.

He now resembled one of the great enduring figures of mythology, which added immeasurably to his popular appeal. Sir James Frazer begins his magisterial compendium of folklore *The Golden Bough* with the tale of the priest in the grove of Nemi, an ordinary man made a priest/king for a year by his community. During this period he is given anything he wants – power, luxuries, women, food – but he knows that at the end of the year he will be eliminated as a fertility sacrifice to the gods. He cannot really enjoy his benefice as he is in constant dread that his assassin-nemesis may be lurking in the bushes nearby.

During the period of his trials in England Castro was in a bind of this kind. He was a Lord of Misrule, a Jack overthrowing the accustomed order for a brief time. But knew the world of wineing and dining and pheasant shooting would soon be brutally stripped away from him. In England the claimant had carried out his dream to some extent – he acted as an English gentleman and acquired the money (borrowed of course) to carry this off in some style. He went shooting as befitted a country gentleman, he travelled around in coaches, he talked to gentry and old soldiers, he used his 'title'. But he had financial and court worries of a pressing kind, which caused him to put on weight rapidly, increasing from 13 to 27 stone (365lb) during his ordeal. He was constantly ill, and his doctors had to cut him back to 20 cigars and two bottles of spirits per day. His mood alternated greatly. In court he could be listless and depressed, but in the evenings when he was on the town, and at weekends in the country, he was much more ebullient. The claimant went through enormous amounts of money, and so did those who opposed him. Tichborne Bonds, subscribed to by the public and of course never redeemed by the plaintiff, raised £40,000. The whole legal process, stretched over a decade, may have cost in the order of £200,000. The public and those private individuals who supported him were also his victims. He duped them and didn't pay his debts, just as he had avoided his financial responsibilities in a much smaller way in Australia.

A SCENE AT THE TRIAL

In the first trial Castro was plaintiff, in the second defendant, both roles he was accustomed to in the many smaller cases he had undergone in Australia. The second trial was at that time the longest in English legal history; it lasted 188 days, from April 23, 1873, until February 28, 1874. It was a criminal, not a civil case like the first one. Castro was indicted on two counts of perjury. In the first case the Crown had to prove he was not Sir Roger Tichborne; in this case it had to show he was someone else, most likely Arthur Orton. Another crucial matter was his claim that he had seduced Roger's cousin and beloved, Katherine Doughty, now Lady Ratcliffe. This matter caused sections of public opinion to swing against the claimant. In the main the same evidence as in the first trial, with the same crucial turning points, was exhaustively canvassed again. Chief Justice Cockburn summed up strongly in favour of the Crown case. The jury found Castro guilty, on the grounds that he was not Sir Roger Tichborne, that he *was* Arthur Orton, and that he did not seduce Lady Ratcliffe. Orton was sentenced to seven years on two counts of perjury, to be served consecutively.

In his *Confession* the claimant frankly revealed that the verdict, though heavy, was the greatest relief he had in his life, as the anxiety and stress he had suffered for over eight years since his initial claim in 1865 had now been lifted from his mind. He served ten and a half years; his weight went rapidly down to about ten stone from twenty five plus, and he became much more healthy. In fact the sentence, though arduous, probably saved his life, as his previous style of living would surely have soon killed him. The agitation by his supporters was kept up during his period of incarceration. But gradually the movement subsided. It was buoyed by hopes from Australia from time to time – the great challenge was to produce an Arthur Orton. The movement was revived on the claimant's release in 1884, when he became an act in a circus, but did not take off.[10] The claimant formed a relationship with another woman and had four more children, all of whom died in infancy. To ease his mind he made his *Confession* in dire financial straits in 1895, retracted it, and died in poverty on April Fool's Day in London in 1898.

We think of the Tichborne saga as a stand-alone case. It was the foremost example of disputed inheritance in the 19th century, but there were many others. Even while the Tichborne saga was being played out, another case with similarities was taking place in Gippsland, one of the places of the residence of the Tichborne claimant. Patrick Coady Buckley was Gippsland's most successful squatter, though born in a Dublin prison of a convict mother, an extreme example of the upward social mobility which the opening up of Australia made possible. When he died in 1872, he left an estate estimated at between £50,000 and £90,000. Two main issues of contention arose: was there a will, and were there descendants or relatives who might inherit the Buckley fortune? Buckley had never married, so he had no direct descendants to leave his money to. He was thought to have died without a will.

The next problem was that a will appeared. A man called Thomas Maher had grown up with Buckley and been a partner of his squatting run in the Monaro in the 1830s. Maher produced a will which purported to have been signed by Buckley in 1843 – 30 years before his death – leaving his estate to Maher. The claimant Maher said Buckley made the will because of fear of death from blacks in the early days. So Maher, like Castro, sued the administrators for the whole estate. Maher told a complicated story of the history of the will. A court in Melbourne directed a Commission to take evidence in NSW before hearing Maher's claim in 1873 (there was a similar Commission in the Tichborne case). The Buckley case turned on the authenticity of the document; in court there were many arguments over Buckley's signature. On 18 March, 1874, after a long-drawn out case which had attracted great public attention, Justice Molesworth found the will was in Maher's writing and was therefore a forgery. The claimant Thomas Maher, convicted of fraud like Castro, was sent to gaol to await trial for making a false will. The lapse of Maher's will left the Crown as claimant to the estate on the grounds Buckley died intestate. But the Maher case had been prolonged and attracted great publicity. A solicitor named O'Brien representing Australian agents, instituted enquires at home and abroad about the existence of possible Buckley relatives. Eventually nine people from around the world (in Ireland, the United States and Canada) claimed to be relatives, and so entitled to a (much diminished) share in the estate.

So ended a series of cases over the Buckley will which had dragged on in the public gaze with a distinct whiff of scandal for a decade. The public made comparisons with the Tichborne saga. The claimant Maher came from Wagga Wagga some years after the Tichborne claimant. Both were suing to gain the estate of a wealthy man, both produced documents to prove their cases, and both were arraigned for false pretences. Maher was found guilty of procuring a false will and charged with fraud at exactly the same time as Castro, the Tichborne claimant, had his claim rejected and was charged with impersonation. So newspaper readers had two legal sagas, both originating in Gippsland and Wagga Wagga, to digest at the same time.

Another famous dispute about inheritance, which had an Australian connection and was a forerunner to the Tichborne case, took place in the British Isles in the early nineteenth century. After the death of the Scots Earl of Crawford in 1808, a man from Ireland called John Crawford claimed the title, saying he was a descendant of a younger son of the family who had disappeared during the previous century. Allowed access to the family papers, the claimant was charged with having forged additions to some of them to help his cause; he was found guilty and sentenced to transportation to Australia. On returning in 1823 as an ex-convict from New South Wales after serving his sentence, Crawford resumed his campaign, and notwithstanding the forgery conviction, gained widespread support from noblemen as well as the populace for his claim, which had some merit, as there had been past connections between his family and the Earls of Crawford. But he died as the case was being heard by the House of Lords, which eventually found against him and his son. Some believed his father was an illegitimate brother of a previous earl. This mysterious cause attracted great public interest half a century before the Tichborne case, which it in many ways resembles.[11]

In Australia before the Tichborne saga, a case of a convict impersonating an English aristocrat, Lord Lascelles, occurred in the 1830s. This man told people confidentially that he was Lord Lascelles sent out by the English government incognito to check on the real condition of the colony of New South Wales, and for them to keep his identity secret. He preyed on country gentlemen, playing up to their snobbery and was feted in grand style. He conducted an extensive and lavish free tour through the colony, at one stage becoming engaged to a wealthy squatter's daughter. He brought fine horses with cheques that bounced, but by then he was gone. He sold the horses he had gained in Sydney but avoided the Governor, Sir Richard Bourke, who knew the real Lord Lascelles. Eventually the imposter was identified by police as a well-known convict. He insisted he was the Lord, but was convicted and sent to Norfolk Island.[12]

The mechanisms of inheritance, requiring proof of death and paternity, meant there were bound to be disputes about succession. There have been a number of famous imposter cases in history, some of which have similarities with the Tichborne case. The

Frenchman Martin de Guerre disappeared in the 1550s and after eight years a man who looked very like him came and resumed married life with his wife. Another case was almost a dress rehearsal for the Tichborne one. The heir of the Sieur de Caille died and was buried. Three years later a man arrived at Toulon claiming to be the dead heir. The case came before the parliament and a vast number of witnesses were heard. Some said the claimant was a low grade ex-criminal. The aristocratic family was opposed to him. He won but the claimant's mother appeared, so another long case was opened. An old retainer had been advising the claimant, as in the Tichborne case. The ruling was reversed and the claimant sent to prison. Michael Gilbert has drawn attention to two cases in India which are remarkably similar to the Tichborne imposture.[13]

There have been similar cases of pretenders to the throne. On the death of King Edward IV, Richard III was said to have murdered the boy King Edward IV and his brother Richard Duke of York on his way to securing the throne. This led to the appearance of a man said to be the Duke of York. He was supported by certain sections of English and French royalty because they wanted a legitimate ruler, and France wanted to influence English affairs. He turned out to be a man named Perkin Warbeck, a non-English speaker from Flanders. Some military forays on British soil in his support were unsuccessful and he was eventually executed. Warbeck was said to be like King Edward IV in appearance, which led some to speculate he was an illegitimate son of the king.

An analogous event occurred during the 'Time of Troubles' in Russia in the decades around 1600 during the reign of Tsar Boris Gudonov. A man claimed to be Dimitry, the son of the late Tsar, Ivan the Terrible, who had escaped an assassination attempt. Some said he was a former monk named Grigory Otrepyev. He gained the support of sections of the Polish aristocracy who used him to put pressure on Russia. While staging a miliary attack on Russia, the ruling tsar died and the False Dimitry was crowed tsar in Moscow in 1605. The former Tsar Ivan's mother accepted him as her son, as Lady Tichborne accepted Arthur Orton as her son. The False Tsar Dimitry was assassinated by a place intrigue a few months after his ascension to the throne.

Last century the case of Anastasia, the missing Russian princess, had some parallels. Anastasia was thought to have survived the murder of the Tsar's family in 1918. In Berlin in 1920 a woman pulled from a canal with memory loss looked remarkably like her. But some said she was a Polish factory worker, Franziska Schanzkowska. She eventually showed great knowledge of the Romanov family and was recognized by some family retainers. After her death DNA samples were assessed, which showed that she could not have been a Romanov and that her DNA was highly compatible with the Polish family from which Franziska came.

A more recent case occurred in Texas.[14] A 13 year old boy, Nicholas Bradley, vanished in San Antonio in June, 1994; his mother searched unsuccessfully for him. In October, 1997, a call came from Granada, Spain, that Nicholas was alive in a children's shelter there. The boy in Granada correctly identified the photographs of several Bradley family members shown to him. The mother accepted him as her son when he eventually arrived in San Antonio. But suspicions grew – his accent wasn't American, his eyes were of a different colour, his scars were not the same, and so on. The boy turned out to be Frederic Bourdin, a French vagrant who had been in trouble with police in Europe. In San Antonio he had pumped family members for stories of the past. He was, in the journalist Nick Davis' words, 'a man who lied in his bones, a chameleon character who had almost ceased to exist as he rewrote himself into a sequence of fictional characters'.

NOTES

1. *The Australian Commission*, op. cit., p. 179.

2. *The Confession*, op. cit., p. 7.

3. *Trial at the Bar of Sir Roger Tichborne*, op. cit., Vol 1, pp. 158-9.

4. *The Confession*, op. cit., p. 8.

5. Ibid., p. 31.

6. Ibid., p. 31.

7. *Trial at the Bar of Sir Roger Tichborne*, op. cit., Vol 1, p. 175.

8. *The Confession*, op. cit., p. 31.

9. Ibid., p.10.

10. In the circus act he was big Tichborne in contrast to a short actor known as little Tichborne, or 'little Tich', a phrase which came to have wide currency.

11. The Crawford case is described in 'The Curious Claim to the Honours of the Earldom of Crawford', in Sir Bernard Burke *Family Romance, or Episodes in the Domestic Annals of the Aristocracy*, Hurst and Blacket, London, 3rd edition, n.d. (c.1870s), pp. 214-21.

12. The Lascelles case is described in William Howitt *Land, Labour and Gold*, op. cit., pp. 421-24.

13. Michael Gilbert *The Claimant: The Tichborne Case Reviewed*, Constable, London, 1957, pp. 219-21.

14. Nick Davis 'The Lost Boy', *The Age*, 2 January, 1998.

14

LITERARY VERSIONS OF THE BASIC STORY

Four major outbreaks of bushranging occurred in the nineteenth century: the depredations of Mike Howe in VDL, the Bogong Jack episode, the Ben Hall gang in the Weddin mountains of NSW, and the Kelly gang in Victoria. Many of the perpetrators were convicts or ex-convicts. Around these events an extensive literature grew up. The relations between events and their folkoric and literary recreations are varied. We tend to think events come first, as they usually do, and are then swept up as folklore and rendered into novels as public mind fashions current gossip into familiar and explicable patterns. But the relationship is sometimes circular – people often act in real life in conformity with preconceived ideas. The Tichborne claimant was a great reader of current sensation novels about people who make a fortune or claim a title, including Kingsley's *Ravenshoe*, which may have given him ideas – literature affecting life, not the other way round.

Kingsley's novella 'The Two Cadets', was first published in February-March 1867, a month or so after the Tichborne claimant's arrival in England. This story is the clearest distillation of the 'gentlemen bushranger' motif in Australia literature. The two principal characters, Horton and Hornsby, are cousins, cadets of two aristocratic English families. They are like each other, but opposites, two potentialities of the same person: Hornsby is a large, loud extrovert, physically strong and brave, but a bully. Horton is 'cast in a gentler and more feminine mould to all appearance...but a most amiable and excellent young fellow, disgusted with his life, and knowing himself fit for higher things'.[1] (This is a self-description by Kingsley). Both cousins fall unsuccessfully in love with their mutual cousin, Alice. Horton kills another man in connection with this love affair and is exiled to Australia, where he becomes a wealthy squatter, and so regains respectable status. Hornsby moves to dissipation, but ends up in Australia as an Inspector of Police. As in *Geoffry Hamlyn*, an outbreak of bushranging occurs, led by an ex-Van Diemen's Land convict known as Marks. Hornsby goes out to hunt the Marks gang, but is captured by the gang and then mysteriously returned to civilization. Horton agrees to pay Hornsby's debts. Then Horton himself shoots the bushranger Marks dead in the bush, only to find out that he is Hornsby in disguise. Horton returns to England and succeeds to a title as Lord Poole.

'The Two Cadets' is important because it is the *ur* story, the fundamental structure around which much other literature, folklore and myth congregates. Once again we have the contrast between two similar types, one who sinks and the other who reclaims his exalted status. This was the basic design of Gerald Griffin's novel *The Rivals*, and of Kingsley's *Ravenshoe*. Kingsley's fictional works relating to Australia have a similar patterning of events. Both Clarke and Boldrewood admired Kingsley's writing and learnt from him. Boldrewood said he knew *Geoffry Hamlyn* almost by heart, and Clarke believed 'the best Australian novel that has been, and probably will be written is "Geoffry Hamlyn" '.

Marcus Clarke became fascinated with Van Diemen's Land's dark convict past, stories of which are recounted in *Old Tales of A Young Country* (1871). Commentators have discussed his major novel, *For the Term of His Natural Life* (1874), primarily in terms of the horrors of the convict system. It was this novel which did much to fix in the public mind the image both of degraded VDL convict behavoir and the barbarous system which produced it. This is the main focus of the novel. But its complicated plot, when untangled, fits neatly into a familiar pattern. In the older generation Sir Richard Devine is married to Ellinor Wade, who is in love with her cousin, Lord Bellasis – once again a woman courted by two men. In the next generation the story is repeated. Two cousins, Maurice Frere and Richard Devine, are involved in a struggle over the will of Devine's father, who is mysteriously murdered. Devine, the suspect, changes his name to Rufus Dawes and is sentenced to a term as a convict in Van Diemen's Land. Frere goes there as an army officer superintending convicts. They often meet as rivals during their respective careers. Both fall in love with Sylvia Vickers in Tasmania. So far this plot is almost identical to Kingsley 'The Two Cadets' – the contrasting careers of two English coevals as convict desperado and policeman in Australia.

A direct Tichborne parallel is evident in the novel, which was published at the height of public interest in the Tichborne case. The heir Devine is thought to have disappeared after a shipwreck. A convict, John Rex, has a mysterious background as a putative son to a valet of Lord Bellasis; this resembles the rumours about Orton being an illegitimate Tichborne. Rex steals a boat called the *Osprey*, the same name as in the Tichborne case. Rex and Devine have both suddenly descended from being gentlemen to convicts. They are both very like each other, practically doubles: 'Mr. North, watching them, was struck by the resemblance the two men bore to each other. Their height, eyes, hair, and complexion were similar. Despite the difference in name, they might be related. 'They might be brothers,' thought he.'[2] In fact Rex is the son of Lord Bellasis and so a half-brother of Dawes/Devine. Rex returns to England under another name, Crofton, just as Orton returned as Castro. Crofton/Rex, like Orton/Castro, has a lower class wife, impersonates the heir and claims the Devine inheritance, having the support of the mother but not of other members of the family. Like Orton/Castro, he learns details of Devine's life: 'With consummate skill, piece by piece he built up the story which was to deceive the poor mother, and to make him the possessor of one of the largest private fortunes in England. This was the tale he hit upon. He had been saved from the burning *Hydapses* by a vessel bound for Rio'.[3] He is eventually exposed as a fraud. Analogies to the Tichborne case are clear. Clarke wrote another novel entitled *Chidiock Tichbourne*, which reveals he was fascinated by the family.

Boldrewood wrote a number of works of fiction on similar lines. In his novel *The Miner's Right*, serialized in 1880 and published in book form in 1890, one character on an Australian goldfield, Jake Challerson, turns out to be an unacknowledged English heir, whose

MARCUS CLARKE

ROLF BOLDREWOOD

real name is Hon. Charles Dormer, son of an earl. In real life the Dormer family was related to the Tichbornes, which may indicate Boldrewood was thinking of them in creating this Tichborne-like character, who leaves England because of a dispute over cards, goes to America, and eventually arrives at an Australian goldfield where he lives under an assumed name and is murdered after being involved in low business. This is the profile of the imagined Tichborne career arising out of speculation on the case (rather than the real life story of Tichborne or Orton/Castro). The novel reflects, as did the speculation about Tichborne, the view that a respectable Englishman can go either way in Australia.

The hero of *The Miner's Right*, Hereward Pole, from a family in social decline, travels to Australia and makes his pile on the goldfields of New South Wales. He acts in a decent way and in spite of certain obstacles, the wealth he accumulates eventually enables him to marry his sweetheart, Ruth Allerton, daughter of a squire, and to succeed to Allerton Hall. Money brings success and status, and allows him to move once more up to gentry rank in England, the same outcome as the Buckley family in Kingsley's *Geoffry Hamlyn*. In contrast Jake Challerson and the novel's villain, Algernon Malgrade, also of aristocratic background, come to Australia and, as a result of moral failings, sink into the morass and fail here. Malgrade gets involved with bushrangers (the Ben Hall and Frank Gardiner gangs lightly disguised), who are connected with horse-stealing and cattle-rustling. There is even a passage reminiscent of the Ballarat Harry saga, where a miner with gold leaves the town and is never seen again. Boldrewood gives his story a twist – like Kingsley in *The Hillyars and the Burtons,* he believes that in Australia it's better to originally be of lower status and to make your way up in society by your own hard work, rather than relying on inherited superiority and wealth.

A great new spur to mythologizing the bushranging outbreaks came when Rolf Boldrewood published his novel *Nevermore* in serial form in the *Centennial Magazine* in 1890, and then in book form in 1892. Boldrewood was Police Magistrate in Albury from 1885 to 1895; it is likely that during this period he picked up the story of the Omeo bushrangers, though he never visited Omeo.[4] *Nevermore* is a melodramatic rewrite of the third volume of *Geoffry Hamlyn*, less fact-based and more gossip-driven. The three novelists had differences in their approach. Kingsley wrote his novel *Geoffry Hamlyn* on the Omeo bushranging outbreak in the late 1850s as it was happening, before any folklore on the event could grow up, so he gives a more realistic, unromanticised portrait of events. In *Geoffrey Hamlyn* the VDL gang are fearsome ruthless thugs, the image of them Kingsley remembered from his Melbourne days in the 1850s. Kingsley was from an earlier generation, with the demeanour of a Regency dandy, a mind formed by the classics, and with an insatiable curiosity for facts. In contrast Clarke and Boldrewood wrote in the high Romantic style. Clarke, writing in the 1870s two decades after Kingsley still shows how awful and vicious Vandemonian convictism with its cannibalism could be, but his convoluted romantic love-line plots blur that effect, and Boldrewood, writing another two decades later in the 1890s has let time gloze over the brutality, and his cardboard cut-out 'villains' are in the Captain Starlight gentleman-bushranger mould. It's the late, bowdlerized, inaccurate Boldrewood version of events, lifted from folklore, which has come down to us masquerading as historical truth.

In *Nevermore* Boldrewood mixed up in fictional form all the main elements previously considered (the Tichborne case, the Toke-Panynter gang, the convict trail, the Ballarat Harry and Cornelius Green murders) and threw in the Kelly gang for good measure. He was the first to offer in fiction a connected account of these variegated events. Lance Trevanion, the son of a West Country squire and heir to the property Wychwood, is clearly the Tichborne figure. He is in love with his cousin, Estelle Chaloner, but leaves for Australia after a quarrel with his father. Like Tichborne, he pledges to be reunited with Estelle after a number of years. On the boat out to Australia he clashes with a fellow passenger, Lawrence Trevanna, who is remarkably like him, a double, and permanent enmity springs up between them. So far the story is identical in outline to Henry Kingsley's novella 'The Two Cadets'. Trevanion

MANARO TO GIPPSLAND

lands at Melbourne, then goes to Ballarat where he succeeds as a gold-digger. But he meets up with the semi-criminal family the Lawlesses (Ned, Kate and others), obviously based on the Kelly family, and forms, against the advice of others, an attachment to Kate. The Lawlesses are involved in horse-stealing, and when Trevanion goes to Omeo with Kate he is arrested by a mounted policeman for being in possession of a stolen horse. The Omeo location and the decade (1850s) means that the Lawless gang is a fictional representation of the Toke-Paynter gang as well as the Kelly one. The rustling operations over the mountains are fully described in the novel. Lance protests his innocence but is returned to Ballarat for trial. Contradictory evidence about him being seen at Omeo previous to his arrest is given, but he is convicted of horse-stealing and sentenced to two years' imprisonment, which is served in the notorious hulks off Williamstown.

However he eventually escapes from the hulk, but is forced now to live incognito as 'Ballarat Harry' Johnstone near Omeo, where he maintains a quiet life as a gold-digger. Kate Lawless is now married to his nemesis and double, Lance Trevanna, who mixes with the Lawless gang. Trevanna represents the Orton/Castro figure. Meanwhile Estelle, worried by his lack of communication, arrives in Melbourne and tracks him to Ballarat and then Omeo. But before she arrives there Lance meets Trevanna and his mate Caleb Coke (clearly Thomas Toke), is shot and tomahawked by them and the body thrown down a mine shaft – a version of the murder of Ballarat Harry. Trevanna then, after taking Trevanion's clothes and rifling his papers, adopts the persona of Trevanion. When Estelle arrives at Omeo she is taken in by the imposter, whom she thinks is her sweetheart, though she does have some doubts. Estelle returns to Melbourne with the goldbuyer Con Gray, who is murdered on the way – a version of the murder of Cornelius Green. In Melbourne Estelle and Trevanna prepare to marry and return home, but at the last minute Kate tells the true story of the circumstances of Trevanion's death, and Trevanna is arrested on a charge of murder. He is tried with another member of the gang (the Chamberlain and Armstrong trial), but Coke turns Queen's Evidence, gets off and returns to the Gibbo, as Toke did in real life. Estelle returns home and marries an acquaintance of her sweetheart from the goldfields. The estate of Wychwood goes to a younger son. At the end it is revealed that Lawrence Trevanna was a natural son of the old squire from a liaison with a lower-class girl. He was therefore a half-brother of Trevanion, which accounts for the remarkable similarity.

Boldrewood employed in his novel the two possible explanations of the Tichborne affair: that the claimant was an illegitimate member of the family, or that the claimant and Tichborne knew each other in the Australian bush. The two then supposedly formed a close alliance, and were involved in shady business, bushranging and perhaps murder. This is why they wanted to hush up their past. Either Tichborne killed Orton (which would explain Orton's disappearance, essential to Castro's case), or more likely Castro/ Orton, having befriended Tichborne, and got to know his life history, habits and background, was involved in killing Tichborne in the bush and from then on impersonating him. Both versions have the advantage that they neatly explain many of the otherwise contradictory aspects of the case. The problem with both is that there is no evidence for them, except a few hazy recollections many years later.

The novel *Nevermore* resurrected the view that Ballarat Harry was Sir Roger Tichborne, both being educated Englishmen seen on the Ballarat goldfields and living under a pseudonym. These explanations had been advanced by commentators before Boldrewood. For example, the journalist 'The Vagabond' (Stanley James), in an 1889 article describing a journey from Omeo down to Bruthen, mentions the Ballarat Harry-Tichborne connection: 'One thing appears to be clear. The real Sir Roger did land in Australia. There is a misty tradition that a miner named "Ballarat Harry", who was mixed up with Sir Roger Tichborne, or who was the real Sir Roger, was murdered by his mates on the banks of this Haunted Stream'. [5] This article appeared before Boldrewood's *Nevermore* was published, so the story had an earlier life. Boldrewood may have used the 'Vagabond' piece as a source.

It was true that the Toke-Paynter gang were participants in the Ballarat Harry and Cornelius Green murders. It was true that Orton knew Ballarat Harry, and that he was implicated in some way with his disappearance near Dargo, as after it he fled back to Boisdale. But there is no evidence connecting these events with Sir Roger Tichborne. The argument became circular – *Nevermore* and folklore promoted the connection, and it was projected back on to the past as fact. Mervyn Pearson in his history of the Omeo Shire, *Echoes From The Mountains* (1969), claims Ballarat Harry was arrested for horse stealing at Ballarat and sentenced to a term on the hulks, from which he escaped.[6] But this 'information' comes from Boldrewood's novel, which is not historical evidence at all. *Nevermore* had the effect of tying up these stories too neatly, and endorsing a mythical version of events. Old timers and newer generations, influenced by reading the novel or having heard of it, then imposed its narrative on to reality, thus confusing fact and fantasy even further.

Similarly with Bogong Jack, who in some folklore versions himself became the Tichborne figure. He was tall, well built, with an aquiline nose, and according to some accounts, such as Eric Harding's, an educated Englishman. So he too came to fill the gap as the proposed heir with a mysterious background. Once again his disappearance and supposed murder would be compatible with the various Tichborne theories, including rumours of Tichborne's bushranging activities. But once again no evidence for these speculations exists, and knowledge of John Paynter's poor Hobart childhood disqualifies this version.

Boldrewood wrote other pieces with related themes. In a novella 'The Wild Australian' published in the *Town and Country Journal* from 30 June to 27 November, 1877, he returned to the 'doubles' motif – an Australian and an English heir, who look extremely like each other, return to England and swop identities to confuse an English novelist, who wants to include a stereotyped Australian in her next book. Like the Tichborne case this shows how the two types can be interchangeable. In another novella, 'The Final Choice', published in *The Australasian* of 19 December, 1885, the heroine's father has been murdered by bushrangers two decades before. She is courted by a number of suitors, including her English cousin. Boldrewood continued to be interested in bushrangers, writing a series of articles on them called 'Wild Deeds of Wild Days in Australia' for the magazine *Life* in 1905, including articles on the murder of Cornelius Green, and on Dan Morgan's holdup of the Police Magistrate Bayliss.

The Tichborne case fascinated other writers. Louisa Atkinson, the first Australian-born novelist, wrote *Debatable Ground or, The Carlillawarra Claimants*, published in 1872 after her death. The novel combines a property dispute, based on one in her own family, with the Tichborne case, which was in the news at the time she was writing. In the novel the Roskell family is wealthy, since Roskell has made money as a miserly Sydney trader. He owns a number of country properties, including 'Woodacres' and 'Carlillawarra'. His sister had married a Mr Animus Woods and they had one son. A mysterious gentleman, Jean Baptiste le Bois, educated in France (as Roger Tichborne was), appears at a neighbouring property and likes the district so much that he acquires the lease of Roskell's property 'Woodacres'. He delves into his own background by questioning some old folk. It turns out, he is led to believe, that he is in fact Arnold Woods, the son of Animus Woods. The Woods family were believed to have drowned in a shipwreck, as Tichborne did, but Arnold survived and was brought up by Catholic priests in France. As the Woods originally owned 'Carlillawarra', he believes he is the rightful owner and heir. Le Bois says to Roskell: 'I am Arnold Woods...I am your dead sister's child; the son that was born in this very house, and it is mine. I appeal to your feelings – to any love you had for your parents – to restore me to my inheritance'.[7] As Roskell will not grant him the property, Woods, alias le Bois, sues Mr Roskell for the property as the Carlillawarra claimant. The court case has echoes of the first Tichborne trail, and the defendant Roskell wins. Woods is too poor to initiate a second case, and goes up country as a station worker, like Arthur Orton. He says to a young girl:

> "I can never alter my name; it is Arnold Woods."
>
> "Oh, you'll change it," persisted she; "every one does; father wasn't called Bill Smith where we came from; and when we get cross country, he'll change again – every one does." This was opening up a new phase of bush life to the shepherd, and brought before his mind some idea of that floating class of beings who, whether from crimes committed, a restless disposition, or the suspicion which springs out of ignorance, and practices making the doer amenable to the laws, are always in a state of transition or incognito.[8]

But Woods, unlike Orton-Castro, is a genuine claimant. After Roskell dies, his daughter Anima, a cousin of Woods, out of charity and justice gives the Carlillawarra property to him, and they eventually marry.

George Darrell's play *The Sunny South* (1883) also makes

use of the Tichborne case. Eli Grup (the name spelt backwards means Pure Guile), described as the son of a butcher, is a vulgar upstart, trying by dubious means to take over the Chester estate in England. For him money means everything, including status. Worth Chester's mother died leaving all her property to a son who died abroad. From Australia appears a 'wild scapegrace', Matt Morley, a digger, who turns out to be Morley Chester, the brother of the owner of the estate, who is about to lose it. One character says of Morley: 'Twenty years in the bush and a gentleman every inch of him! It's knocked off his West End polish but it hasn't touched his heart.' Morley has changed his name on the diggings and hasn't bothered to alter it since. On his return Grup disparagingly refers to his claim of the estate as 'Ha! Ha! Sir Roger the second!', drawing attention to his similarity to Sir Roger Tichborne's position. Morley retaliates by describing Grup as 'the false steward who robbed from his master, the lair who lied to the judge, the thief who lived and fattened on the proceeds of his crime!'[9]

Many other novels of the period, though not directly about the Tichborne affair, focus on the retrieval of lost titles, patrimony or lands, or associated themes. Rosa Praed's novel *Policy and Passion* (1881), a study in changing social status, is a version of the basic story in which the action is confined to Australia. The hero Longleat rises by his own exertions from humble origins to become Premier of his state, only to lose his position when his convict past is revealed. His daughter has to choose between an Australian suitor and a reprobate English aristocratic one. Ada Cambridge's *The Three Miss Kings*, serialized in 1883, is a variant of the fable in which women play the key roles. The Misses King, orphans from England living in straightened circumstances in Melbourne, attempt to regain gentry status through marriage. But it transpires they are heirs to an English fortune, and in the end one of the sisters returns to the family seat married to a cousin.

NOTES

1. Henry Kingsley 'The Two Cadets', op. cit., p. 339.

2. Marcus Clarke *For the Term of His Natural Life, 1874,* repr. Oxford University Press, London, 1952, p. 344.

3. Ibid., p. 482.

4. In one of his first published articles Boldrewood wrote an account of a trip from Monaro to Gippsland in the *Town and Country Journal* of 29 September, 1870. The engraving which accompanied this article, entitled 'From Manaro to Gippsland – A Scene in the Australian Alps', which is reproduced in this book, is in fact an adaption of Nicholas Chevalier's painting 'The Buffalo Ranges'.

5. The Vagabond 'Across the Main Divide', *The Age,* 4 May, 1889.

6. A. Mervyn Pearson *Echoes From the Mountains,* Omeo Shire Council, Omeo, 1969, p. 74.

7. Louisa Atkinson *Debatable Ground or, The Carlillawarra Claimants,* 1872, repr. Mulini Press, Canberra, 1992, p. 75.

8. Ibid, p. 75.

9. George Darrell *The Sunny South,* 1883, repr. Currency Press, Sydney, 1975, pp. 22, 29 & 30.

15

A VICTORIAN FABLE

In their incarnations in literature and folklore, the Tichborne, Bogong Jack and similar stories were based on the belief that life in Australia just a sideshow, where one could redeem oneself and return to an enhanced life in the British Isles. The choice of subject matter was not arbitrary. In English fiction, there is a common thread from James Hogg's *The Confessions of a Justified Sinner* (1824), Gerald Griffin's *The Rivals* (1829) and Henry Kingsley's *Ravenshoe* (1862) to David Malouf's *The Conversations at Curlow Creek* (1996). It is the story of two men, one of whom succeeds, and the other who loses his loved one and his inheritance. The Australian variant is that the disappearance or exile takes place here. The two characters take the contrary paths which the country offers them. In some versions it is a story of two warring potentialities within the same personality, both of which are given new rein in Australia. Captivity narratives in Australia repeat the pattern, with Aboriginal society as the new sub-stratum.

The basic story can be broken down into sub-divisions:

The Orphan and the Heir. The foundling finds himself in Australia, makes his fortune and establishes an identity. The heir sloughs off the burden of his English inheritance, goes incognito, and rejoices in his newly found absence of responsibility. The venturers are doubles, secret sharers in the same quest, but temperamental opposites (eg. masculine versus feminine, active versus reflective). Some residual mystery often attends their eventual fate.

The Quest. Both travellers are like troubadours, venturing into the badlands or unknown lands to win by feats of enterprise the hand of their idealized lady – their muse – when they return. But one may not come back, since he has found a new love which he fully embraces, Australia. In some versions (for example, in Rolf Boldrewood's *Nevermore*) the loved one herself travels out to Australia.

The Gentleman and the Rogue. One character becomes a gentleman and may even achieve here a quasi-aristocratic status, not available to him in England, by keeping up respectable ways, and making his fortune through land, labour or gold. The other voluntarily renounces his exalted status, and embraces low life and the attractive levelling spirit of early colonial life. This reflects the fluidity of the Australian social order. Frustrated by social advancement in England, a period in Australia could become a roundabout mechanism for improving one's status and financial position in England. On the other hand Australia could be a welcome escape from the tightness and constraints of upper-class English life.

The Descent and the Rise. The Romantic urge to break away from society, to go down into the mire, was a very powerful urge in both life and literature. Lionel Trilling has described this urge as 'the idea of losing oneself up to the point of self-destruction, of surrendering oneself to experience without regard to self-interest or conventional morality, of escaping wholly from the societal bond'.[1] Then to resurrect oneself was to reverse the cycle, and to improve on one's former position.

The Policeman and the Bushranger. One of the two may become a soldier or policeman, asserting the need for order, restraint and established structures in a new, unformed world which constantly threatens to descend into anarchy. The other gravitates to the opposite end of the social spectrum, the convict-bushranger fraternity. (One can compare the divergent paths taken by the Belgian overseers and Kurtz in *Heart of Darkness,* and the Shillingsworth brothers in *Capricornia.*) The antipodes is not just the other, but the opposite, the overthrowing of the old moral order.

The Outbreak. Antagonisms stifled for centuries in the British Isles could now be fought out in Australia, where the social mixture was different, and the contention between authority and dissidence more evenly balanced. Life in the bush and mountains, where untrammelled freedom reigned, was welcomed as wild and liberating by many of its denizens. The colonial authorities believed the nomadic life of the frontier was potentially barbaric, and lived in fear that convict-bushranger disturbances could trigger a wider outbreak of civil disorder. Some mixture of adversary elements (convict, bushranger, Irish and Aboriginal) would constitute the forces of rebellion. From Castle Hill through Eureka to the Kelly saga, actual outbreaks occurred.

Mountains and Plains. Criminal activity takes place in the seclusion of the mountains, where things can be concealed and social bonds are more rudimentary. In contrast, life on the outback plains on squatting properties is more open, respectable and transparent.

The fable flourished in the nineteenth century, but, as the novelist David Malouf suggests, 'each time in a slightly different form as it suffered the slippage of a detail added here, a suggestion there, according to the narrator's flair for story-telling or capacity for bold magnification...and his own sense of what was not but ought to have been true.'[2] In all the stories, there exist neat opposites, but also the possibilities of the opposites changing places or coalescing, the characteristic of the double. Tichborne and the claimant are opposites, but can change places. The colony of Victoria was settled by respectable families, but was contaminated by convict-bushrangers from adjacent colonies. Toke, the unprepossessing VDL ex-convict contrasts with the more romantic and appealing 'Bogong Jack' Paynter of the same gang. On pastoral runs, squatters appear to have opposite interests to their rural workers, but in Australia the latter can become landholders in their own right.

Folklore from around the world abounds with the motifs of twins, lost brothers, doubles, imposters, and false, hidden and changeable identities, all of which are apparent in the Tichborne and related stories. In the 'Sinbad the Sailor' story from *The Thousand and One Nights*, Sinbad the porter is a poor man working in the house of a rich man, Sinbad the seaman, and envying his wealth. Sinbad the seaman goes on perilous journeys in remote and exotic places to exorcise the 'old bad man' in him. It is implied that the two characters are both similar and opposites, 'brothers under the skin'. In the Grimm's Fairy Tales story of 'The Goose Girl', a princess and her maid go on a journey. The maid forces the princess to change roles, so in a faraway country the real princess works as a goose girl, and the maid becomes a pretend princess who is betrothed to the king's son. But the usurper is eventually unmasked, and the real princess marries the prince. In some versions, it is a prince and his servant who are the main characters and who undergo a reversal of their social roles. In the story of the two brothers in Grimm's Fairy Tales, the two brothers are opposites and have different fates. One (the heir) wishes to stay attached to the past and the other to break away to reach out to a new future. He goes to a strange, unfamiliar place where he undergoes trials before returning home. In some versions they are rivals for the love of the same woman. It is implied that both, not just one, aspects of our personalities need to be satisfied for a person to be an integrated whole.[3] The novels and the Tichborne case therefore reinforce deep folk stereotypes.

The experience of going to a strange country is a common one in folklore. In the 19th century Australia often fulfilled the role of that faraway, exotic and even inverted place. In *Geoffry Hamlyn* Kingsley quotes a stanza from the old Scots border ballad 'Thomas the Rhymer':

> Oh see ye not that pleasant road,
>   That winds among the ferny brae?
> Oh that's the road to fairy land,
>   Where thou and I this e'en must gae.[4]

In the ballad a spirit figure lures Thomas away to faery land for seven years. It is an enticing place, but after some time he longs to return home. This reflects Kingsley's and others' time in Australia – an exotic adventure which must come to an end. The first Bogong Jack, after four years in the alps, yearns to return to his family in the Ovens valley.

In his study of mythology *The White Goddess* Robert Graves combines many such dominant folklore motifs in a foundation myth which he claims underwrites much of our heritage. Its main figures are two equal but opposite males, the God of the Waxing Year, the God of the Waning Year, and the all-powerful Threefold Goddess:

> The poet identifies himself with the God of the Waxing Year and his muse with the Goddess; the rival is his blood-brother, his other self, his weird. All true poetry celebrates some incident or scene in this very ancient story, and the three main characters are so much a part of our racial inheritance that they not only assert themselves in poetry but recur on occasions of emotional stress in the form of dreams, paranoiac visions and delusions.[5]

In the penny dreadfuls and broadsheets which poured out on the Tichborne case, we again witness the popular imagination selecting and manoeuvring the facts to fit them into common patterns.[6] The journeying Tichborne is liked to Sinbad the Sailor and Robinson Crusoe. He accosts people in the street like the Ancient Mariner to tell them his story. The claimant is heroicized as 'Jolly Roger' or 'Roger the Dodger'. He is depicted as having been dealt a hard deal by life, a victim of injustice, especially by the English establishment and the lawyers, who get all the money. Love and sexual aspects are highlighted – he is depicted as a great lover, but unfaithful, going from one woman to another. Salacious details of tattoos in intimate places are repeated, as is 'dancing the can-can in the mill', a reference to Tichborne's supposed dalliance with his cousin Lady Doughty before his journey overseas. In all cases the appeal of these stories is that they are skewed to fit in with deeply embedded folk myths.

For many people in Australian in the 19th century, England was seen as the source country, the central force in their lives, the place around which they oriented themselves ('home'). Australia was not then regarded then, as it is now, as an autonomous realm, but as a peripheral dependency of England, and a new way of improving one's British credentials. One came to Australia to strive in a lesser world, surrendering many comforts and certainties, in the hope of improving one's situation in life. A sojourn in Australia provided a roundabout, back-door way of making a pile so that one could regain one's patrimony in English society, the main aim. Its basic drive was to reconcile the British and Australian experiences into a new amalgam. This idea was immeasurable strengthened by the discovery of gold here, and it was also the way many in England itself saw Australia, as the novels of Dickens, Braddon and others attest. This was the central narrative of colonial Australia. The interconnected mystery stories of the south-eastern corner of the continent were easily shoehorned into the familiar mythic sequence of exile, descent, struggle and trial, and finally ascent. The lost aristocrat down under, the gentleman bushranger, and related themes, became the organizing principles of much Australia colonial literature, and the first defining myth created by Europeans here.

The basic story did not however retain this status, as it easily might have, but faded after the first century of European settlement. The originally settled fertile crescent area of the east coast became suppressed in the Australian consciousness. Its folk hero, the Man from Snowy River, could not compete on the national canvas with Clancy of the Overflow. The earlier fable has not come down to us in any clarity because, after the Kelly outbreak, it was overtaken by the late nineteenth century vogue for exclusive nationalism. The earlier myth celebrated duality and its mysteries – going up and down in society, being both pro-Australian and pro-British, being both savage and civilized, and merging them at the same time. In the classic fable, ambiguity and shape-changing reigned; people could adapt to new modes very easily and quickly.

But in the mateship nationalist version the two sides, England and Australia, were put rigidly and forever at war with each other; the possibility of duality and coalescence was eliminated. Nationalism removed these variations and promoted a monochrome view of society. One side of our existence (British Isles background, genteel status, and one's past in general) was elided in an attempt to make the Australian experience a clean break with the past, a new start. The other side of the duality (egalitarianism, isolationism, and demotic behaviour) was emphasized, with the result that an unvariegated version of life here was held up as exemplary.

The Kelly saga was a point of transition whereby the earlier myth was recast into the later one. The earlier myth was focussed on one's station in life. The Kelly saga transformed the myth from one of status to one of class, just as Kenealy QC had attempted to do during the Tichborne trials. Kelly's overt anti-Britishness introduced a new element – an alternative Celtic folk memory of long duration:

> [An Irish Australian policeman] is a traitor to his country ancestors and religion as they were all Catholic before the Saxons and Cranmore yolk held sway...more was transported to Van Diemand's Land to pine their young lives away in starvation and misery among tyrants worse than the promised hell itself.

The Queen of England was, in Kelly's Jerilderie Letter, as guilty as the horse stealers. Class struggle, in which poor selectors vied with a rapacious establishment, was a dominant motif in the Kelly outbreak. The earlier myth was able to combine respectable and quasi-criminal behaviour in the one personality. The Kelly outbreak separated these two activities. It announced clear-cut political, ethnic and societal dimensions, with which the early events could not compete. The aim of turning oneself into an English gentleman was no longer achievable, nor even desirable. The archetype was changing. Mateship nationalism took off in the public realm in the way that the earlier story, which was more complicated and mysterious, never fully did.

But Australia was not a meeting of two blanks, as nationalism pretended, a scrubbed-out past meeting an Australian *carte blanche.* Two existing entities, a European past and an Australian presence, were coming into contact here, sometimes at odds but more usually mingling in complex ways. In recent decades novelists have revived older mystery stories to present a view of the Australian experience which reconciles origins and environment. Patrick White has retold the Mrs Eliza Fraser story in *Fringe of Leaves* (1976), novels on coastal wrecks like the Batavia and the Mahogany ship abound, Liam Davison has written *The White Woman (*1994*)* retelling the story of lost white woman of the 1840s, and Mat Schulz's novel

Claim (1996) is an imaginative retelling of the Tichborne saga, emphasizing the claimant's sexual duality. White's *The Twyborn Affair* (1979), with the word 'twyborn' a play on 'twice born' and 'Tichborne', celebrates identity changing and duality in all its forms. Janet Turner Hospital's recent novel *The Claimant* (2014) is also influenced by the Tichborne case. The Australian public is still fascinated by stories of ordinary Australians like the postman from northern Tasmania and the pensioner from Western Australian who have inherited English earldoms. A dispute over the inheritance of the dissipated Lord Moynihan, who ran seedy bars in Manila after an Australian sojourn (a classical case of the fallen aristocrat), was resolved some years ago in England. An English aristocrat, Lord McAlpine, revived Broome.

It needed a major novelist to bring the archetype to life again in its elemental form. David Malouf's novel *The Conversations at Curlow Creek* is written in the style of a fable, a story whose basic structure is familiar to us from fictions like Kingsley's *The Two Cadets*. Two boys grow up together in a great house in Ireland around 1800. One, Michael Adair, an orphan, is fostered in the home of the second, Fergus Connellan, the heir to an estate. A close bond develops between them, and with a neighbouring girl, Virgilia, with whom they are both in love. But their temperaments gradually diverge; Fergus immerses himself in the plight of ordinary Irish folk, while Adair remains more reflective. Their personal and political attachments remain unresolved at home. As men, both come to Australia. All the cards are reshuffled on the great inland plains of New South Wales, where their divergent life histories are played out. Fergus, having discarded his upper class heritage, reappears as the bushranger-rebel Dolan, who has moved away from society into the high plains, perhaps to lead an insurrection. In contrast, the more austere Adair has improved his position in the world. Now a soldier-policeman, he seeks out his former companion.

One source of Malouf's *Remembering Babylon*, a captivity narrative, may be the story 'The First Queensland Explorer' from Marcus Clarke's *Old Tales of a Young Country* (1871). This suggests Malouf may have been exploring colonial accounts in order to capture the essence of a story which obsessed many early Australians. But Malouf is not, like the nineteenth century novelists, interested primarily in the story, action and external appearances, in the romantic self-pity of the hero, in the loss of title and loved one, nor in social mobility patterns in Australia. He has stripped down the fable to an essential interest in how two human beings from similar backgrounds, 'pushing off from the edges of consciousness into the mystery of what we have not yet become', can turn out so differently.

NOTES

1 Lionel Trilling 'On the Modern Element in Modern Literature', *The Idea of the Modern*, ed. Irving Howe, Horizon Press, New York, 1968, p. 82.

2 David Malouf *The Conversations at Curlow Creek*, Chatto & Windus, London, 1996, p. 205.

3 A discussion of these folktales can be found in Bruno Bettleheim *The Uses of Enchantment*, 1976, repr. Penguin Books, Harmondsworth, 1978, pp. 83-6, 90-6, & 136-143. Christopher Booker *The Seven Basic Plots: Why We Tell Stories* (2006) provides a much more detailed account of recurring story lines in literature and film.

4 Henry Kingsley *The Recollections of Geoffry Hamlyn*, op. cit., p. 248.

5 Robert Graves *The White Goddess*, Faber and Faber, London, 1961, p. 24.

6 These examples come from *Baronet or Butcher?: The Trial of the Tichborne Claimant,* ed. Hugh Anderson, Red Rooster Press, 1999.

ACKNOWLEDGEMENTS

Paul De Serville's immense knowledge of early Victoria has been essential in completing this project. Working with Stan Mellick, the biographer of Henry Kingsley, on the Academy Edition of Kingsley's *The Recollections of Geoffry Hamlyn* provided me with a lot of the information on which this book is based. Vic Webber's and Peter Gardner's knowledge of Omeo, and Jane Cowans of Thomas Toke, were a great help to me in the early stages of my research. The 1869 Australian Commission on the Tichborne case, and the early Gippsland Police files in the Public Records Office of Victoria, both produced large amounts of original material. Dr Victor Crittenden of Canberra, who edited the magazine *Margin* on early Australia literature, published some pieces of mine on topics connected with the present book. A version of the chapter on Bogong Jack appeared in *Quadrant* magazine.

The collections of the Public Records Office of Victoria, the State Library of Victoria, and the National Library of Australia have once again proved invaluable for research purposes. The manuscript of this book was largely completed before The National Library of Australia's 'Trove' became available. I had read the relevant newspapers from Beechworth, Port Albert and Sale, but when I entered the name Bogong Jack on 'Trove', I found in the *Ovens Constitution* of Wangaratta an 1857 reference to a horse-stealer, John Andrews, known at the time as Bogong Jack, the first appearance of the name in print.

Illustrations reproduced with permission included the portraits of Marcus Clarke (H 12992) and Rolf Boldrewood (H84. 322) from the State Library of Victoria, the photographs of early Omeo and Cornelius Green from the East Gippsland Historical Society, and the file of Thomas Tookey (Con 31/4/44 p. 126 (Convict Record)) from the Tasmanian Information and Research Service. Alexander Barr, a librarian of the Research Service, kindly located the last item for me. Other illustrations (Liverpool Street Hobart, From Manaro to Gippsland, A Scene at the Trial,

Tom Castro's House at Wagga Wagga, The Tichborne Claimant, and Henry Kingsley) come from the author's collection.

I am grateful to Debbie Squires who drew the maps, and to Ann Synan who digitalized the illustrations. Finally I wish to express my indebtedness to Anthony Cappello of Connor Court for publishing this book.

www.ingramcontent.com/pod-product-compliance
Lightning Source LLC
Chambersburg PA
CBHW070352240426
43671CB00013BA/2472